LAURA
MEETS
JEFFREY

LAURA
MEETS
JEFFREY

BOTH SIDES OF AN
EROTIC MEMOIR

JEFFREY MICHELSON
and LAURA BRADLEY

NEW
BLUE
BOOKS

Lehigh Valley, Pennsylvania

2012

NEW BLUE BOOKS
a division of Blue Mountain Marketing Inc.
www.NewBlueBooks.com

For information about permission to reproduce selections from this book,
please contact Andrea Loog at Blue Mountain Marketing, 610-737-9210 or
AndreaLoogBMM@gmail.com
To reach the authors: LauraMeetsJeffrey@gmail.com
LIBRARY OF CONGRESS CATALOGING-IN-PUBLICATION DATA
Michelson, Jeffrey.
    Laura Meets Jeffrey : both sides of an erotic memoir / Jeffrey Michelson
    and Laura Bradley — 1st ed
ISBN: 978-0-9850098-4-7

Other available versions:

Digital Distribution
ISBN: 978-0-9850098-1-6

Audio Book
ISBN: 978-0-9850098-3-0

Manufactured in the United States of America
First Edition

COVER AND BOOK DESIGN BY JOHN LOTTE FOR BLUE MOUNTAIN MARKETING
WEB DESIGN BY BLUE MOUNTAIN MARKETING

LauraMeetsJeffrey.com

To Joanna and Andrea

The last prejudice man will overcome is our prejudice toward beauty.

—Malcolm Braly

Contents

A note to the memoir police

Some names and places are changed to protect both the innocent and the guilty. Otherwise only minor liberties have been taken.

Norman Mailer wrote his foreword after he read my first draft. A few weeks before he died in November of 2007, he suggested that when I was finished I give the book to Laura, whom he knew and loved, to get her side of the story.

She agreed.

Three years later when my part was done, Laura read my manuscript and relayed her version to Legs McNeil in a series of interviews.

Mailer's commentary on my boxing matches with Ryan O'Neal was first published in *Esquire* magazine in 1993. The interviews that Laura and I did with Mailer and Timothy Leary first appeared in *Puritan* magazine in 1981 and 1982.

Foreword

Norman Mailer

Between the appearance of the Pill in the late '60s and the first onspread of AIDS in the '80s, there was an opening—call it a broad highway—into a wide-open world of sexual experiment and laissez-faire promiscuity.

A great many Americans went off on a non-stop gymkhana of libido exercises and group excursions. Jeffrey Michelson's book captures the heart of that fifteen-year period with a directness and candor that lifts his work above the directly pornographic.

The result is most readable and, considering his own involvement, surprisingly objective and funny.

A subtle pathos mixes with an unquenching optimism and the result—no matter what a plethora of the salacious we have here—is perversely—dare I say it?—Uplifting!

The difference between writing and literature is agreeable style and irony. This book has both.

To Jeffrey
dear friend — you are sui generis
and don't ask who Sney is.
Salud!

Norman

Introduction

Legs McNeil

Jeffrey Michelson has achieved the impossible—he has written about extreme sex in an objective, factual and funny way—with a raging hard-on—yet he's neither bragging nor a jerk about it, and writing about sex is one of the hardest things in the world to get right and not sound like an asshole.

Michelson's articulate style, like a veteran sportscaster enthusiastically calling out the play-by-plays with candor, humor and an unerring eye for all the details, invites the readers to stand over the bed and observe all these debaucheries, smell the sheets after the deed is done and not have to get any of the mess on themselves.

Be warned: This is a dirty book, an odd romantic S&M love story bathed in bodily fluids.

And be invited: This is one of the best-written nonfiction works I've ever read.

As Norman Mailer pointed out in his foreword, there was a very short window in world history when it was safe most of the time to have indiscriminate sex with anonymous partners without having to worry about unwanted pregnancies, gonorrhea, syphilis, herpes, or AIDS.

Penicillin was the first breakthrough; before the invention of penicillin, people died or went insane from "social diseases." And with the advent of the Pill in the early '60s—the first modern form of birth control—this duo created, for about twenty years, true sexual freedom for anyone daring enough to experiment. Then came herpes and AIDS in the '80s and the window closed.

Thank the Lord someone finally had the balls to write down those swinging times, because I don't think future generations would ever believe the stuff that happened in those good old days. It came and it went just like that and I'm not sure that window will ever open again, at least not while my dick is still working.

LAURA MEETS JEFFREY traps that era's Zeitgeist and though other books document that time, none are as sexy and make you wish you were part of it more than this one. It took Michelson over thirty years of separation from that period to look back at a man he no longer was and have the comfort of neutral insight to write about it.

Laura—Jeffrey's object of desire, lust and obsession—was truly the woman of most men's dreams. The only complaint from her lips was the demand for "More!" I knew her and like most men, and many women, I wanted her. I knew Jeffrey and Laura socially but didn't know Laura was a hooker. If I had known, that would have been money I would have spent.

Surrounding our unknown libertines are some of the era's biggest icons: John & Yoko—who kick-started Jeffrey's design career; Jeffrey's boxing nemesis Ryan O'Neal; plus Jerzy Kosinski, Al Goldstein, Tim Leary, and Norman and Norris Mailer... a sprinkling of famous porn stars; cameos by Steve Van Zandt, Little Richard and Bruce Springsteen; and a Whitehouse speechwriter or two.

Reading about Laura is like watching one of those incredibly beautiful porn stars getting gang-banged, and thinking, "My God this woman is sooo beautiful; she doesn't have to be doing this!!!!"

Then it hits like a lightening bolt! The reason is even more sinful—she's doing it because she enjoys it!

Norman Mailer's suggestions to have Laura read Jeffrey's manuscript and add her side of the story is a wonderful literary, marketing and fact-checking device, a great parting gift from the old master to his friend. Laura completes the pictures and makes this book a richer history. She wrote some of her commentary, and most she gave as candid monologues of oral history. It was my pleasure to interview her several times and record her shameless well-aged reflections.

So enjoy the ride. Take a trip with Jeffrey Michelson and Laura Bradley, who had as much sex, drugs, and rock & roll as any two people who aren't Keith Richards!

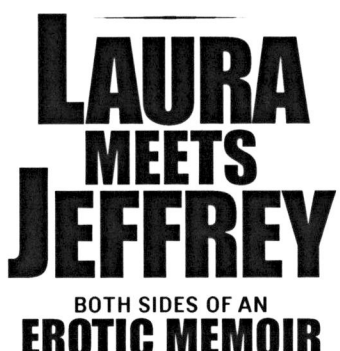

LAURA MEETS JEFFREY

BOTH SIDES OF AN
EROTIC MEMOIR

It was sexual liberation primetime in New York City.

1

The world before Laura, part one

October 1979

The Legend of Laura Bradley starts with Sherry, and Sherry deserves a few minutes if just for her skin.

Sherry was a fiery blonde with thrilling-to-the-touch white buttermilk flesh and a rattlesnake disposition. We'd been seeing each other for about half a year, spending several days a week together, some in her apartment in New York City and some at my cabin in the foothills of the Poconos, even though we shared nothing except thermonuclear chemistry.

She was a former Texan—proud, loud and stubborn. But you can't really be a former Texan. You can only move out of Texas. To be a former Texan would be like growing up in Italy, moving out, and being formerly Italian.

Sherry's father had abandoned her mother and her when she was a baby, and Sherry was going to make sure all men received payback. At first I tried to understand her hostility, but I developed compassion fatigue.

I met Sherry one autumn night in 1979 in Manhattan when Freddy, my whoring buddy and I were driving around, smoking pot and deciding which whores to visit. I was between main squeezes, dating a lot, none of it great, and garnishing my sex life with the occasional hooker.

I saw a sparkling blonde vision in high heels and a white fur coat unsuccessfully hailing a cab at 23rd and Lexington. From one hundred yards away I wanted her. I pointed her out to Freddy and he said, "Wow! Let's offer her a ride."

Freddy coached me while he hung a big U-turn on 23rd. "Take a deep breath and let it out before you start," he said, "like snipers do."

Freddy, forty-five, and twelve years older than me, was married and not looking for any relationship with a woman who wasn't his wife except those that lasted less than two hours, cost more than $50 but less than $200, involved women who were about half his age and were already wearing lingerie. As we pulled up he said, "Relax. We're two nice-looking middle-class Jewish guys in a big new Mercedes. We don't look like trouble. Just put on your game face."

Game face. Not so easy. My heart had been broken less than a year before when my fiancé, after a three-and-a-half-year relationship, left me for another guy. I was past being a mess, just getting past missing her every moment but not even halfway out of the pain from rejection, so I was not oozing confidence.

I didn't do as well as many guys getting girls but I did okay. I wouldn't classify myself as good-looking: I'm too Semitic, my nose is big and my forehead is a little too caveman. But I did have some decent attributes for a bright Jewish kid from Boston with lots of energy: I was just under six feet tall with broad shoulders, I had a healthy curly dark brown Jewfro, and even though I carried five, ten pounds too many, I was in decent shape. I was an amateur boxer, very amateur, but a real weekend warrior.

In the Penis Department, I was a notch bigger than average according to *Cosmopolitan* and *Playboy* but only half a notch larger than what I saw as average in the gym showers, a notch or two smaller than some of the guys, and three to four notches smaller than the salamis you see in porn films. There were some women who liked my hippie/biker/rabbi look, but most of the women who would get naked with me did so for other reasons.

It's said that men fall in love with what they see and women fall in love with what they hear. Thank God, since I wasn't blessed with the gift of handsome, at least I got the gift of gab. And once in bed, if a girl is into talking dirty, I'm DJ Eros with sex rap, play-by-play, color commentary, and fantasy scenarios. I love a dirty audio track. Plus I love to direct in bed. I love telling women what to do sexually and many crave to be told. I am a natural dominant and submissives need that.

Another gift—and one that only shows up after the deal has been at least opened and on the road to closing—is that it takes me forever to climax. As far as orgasms go I was an ugly duckling. In my late teens I suffered from an affliction: I was horny enough for three guys and I got hard as a rock, would fuck, stay hard forever, and not achieve a climax. I couldn't come fucking. I couldn't come being sucked. I would have to stop fucking and have the girl touch me or suck my balls while I jerked off. Maybe I jerked off too well and that's the reason why I had the problem.

This condition was hell to me but a gift to the many girls with boyfriends cursed oppositely with premature ejaculation. Some times I'd be passed around from a girlfriend to her girlfriend as if I was something between a miracle cure and a circus act. By my mid-twenties this problem worked itself out but it was still difficult for me to climax fucking. It took a long time, sometimes thirty or forty-five minutes of concerted effort, sometimes longer. I was also, and not to my choosing, the horniest man I ever met, read about or heard of. I didn't sign up for it: it was just the way my hormones lined up.

The main reason I pulled women is that I truly love women. There's the old sexist saw that if girls didn't have vaginas there would be a bounty on their heads. I disagree. Even if you couldn't fuck them, I would still wander over to their caves occasionally just to smell them, look at their bodies, and listen to them talk. They don't work the same way men do, and I find that a constant source of amusement. Often exasperating but seldom boring.

Okay. Game face. Overrule my emotions with my intellect. Ready to bring it. If self-confidence has its own pheromones, for the first time in a long time mine were turned on. If you're not afraid to lose, you are more likely to win. I was ready to win.

I'm starboard, nearest her, as she continues to wave her arm although there were no cabs in sight. I lean out the window and say with a blend of warmth and confidence, "Where are you going? Can we give you a lift?"

She bends over, cautiously looks all over inside Freddy's Mercedes, checks us out like a seasoned detective, pauses, then smiles. Up close I want her even more. She is thirty-something with an air of sophistication and big blue eyes, high forehead, striking blonde locks, and a cheerleader smile. She is a dish.

"OK. I'm going to the UN Plaza Hotel. Can you do that?" Her Texan accent completes the package. She's more than a dish; she's a peach.

"Sure," I said. I jump out, open the back door and when she settles into the back seat, I ask what she's doing tonight.

"Going out on a date with a diplomat."

"Is he your boyfriend?" I ask.

"Just someone I see from time to time."

I ask her lots of questions about herself, the most seductive tack a man can take. She's a nurse. She loves her dog. She lives in a small studio in a fancy building on Lexington near Gramercy Park. She was a beauty queen in Beaumont, Texas. At the hotel I walk her into the lobby. I ask for her number and to my great surprise she gives it to me.

Freddy and I continued on to the Upper West Side where we were entertained by two lovely co-eds he knew who were earning next semester's tuition. We both contributed $100 to furthering their education, a decent sum in 1979 when street hookers were $10 to $25.

I called Sherry the following week and on that phone call we had our very first argument. She wanted to go hear country music. I wanted to go dancing. How much more of a warning sign do two people need? I wanted to get into her skirt but what was her reason for staying on the phone? We compromised. If I got a limo she'd disco.

2

The world before Laura, part two

October 1979–April 1980

When I picked her up she looked hot, tall, maybe 5'11" in heels—almost my height—dressed country-sexy in a short cowgirl miniskirt, tight plaid western shirt with one more button open than one would expect, and a white cowboy hat. She was either wearing a padded push-up bra or had the same tits she had when she was seventeen. She had the clear super white skin that Neo-Nazis revere. She was every Jewish boy's dream.

We went to a dinner-dance club and ate an overpriced meal. She was bitchy and ill-humored. I asked her why she accepted the date. She said she'd been going out with older men for years and wanted to date someone around her own age. We discovered we didn't like any of the same books, movies, restaurants, food, vacation destinations, colors, flowers, trees, poets, toothpaste, comedians, TV shows, politicians, or music. She said maybe she should stick with older guys. I was pissed. I'd wasted all this money and wouldn't be getting laid.

Then a miracle! I asked for a dance. She said yes. The first moment we touched I got hard. I looked in her eyes and it was also happening to her. Bam!! Some cheeky angel was fucking with us. Right there next to the table not even a foot toward the dance floor we started groping each other's flesh. Her skin. Silk. Satin. Baby bottom. Butter lamb suede. Electric.

"Lay-its go back to ma place," she drawled.

We started in the limo. As for the tits question, she wasn't wearing a padded push-up bra. We finished in her apartment, exchanging a volley of compliments. She said: "I like that you have a hairy chest and not a hairy back."

I said: "I love your tits."

"I like being naked with a younger man."

"I love your ass."

"Your cock tastes like dessert."

"I love your tits."

"I really like the way you smell."

"I love your ass."

We stopped talking and made love for hours, that cheeky angel's gift to keep us from arguing and/or killing each other. I came three times. I think she beat me by double.

Next morning we started fighting immediately. It seemed whatever I did was wrong. I put the coffee mug in the wrong place. I left the toilet seat up. I used the wrong spoon.

Each date we would bicker for foreplay, have wordless blinding sex that we both considered the best of our lives, sleep like angels, greet the morning with a royal fuck, and then get up and fight. I'd ask her to turn down the country music; she made it louder. I'd buy flowers; they'd be "ugly and cheap." My patched hippie jeans were an embarrassment. She hated that I smoked "illegal" pot, but she defended her Dionysian consumption of alcohol, Valium and Percodan, even though she was a nurse.

Even our dogs fought. She had an expensive pedigreed Lhasa Apso male, scarred by being named Muffy. I had Necort, also a male. Necort (pronounced "knee court") was a forty-pound sweet apricot fluffy mutt who got along with everyone—humans, cats and other dogs—but had a low tolerance for hostility.

One day while Sherry was bitching at me, Muffy attacked Necort, biting and growling abusive insults about his mixed breeding. Necort was about three times as big as Muffy, and would have killed him right there, but I stopped him because I wasn't yet ready to give up the hottest sex of my life.

This polarity of fucking and fighting went on for months. Our attraction was a diabolical Darwinian prank. She never wanted to break up. She said she loved me and love was hard. This was a woman who listened to way too much country music. I stuck in there because Mr. Penis overruled Mr. Brain. We spent New Year's Eve 1980 together, but my half-filled champagne glass was half empty.

The Greater National Ugly Mood amplified my homegrown funkitude. Americans were hostages in Iran and we all felt a bit like a bully was beating us up and stealing our lunch money every day in the schoolyard. The Soviets had just invaded Afghanistan. In February, Congress was rocked by Abscam, the FBI bribe sting that confirmed that my worst cynical fears about government weren't cynical. Then it got worse.

In early April 1980 one of my best friends, Malcolm Braly, writer, screenwriter, noted ex-convict and the world's funniest giant leprechaun, died in an alcohol-fueled automobile accident. I went to Baltimore for his funeral and cried for three days. I didn't know a person could cry that much.

Later that sad month I watched the news on TV of the failed Iranian rescue mission and felt embarrassed, humiliated and sick in my stomach.

3
Enter Laura stage left

Late April 1980

It was a Friday morning in late April. Sherry and I had rotted to more venom than heat and on that particular morning we did not have sex. Sherry went off to work her shift. I took both dogs out for a walk. Muffy, having read Necort's riot act, didn't cross the line again, and our dogs were getting along better than their owners. The sun was shining, and it was one of those rare, clear, pollution-free days in Manhattan when you could actually smell the salt from the ocean.

I'd recently stepped down as creative director of *Puritan*, the nation's first—and for years the only—porn periodical with literary aspirations. We published Norman Mailer, Tennessee Williams and Hunter S. Thompson cheek-by-jowl with full frontal photos of people fucking. "Art you can jerk off to" was how I described it.

I was once again a freelance art director, copywriter and journalist. In addition to regular clients, my penis still led me to do projects in the porn business.

The best thing about the porn biz was that they paid C.O.D. By noon I was walking out of a porn mag publisher's office with two grand in my pocket for some magazine work and for designing a label for a famous brand of butyl nitrate, a popular recreational legal drug at the time. The second-best thing about the porn biz was that once in a while I got to fuck a porn model.

Here's the deal on fucking porn models and porn actresses. They are the core of the very few women who wake up in the morning and say, "Today I am going to look fabulous, smell wonderful and be the best fuck I can be." Some of these women are in it for fame, some for the money and some, my personal favorites, are driven by pathological lust.

If you eliminate the many porn babes who are not promiscuous off the set because they are married, they just aren't sex-driven, or they only fuck guys for the money, what's left is our control group. Now, if you're a guy who is better looking, more charismatic and/or wealthier than me, and we both meet twenty of these most eligible hotties with willing vaginas, you might get to fuck five of them whereas I might only get to fuck three. I got to meet 100 of them, however, and you probably never met any.

I had sex with a dozen second-and third-billing porn actresses and a few porn stars. Serena, Samantha and Gloria Leonard pop into my mind. Serena, my first, in 1976, was a big star at the time and at our first meeting, to my utter amazement, she seduced me.

Samantha was a hot quickie in the empty *Puritan* office on the afternoon of the night in February 1978 when Ali lost to Spinks. She came by to pick up some copies of pictures from a shoot she did for us, and we did it right there in the art department. Afterward when I suggested we get together again she said, "No, but thank you. I have a boyfriend and our deal is I can only fuck a guy once. And you just had yours."

Gloria Leonard was the most notable because I never felt anyone have orgasms as intense as hers. At first I thought she was faking but then I thought, no, she's too smart and too good an actress to think she could get away with this much overacting.

And she wasn't acting. Her body shuddered and her eyes rolled like she was shocked with electricity except it was all pleasure and no pain. I'd like to think it had something to do with me and it probably did but only a very little. This woman was just wired like this, which is probably why such a bright Jewish girl would become a porn star in the first place. Her climax was so big it made me jealous. In my head I was whining, "I want one, too."

I'd always fancied her and one night leaving a reception for some porn thing, we smiled at each other at the same time and soon were in her bed. She liked me enough to invite me back a few times. She kept having these 20-megaton nuclear blasts, and I got over being jealous and was just happy to be there having my own using conventional explosives.

I'd been monogamous with Sherry since we met, but as I walked past 54th and Madison, the home of Eureka!, my favorite whorehouse in New York, my penis tapped me on the shoulder and suggested I go upstairs and have a peaceful, relaxing massage and fuck someone I didn't hate.

Eureka was on a high floor in a tall modern chrome and glass building. I got off the elevator and walked through a door marked "Executive Offices" and into a bland reception area with modern art on the walls, cushy leather sofas, a coffee table covered with finance and sports magazines, and a few high-backed expensive men's club chairs studded with brass tacks. It could have been any other business in New York City that rented space and secretaries by the hour, day, week or month, with lots of different men coming and going. The girls were instructed to dress modestly, preferably in business clothes, until they got there and changed into their slutwear.

Liz, the madam, sitting behind an antique desk, welcomed me warmly. "Well, hello, Jeffrey, it's been a long time. And have we got a treat for you. A new girl—Laura—and we know you're going to love her. Jeffrey…trust me…you must meet Laura. She's an artist, you know, a bit crazy. Like you!"

Liz was an attractive, late-thirties Polish blue-eyed blonde who passed herself off as late twenties and Swedish. She always spoke in the first person plural; the practice Mark Twain said should be limited to editors, royalty and people with tapeworms.

Two years before, the first time I walked into her establishment, I found her struggling to design her Yellow Pages ad, business cards and matches. I offered my help and performed my skills right there in front of her. I wrote copy she loved, designed a logo and added the exclamation point. She was so impressed she gave me a girl for two hours for free (whom I tipped), and even invited me out to dinner. We had a short affair (we both wanted control in bed), but remained on good terms. I remained a good customer.

I introduced lots of men to Eureka and steered some suitable working girls toward Liz, for which she would give me an occasional freebie. This was 1980. Pre-AIDS. Pre-herpes. Today if you hire a whore—and I haven't in about three decades—I'm told it's no kissing and mandatory rubbers. No kissing? Rubbers? That's like being hungry and eating vitamin-enriched cardboard with protein powder and soybean oil, and calling it dinner.

No, this was a different era. It was kissing and hugging and oral and anal and skin-to-skin and it was just like having sex with your girlfriend or wife except without the aggravation. The girl's enthusiasm level was high, she always acted horny and she appeared to care about you. That's the package you get from a real professional.

I was led into one of a dozen stark, clean, small rooms, each with a double bed resting on a low platform and a large mirror and an innocuous landscape print on the wall. I sat down on a cheap Danish Modern wooden chair. The bed was made with clean sheets, two pillows and one light blanket. Eureka was always spotless, with a Eucalyptus aroma that gave me the feeling that in the event of an emergency it would be a safe place to have open-heart surgery.

A parade of girls in lingerie began. Each smiled seductively, told me her name and promised with her body language to give me a good time. The ambitious ones came over and touched my arm or cheek. As usual, it was an unusually attractive and diverse group. Diversity is basic whorehouse marketing. Not every man wants a tall thin young blonde with big tits. Some prefer little brunette spinners, some want mature, some want Hispanic or black or Asian or punk or biker or redheads or small-breasted librarians with glasses. Not every whorehouse covers every base, but they try.

New girls are necessary no matter what their look, so in addition to franchise players, there are lots of free agents. Some guys love going back to the same girl every time. They like the relaxation and security, but many guys are always looking for someone new.

You see everyone and choose the one you want. It's a very powerful feeling and one of the reasons there have always been whorehouses. I bet there was a cave in France with drawings of horses on the wall where you could choose between Cro-Magnon and Neanderthal.

The Pussy Parade featured a few girls I had been with before: the lovely light mocha Thai girl who always smelled of coconut oil and loved to kiss and could squeeze your dick with her vagina so hard you almost couldn't pull it out. She timed her squeezes to your climax. She was a favorite of mine.

Then there was the redhead with nearly transparent white skin, who always smiled, always had pot, used to work on the streets, and now had three kids who were taken care of every day by her househusband, who, with all due irony, had originally been her pimp. She was fun and loved being fucked really hard.

There was the tiny Chinese woman of indeterminate age who always cleaned your asshole with Lavoris and would then suck it; the fabulous-looking, elegant, middle-aged woman who specialized in first-timers, and the 6'1" black girl with slender hips and shaved pubes who always wore 6"-high heels, loved to do it doggie style, and wouldn't kiss.

Then a girl stumbles in. The day is young and already she's drunk or stoned or both. She's laughing like someone just told her the punch line to the week's best joke. She's holding on to the doorway to keep her balance. She has long, wavy, light brown hair, twinkling green/hazel eyes that look blue at some angles, luminous light olive skin, and enough cheekbones for three Cherokee Indians. She looks like Margo Kidder with Brooke Shields eyebrows.

She's wearing dime-store-tacky pink negligee and panties, with pink ribbons in her hair. Her breasts, medium with giant, disproportionate nipples, are falling out. Her makeup is minimal, just pink lipstick, quite unlike the other more painted ladies. Standing barefoot she must be about 5'8" if she could stand up straight. Her smile is infectious. She is not like any whore I ever met. I want her.

"My name is Laura. Liz said I had to meet you. Do you have any drugs?"

"No," I laugh.

"Well, Liz says you'll probably choose me, so I'll bring my own. Just please don't tell her." And Laura somehow does a pirouette and manages, almost gracefully, an exit. Her bum, although not a bubble, is fleshy enough to make my eyes happy.

I pay my $35 and choose Laura.

4

Falling in love in a whorehouse

Ten minutes later

Laura is undressing me in the huge bathroom down the hall. We're smoking her joint. She draws my bubble bath and I get in the oversized claw-foot tub. Instead of washing me from outside the bath, which is customary, she strips and climbs in. Her body is long and lean. Her nipples are big as organ stops, and her ass is round and childlike cute.

I lie back in the tub with her between my legs. All of a sudden her hands are under my bottom pushing me up so my dick is out of the water and in a flash her mouth is on it. This surprises me as the cock-in-mouth stage usually comes later in the session. She starts at the tip to squeegee the bubbles off, quickly making it hard with short sucking bursts.

My God! What a warm mouth.

Laura takes a break and asks, "Oh, what's your name?" It was right there that I felt the first lightning bolt of love. Here was a woman who sucks your dick first and asks your name second.

"I'm Jeffrey." We kiss and the same warmth that was on my dick is now on my mouth. Either this girl has a fever or her normal temperature is above 98.6.

We put on robes and scoot down the hall to the little room. We throw our robes off and flow onto the bed. We lie down next to each other completely naked. I am overwhelmed by the magnetic texture of her flesh. I can't believe that right after meeting Sherry, and encountering the best chemistry ever, I surpass it with the next woman I meet. My life must be going in the right direction.

Laura and I skip the massage that usually starts these sessions, kiss wet and deep and feel each other all over, as frenetic as if our lives depend on how much surface we can cover. From this fast-forward appetizer, we get into real time as I steer my cock inside her. Then everything gets slo-mo. Her pussy is even warmer than the rest of her! Through the biochemical fog of lust that part of me in charge of self-preservation stops to ask if, in fact, she does have a fever. She chortles and speaks broken English as if it's her second language, "No fever, please kiss more."

She smells great! Not perfume great but girl great. Her aroma and flavor jolt my emotions. The taste of her kiss tells me her pussy will be delicious. I know she is a whore, but I have to taste her. I am selective eating pussy even outside of whorehouses, but this I must sample. I pull out, instruct her to just lie there, and dive between her legs. My tongue and lips are delighted. It's dessert! Her natural lubrication is thick and it's sweet. I could put it on strawberries and serve it to my mother.

I turn around and get back on top, squeeze my cock in, and look down at her. I'm on my elbows. I hold her head in my hands and arch up to keep my weight off her. I slide in and almost out, not straight like a piston but in wide looping orbits like a connecting rod to a camshaft. Laura turns her head to the side, kissing and sucking whatever part of my arms and hands she can reach, moaning and grunting.

I take my hands from her head and restrain her wrists. She whimpers and submits. I never felt more desirous of controlling another woman.

She says, "No one ever fucked me like this. I want it in my life."

She is long-limbed. Her legs are not shaved and I don't mind. The hair is fine and sparse, feels nice and doesn't tickle.

We move, two tango dancers.

The fuck gets fast.

Harder.

Tighter orbits.

Pheromones rage.

Hormones rule.

I am a stallion.

The part of me that decides when to have an orgasm says, "Now." I start to come. Orgasm feels different from the first blush. Jumbo. Super jumbo. Every increment grips. It builds. Builds. BUILDS. Halfway there. Most intense ever. We are wired together though our eyes and the fuck. Breathing in synch. Gasping harmony. Her eyes so big. She starts to come.

Poetry and fireworks.

No one blinks.

I can't hold it.

She/I erupt.

She screams.

I bellow.

We are a duet of pleasure noises from before our species walked upright.

I forget what I was thinking about. My head is empty.

* * *

If there is a God, it feels like this.

* * *

We don't move.

We still don't move.

We are silent.

My cock surprises me by staying so hard it could cut diamonds. However big my penis can possibly be, it is. I roll on my side and she moves with me. We face each other. I return from the fuck to earth with hunger for attachment. I know she is a whore, but I want her forever. I found The Holy Vagina Grail. My nose lobbies for me to marry her immediately.

This is the single best sex I ever had. Ever. More muscular. More pumping. Shakes me from the inside out.

My connection to Laura grows every moment. The warmth, the smile, all the stuff you hear about in top-40 pop songs. They wouldn't write about love at first sight if it didn't sometimes happen.

"You are wonderful," I say.

"You are wonderful," she says.

That's what this is: love. Not just great chemistry, like I have with Sherry but love, like on a Hallmark anniversary card, like in the last scene of a chic flick, the feeling deep inside me that makes me know if need be, I would die to save her.

I'd fucked many hookers in my life. Some encounters were terrific, mind-boggling, ultra-satisfying releases. I'd had many girlfriends. I'd been married and loved my wife. At orgies I'd fucked women I hadn't even been introduced to, some whose names I never learned, some whose faces I never saw. I was thirty-four years old and I knew which end was up.

I knew what it was like to fuck on acid, mescaline, peyote, mushrooms, grass, coke, Quaaludes, poppers and most of the chemical enhancements known to man. Or even Hunter Thompson. I'd used opiates and speed, which give you a lovely bone but make it nearly impossible to climax. This was different from all of that, and all I'd had were a few tokes.

I'm lying there with Laura stroking my short beard, kissing my cheek, touching my brow, moving on my chrome molly cock. "Fuck me again from behind, please," she requests. I stay inside her as we articulate into doggie style. I'm on my knees and hold her hips. She fucks in half time. I stop moving and watch her slow rhythm. My vision widens and again I see where I am. I'm finding romance in a sex marketplace.

She charms the next orgasm out of me. We come together again, both too loud. We freeze, a snapshot of dogs fucking. A minute later a knock on the door means my time is up. We crumble into a double spoon cuddle, my dick finally softening. I stare at the back of her long aristocratic neck. What the fuck is this wonderful creature doing in a whorehouse? Is she like this with every man? Am I special? Is all that I feel one-sided?

* * *

A month before he died, Norman Mailer suggested I ask Laura, whom he knew, to add her side of the story. She agreed, read the manuscript, and revealed her thoughts in a series of interviews with Legs McNeil.

"How did I get to the whorehouse?" Laura laughs and begins to explain. "Well, it's kind of a long story. You see, my first husband, Sandy, and I had a very open relationship, and actually, I didn't really have much sex with him. Sandy had a really giant cock. It was uncomfortable. He was so obsessed with his cock it was disturbing, so I didn't even want to suck him off. So, no, we didn't have much sex for the first five years.

"Then he started having sex with other women. And then I started having a lot of sex with people. That was kind of my *modus operandi*. That's what I would do—I would go into a club and find the most attractive guy or whoever got me hot at the time, and say, 'Let's go fuck.'

"So I was picking up guys—a lot—and being very wild and promiscuous.

"Then Sandy and I went to California," Laura continues, "and on the way we stopped in Reno, Nevada, and he gambled away every single penny we had. Every single penny! I was stoned and goofing around and having a good time and came back and discovered that Sandy had a gambling addiction. I don't even know if he knew he had one. Sandy used up our entire credit card and the only thing we had was the van—and the gas in it. And that was it.

"Sandy had gambled away $10,000 in like two hours playing blackjack so now we are $10,000 in debt. At that time in my life being $10,000 in debt was gigantic. I couldn't even imagine it.

"We made it to California and our friends gave us enough money to get back home.

"So then I said, 'Okay, how are we going to get out of debt?'

"Sandy said, 'Well, you're *fucking* guys all the time anyway, why don't you go work in a whorehouse?'

"I thought that being a whore held a certain nobility," Laura acknowledges, "and I thought I just had to pay back that $10,000. I knew Sandy could never pay it back, so that was my goal.

"So Sandy set up an appointment for me at a whorehouse in New York City that he went to all the time—I found out later—and he took me there and dropped me off. They were waiting for me, they liked the way I looked and gave me a job right away.

"I mean, I was already having great sex with lots of guys. The idea of charging for sex seemed completely absurd, and when I was in the whorehouse, most of the men, I made them make me have an orgasm, ha, ha, ha.

"I was like, 'Wait, wait, I'm not done. Let's keep going....'"

Most hookers don't have orgasms with their clients. Some occasionally do. I've spoken to many hookers and the truth is that most get as emotionally involved in the fuck as a mechanic does driving home lug nuts with his Snap-On pneumatic impact wrench. It's just a job, man.

Many fake it, and if they're good whores, the kind that care about their industry's reputation for quality and service, they fake it with every client because that's what most guys' egos need. It's part of the show.

It's hard to tell the real from the fake. The CIA, Mossad and the KGB, with all their resources and black-ops, working for decades in conjunction with the finest doctors in the world, some of them ex-Nazis who were working on the problem for Hitler, have been unsuccessful in ferreting out a litmus test for fake orgasms, so don't feel bad if you can't tell.

There are some, like Laura's—so blinding, so huge, so spastic— they must be authentic. I know her orgasm is real.

The knock again, this time louder. I hold her tight so she can't move. The stronger I hold her the less resistance she offers. Until she turns her head toward me and says, "I'm sorry I have to leave. I have a regular waiting for me."

I watch Laura put on her pink negligee and fix the ribbons in her hair. "I'll be right back," she says, "Let me get him settled."

I stand at the door with it cracked open and hear her down the hall say, "Hello Rob" to her waiting customer. I am wounded. Then it all comes into perspective. I just had this blinding sexual and emotional experience with a hooker but the bottom line is that she's a hooker and it is her job to give me a blinding sexual experience so I must leave my emotions in the room and go back to my life.

I get dressed. She returns and I give her a $50 tip, twice what's expected and say thanks. She doesn't look at the money, kisses my cheek, then slowly and tenderly my lips, and then she disappears.

I procrastinate. I don't want to leave our scent. I can still taste her, sweet with an accent of umami. I'd never tasted a sweet *and* umami pussy before. Umami means savory. It's the full-flavor taste we get from things like Parmesan cheese, mushrooms and red wine. It's the fifth basic taste, added by the Japanese about fifty years ago to the other four: sweet, sour, salty and bitter. It's said the reason Coca Cola and ketchup are universally loved is that they contain all five flavors.

I like women who taste sweet. Some are salty, which I don't prefer, and some are sour or bitter, which I don't like. There are variations in receptors and preferences. A woman I taste as sweet might be bitter to another man. Or maybe he likes one I taste as bitter.

Laura has the bottom note I love in patchouli or "Opium" perfume. She's flowers with gravitas. She has meaning. She's important.

"I loved sex and was willing to fuck every man that chose me," Laura remembers about when she first met Jeffrey. "But sometimes I'd get numb by a stream of men coming to the whorehouse pretending to be men. They had hard cocks and flaccid attitudes. No matter how old they were, some seemed like self-conscious boys with an adolescent desperation to find a moment of stolen ecstasy.

"Some of the men who frequented the whorehouse were really attractive. Some weren't. A few were gorgeous. Some were assholes, some were sweethearts. Lots of guys were just horny guys who had wives who weren't giving them what they needed. Some guys just need extra sex. Some had quirky kinks they couldn't do with their wives or girlfriends. Some guys just couldn't find women to fuck them and so they paid us. Some were away on business and needed to get rid of their stress. Some who came in were neurotic, or desperate or something. Some of the guys who came in were damaged goods in some way. There was some of everything. It was like Russian sexual roulette. You never knew who would choose you.

"Then Jeffrey came in," Laura recalls. "He had an open smile and didn't wear a mask. He was a real man. He was different. He was totally at ease. We had sex right away.

"When I met Jeffrey I had just realized what I wanted my life to be: I wanted to experience ultimate pleasure and joy, that really the whole pursuit in life—the ultimate focus and movement in life—was about joy and bliss. So I went directly from understanding this to meeting Jeffrey.

"Jeffrey was a great fuck," Laura continues, "Oh God could Jeffrey satisfy me! Yes! OH YES! I felt this man's passion from both his hands—fucking him was as much as anyone could ask from sex! I didn't want to loose a single drop of this initial attraction. I am a junky for passion and this man was an opportunity I didn't want to miss."

That afternoon as Sherry and I and our dogs drove to my cabin in the country for the weekend, I knew I had to break up with her.

That night I went through the motions with less energy than usual. I couldn't get Laura out of my mind. I kept thinking, "She's a whore, I can't get involved." But I was.

Sherry knew something was up. She asked why I was so quiet. I told her I was tired. Instead of her nagging, bitchy selfishness, she was deferential. I didn't know how to end it with her but I knew one thing: with hostile bitches you have to get them to leave you.

If you leave them, they'll machine gun your life, fuck your reputation, annoy your friends, steal, break things, call you in the middle of the night, and cause endless trouble. They'll turn you in to the I.R.S.

But if you can manipulate them to leave you—you're safe. Their ego will be intact. They won't have rejection to fuel their anger. They'll feel sorry for you. They'll be comfortable with you being the victim. They'll feel they won. They won't call the I.R.S.

All next week in New York City I did whatever Sherry wanted. We listened to her country music every day. I let each snide remark pass unchallenged. I swallowed my words when she served my medium rare steak well done. Whatever ridiculous thing she was offended by I apologized for. Deprived of the combat she so dearly needed she focused on my lack of financial ambition and said, "Jeffrey, this isn't working anymore. You're too comfortable with too little. I think I need some space." I needed a sharper resolution so I begged her not to leave me. I continued being obsequious. The next day she threw me and Necort out.

5

My heart gets flushed down the toilet of love

Early May 1980

Now that I wasn't with Sherry anymore I needed a place to live in New York. I hated commuting two hours each way from my cabin.

A country neighbor and friend, Susan came over to stay with Necort while I looked for a place. He adored her and I'd come home to a clean cabin, a happy dog and lots of delicious food waiting for me. And if either one of us needed sex, neither of us was shy about asking.

I had about $850 a month to spend and in the spring of 1980 that still got you a decent place, but there were not many vacancies and I was not having any luck.

Three weeks to the day after I met Laura, with every day a losing battle to not think about her, I was in a cab late one morning on the way to check out an apartment when we passed 54th and Madison. I told the cabby to stop. I had to see her.

I enter Eureka and ask if Laura is in. Liz is off but Theresa, her assistant, says Laura just went into a session and won't be available for fifty minutes. She asks if I would like to see another girl. I tell Theresa that I only want to see Laura and only want to talk to her a minute or two. I ask if it's OK to wait. Theresa smiles, "Sure, go in room five and I'll send her in as soon as she's out."

I wait. Not scared, not frustrated. Empty of anxiety. There is nothing else I can do. I am as emotional, hot, driven as I have ever been, close to exploding, so I dig down deep into my pool of cool. If there ever is a moment outside of the boxing ring to overrule my emotions, this is it. I don't want to come off as a needy jerk or a desperate lunatic. I find the still place and jump in. I am Billy Jack, Hud and The Outlaw Josey Wales. I feel thinner. I stare in the mirror and instead of the chump I sometimes see, I see a face full of character.

Forty minutes later, Laura rushes in wearing only a towel. She is stoned. There is just a trace of lipstick left. "I heard you were here. I've got to finish up. I'll be right back. Don't go anywhere!" She rushes out.

She looks beautiful, wild. She smells like fucking. I'm so excited, I'm no longer cool. Josey Wales and Billy Jack desert me.

After what seems like a week, she's back. Again her pheromones call to me. She smiles with her eyes and her mouth. I keep myself from ripping off her towel.

"I can't stop thinking of you," I blurt.

"I can't stop thinking about you," she answers, answering my prayers.

"I've got to see you soon," I say as we fondle each other's arms.

She stuns me with, "I need you to fuck me right now."

"I don't have enough money." I only had about $30 on me. I'd planned to go to my bank just before I checked out the apartment.

"I've got money. I'll pay," she says, blowing me away with her urgency.

She runs out and sixty seconds later she rushes back. "I took my last two tips and gave $35 of it to Theresa for your session. I'm glad you came back. I think about you every day."

She rattles off, "I love the way you hold my head when you fuck me. I have to have more of that in my life. I need you to fuck me. Fuck me, please."

Her body is wet from the last fuck and her pussy is lubricated with another man's come and I love it all. We are groping animals acting out preordained genetic code. First me on top, then intoxicating, wet, together, slippery sixty-nine; I taste her previous client. I don't care. Next, pounding doggie style, then elegant missionary with her long legs wrapped around me. We change positions frequently, flipping through the *Kama Sutra*.

Now standing up on the floor, with her bent over holding her ankles.

Now her legs spread and her hands up against the wall in cop/ frisk position.

Back in bed, her on top facing me. Laura is not on her knees but on the soles of her feet, touching me only where the fuck meets, slow milking, sucking me with her pussy.

Now she leans over with her hands on my shoulders so we can kiss. Then rolling over in perfect unison with me on top responding to her barely audible, "harder," belting into her, jet-propelled bursts, an offensive guard lunging at the snap, harder and harder until we're crunched up against the headboard and I'm holding her head in my hands, her back curving slightly, and we come in the shuddering frenzy of divine spasm.

Even now, nearly thirty years later, I can still feel my shooting— creamy soft blasts in her belly again and again and again, giant throbs convulsing inside me so many times I fear I might run out of jism and pump blood.

My spasms stop. My dick slithers out and I fall to the bed. We lie there staring into each other's eyes. No one moves. Then with a knock at the door—reality seeps in through the cracks. My vision expands beyond Laura to include the rest of the world. "I'll be back," she purrs.

Five minutes later Laura walks back into the room with determination. Something is wrong. "How much of a tip are you going to owe me?" She demands. "When are you going to pay me back for the session and drop off my tip?"

"What? What?" You could drive a nail into my skull and I wouldn't blink. "What are you talking about?" I bumble.

She softly repeats her demands—an accounts receivable manager coolly dunning an overdue bill from a good customer.

"I'll, um, repay you this afternoon and drop off your tip." I get dressed feeling ashamed of my nakedness. I avoid her eyes and split.

I walk the streets punch drunk. The quizzical mantra of "What?" is the sole noise in my head. Then, finally, "What the fuck is going on? How could I travel through ecstasy to the toilet?"

I felt betrayal, not only by Laura but also by my own self-defenses. How could I have misread her? Was she a conniving hustler the whole time? Was I just another trick? I was so out of balance that if I'd broken out with pimples, boils and festering sores right there on the street it wouldn't have been a surprise.

Later that afternoon I went back with $85 in an envelope and dropped it off at the receptionist's desk. I didn't ask to see Laura.

6

Shake it off.
Get back in the game.

Twenty minutes later to three weeks later

I got my car and drove back to my cabin. Sometimes Susan left when I returned and sometimes she stayed. I called and asked her to stay because I did not want to be alone. I got home and I cried in her arms. It was one of the very few times in my life I couldn't get it up to fuck. She made me herb tea, I took a couple sleeping pills and she rubbed me to sleep. I never heard her leave.

The next morning I recovered enough to want to know what the story was. I called Eureka three times until I got Laura. I had no pride.

"What's going on? You tell me you miss me and you need me to fuck you right away and you'll pay for it and then you leave and come back in the room like I'm a regular john. I don't get it."

"Look," she said, "I have a husband and a mortgage and a huge debt to pay back. As long as I'm in debt my focus is to get out of it and I can't just go off and have a good time. If we're together again I'm sure it will be magical but I need to get money."

"Well, I'm sorry you feel that way. I thought something else was going on. I must have misled myself. If you change your mind you can reach me through Response answering service. They're listed and you know my name." I said goodbye and hung up.

I felt stupid. I fell for a whore. What an asshole. I told my friends the story, making it funnier each time, purging Laura from my guts with each telling. Self-denigration is the soul of Jewish humor. In a week and a half the incident was dim headlights in my rear view mirror.

> "I'm an excitement junky," Laura explains, "I love extreme orgasms. I love orgasms that never stop. I love being adored beyond limits. I love taking everything to its limits. I couldn't pass up this experience with Jeffrey—but I had huge financial troubles and I still had to pay back Sandy's ten thousand dollar gambling debt. I don't think Jeffrey understood..."

I went about my life. I had fun with Susan and Necort. I got my sex drive back. I hung out with my buddy and long-time occasional fuck, Erika, a foxy, six-foot tall self-styled "Cum Junkie" whose Friday night hobby was to gang-suck entire barrooms of men. I'd watch her get drunk, sit in a men's room stall and give a rousing suck-off to a quickly moving line of maybe a dozen or more guys. Sometimes she'd get a little too drunk, and I'd walk her home and hold her over her toilet as she vomited a most unique collection of sperm and imported and domestic beers. Knowing what she was about to do in the evening, I'd have sex with her before we left for the bar. Even I had some limits.

Until I could find my own place in New York, I made a deal with a client to pay part of his rent on a slickly furnished expensive flat. Lots of light woods and glass, lots of mirrors, good for both business and for impressing New York pussy. The only problem was it was a no-pets building so I couldn't take Necort.

A few days later I started having an affair with Becky, an extremely attractive, WASP stock analyst I meet in the elevator. (My rent money was already paying off!) She was a Virginia Tidewater Aristocrat, one of the kinky, trust fund, Protestant old-money rich.

Becky was very tall, nearly as tall as me, and a lot taller than me when she wore high heels, which I encouraged. Some men hate being with taller women. At just under six feet and comfortable with my height, I love when the woman I'm with towers over me. It says, "I'm the guy who caught the big fish."

She was also slim, a Wharton grad, a middle-level manager at a very big brokerage company, a lady "suit" and my first real adult, with a hairdo, golf clubs, money market fund, a condo in Florida, a refined appreciation of art and theater, a closet full of Perry Ellis and Albert Nippon, a Mercedes, nouvelle-French cooking skills, and to top it off, as many handcuffs as the Sixth Precinct.

She loved smoking pot, being handcuffed to her huge four-poster bed and being fucked while struggling against her bonds. I got the feeling she was consciously slumming with me, which made it sexier for both of us. I was Stanley from *Streetcar*.

She liked it when I talked like a street punk and acted tough. Sadly, she was also one of those people born without a sense of humor. Worse than not being funny herself, she didn't get my jokes.

But Becky did have compensations: skin that felt the way expensive wine tastes, a pussy so delicious that it must have taken several generations of refinement to breed, and long, long legs. What a fuckin' set of wheels!

And could she ever suck dick! She was the girl who literalized the proverbial remark about orally removing the chrome from a '55 Buick Roadmaster. I made myself think of that every time one of my witty bon mots went flat.

She also did something that I have only heard of once before and that was in the movie Deep Throat. She came when she sucked cock. I don't mean small mini-swells of pleasure; I mean thrashing, screaming, major-league, exploding climaxes. Quite impressive.

The second time I visited her I tried fucking her ass but it she would have none of that. Until she said, "If you want that you'll have to take it!" I understood. She wanted fake rape. Not at all my trip, but I'd known other women who loved anal sex but considered it a perversion and needed to be pushed over some psychic wall in order to allay their guilt.

I handcuffed her wrists and ankles to her four-poster and Vaselined the entrance. I readied the target by working in one, then two, then three fingers. I was gentle enough not to hurt her and hard enough for her to feel she was being forced. I slid in slow. Then faster. Then jack hammer. I came in her and she came again and again.

Then she begged to clean off my dick with her mouth, a request that separated the moderately kinky from the truly perverted. She relished the humiliation and moaned drunkenly as she did the deed. "Got to lick my shit off the dirty Jew's dick," she chanted like a hammer-swinging member of a chain gang. It was the only pleasant anti-Semitic experience of my life.

7

Anal sex

Anal sex in all its forms is either the most disgusting thing you can imagine, and the anus is a place used only for elimination and to be avoided for all and any other purposes—or anal sex has a rightful place in the realm of pleasure, is way out there erotically and is a source of prodigious hedonistic euphoria.

I'm in the prodigious hedonistic euphoria club.

Some people, male or female, like the anus touched gently, some like it rough, some not at all. Some like it entered, some like to enter. Some like to lick or suck and some like to be licked and/or sucked. Just choosing one activity doesn't mean you can't play another.

On purpose I skipped a lot of anal antics, the ones with just men, all of them that have to do with cucumbers, zucchinis, fists, and anything with batteries or any that can only be done with a forklift.

Like oral sex, anal sex is pure sex, total recreational sex. The only thing it has to do with procreation is avoiding it. Many heterosexuals go through their entire lives without doing it or wanting it or thinking about it, and that's perfectly all right. For them.

Sodomy is a biblically proscribed act. It's still illegal—even for husbands and wives—in a dozen states. (Is there a marketing opportunity selling packaged tours to those states to married couples for the purpose of turning their sex into criminal activity they get away with?)

Anal sex is fundamental because, at the risk of committing a tautology, it's the fundament. (Fundament means "the anus," as well as "the founding principle," "the foundation.") It's raw, lascivious, carnal, licentious, lewd, coarse, profane, bawdy, provocative, and wanton.

For health reasons I suggest you wash thoroughly, use mouthwash or vodka as an antiseptic, go slow in whatever direction you are heading into or is heading into you and avoid anything that smells bad and is obvious hygienic suicide.

Anal sex is as much about power as it is about sex. All the aphorisms about it show a demarcation of supremacy: "kiss my ass," "he's an assfuck," "he's an asshole," "bugger you" (and all its buggerful variations), "I'm not going to bend over and take it up the ass," "brownnose," "eat shit," and "don't drop the soap."

The act physically necessitates submission on the part of the female or male bottom. The bottom has to let go and relax, open up and be taken. It's a power tool trip—and—here's the closing pitch for you boys—it is very tight, usually much tighter than a pussy and it feels—if not better than a pussy—then at least different enough to deserve its own brand name. It's a whole other place to explore when you want to go someplace else on the weekend.

Many women don't like it—that's a fact. On the other hand, most horny sluts come pre-packaged with anal "interest" bundled on their hard drives, and I have always been attracted to horny sluts.

A few select female gems actually prefer it. They are not only diamonds; they are D-color internally flawless. I have only met a few in my life. The one I remember most, Rochelle, would hustle me through all the preliminaries to get me to her back door as soon as possible. She was a California Jewish Princess, which is either ironic or obvious and I don't know which.

As far as rimming, licking and sucking assholes: Where else can you go farther if you want to give or get adoration? In the world of wild sex a prude is anyone who never sucked an asshole because that's the dividing line between aficionado and the truly committed.

Most really slutty females that go crazy on you in bed like to lick your ass. Almost all of them. Like they can't do enough. They suck your cock, they lick your balls, they make grunting noises and speed things up and lick and touch and kiss everywhere but especially your asshole. It's the center that the whole thing rotates around.

It's great as horny foreplay, treading transitions between orgasms, or after fucking as mellow down time.

The most amazing data point about assholes comes from an ex-girlfriend of mine who was Korean. She was taught by her mother that cleaning and then sucking a man's asshole was the key to having power over him in a society where women had no power. And also by letting him fuck you in the ass or better yet by begging him to fuck you in the ass. I really don't know whether it was just my girlfriend's mother or a Korean cultural norm, but I liked that she taught her daughter that anal sex was how to control a man.

After three trips back to Korea and several thousand hours of negotiating with her father and mother she went back to marry some guy her family wanted her to marry to bring their families closer together. She knew the guy and thought he was sexy and didn't mind the arrangement. She's probably sucking his asshole as you're reading this.

A mellow version of anal sex, suited to all ages but fitting in well with senior citizens, is anal massage, preferably while watching a football game but any favorite TV program will do. Have your lover get a warm wet towel and wash your face and hands and package and crack, and then oil your junk and butthole. Weed enhances this by a factor of ten and falling asleep for short naps and waking up to this has a kinship with the euphoric rush of opiates.

Anal sex is a staple of porn films and usually comes at the end just before the cum shot. It's penultimate—the dirtiest part of a dirty movie before the climax. I always thought there should be T-shirts for men who really like it that say: "I Fast Forward To The Anal."

8

The return of Laura

A Friday afternoon in June 1980

Exactly three weeks after our last meeting, Laura calls my service and leaves a message asking me to please get in touch with her.

I call back and catch her on her way into a session. She is near to crying. "I can't stop thinking about you. I'm sorry about what happened. I need you. Can you please come by after work and meet me?"

"You bet!"

"Can I spend the weekend with you?"

"Yes," I tell her, "but you buy dinner."

"You're on."

Of all the whorehouses in all the towns in all the world, I walked into hers.

9

Emblematic mojos rising

My mojo was working again! The shock of winning, then losing Laura had knocked me down. Now this extra-innings, sudden-death, come-from-behind score refurbished my pride.

In addition to the normal ups and downs of life, I've been the beneficiary of flukes. When I was nineteen, I worked as a pool boy at Sydney Hills Country Club in Newton, Massachusetts. It was the summer of 1966 and most of what was great was English. Nearly all the music I listened to was English except for Elvis, Bobby Vee, Chuck Berry, the Beach Boys, The Beau Brummels, and Gene Pitney. The clothes I wanted were English and the women I wanted were English. I had to get to England. I decided not to go back to the University of Bridgeport for my junior year but to move to London instead.

I worked every day that summer and saved every cent. I bought a round-trip ticket to London and had enough money left over to live there frugally for a year. (This was $1,250, or about £10 or $25 a week—all you needed in those days.).

I packed up my camp trunk, a large duffel bag, plus a large and small suitcase with clothes, books, and my favorite blanket, even my favorite pillow. I said goodbye to my family and girlfriend and boarded the plane one late September night in 1966 at 10:10 p.m.

I was too excited to sleep all night and landed at Heathrow the next morning. I wrestled through customs with my abundance of baggage, cashed about $100 into English pounds and found the London bus. It dropped me off at Victoria Station, where I checked all my stuff in Left Luggage except one small suitcase with a few days' clothes. I was sweaty and beat.

Then I stood in a long line to get a cab. When my cabby pulled up he asked, "Where to Guv'nor?" Only at that moment did it occur to me that I had no idea where I was going.

I left the line and sat on my small suitcase next to the cab queue and thought about his question. Where the fuck was I going? I had no plans. I guess I operated on a need-to-know basis with myself. I was totally astounded at my short-sightedness. I put all that drive and effort into getting to London but I never gave a second thought to what I would do once I got here.

It was a wake-up call. For the first time in my life, I suspected I just might be missing a few socks in my dryer. From then on, I knew I had to pay better attention to what I was doing.

As it happened, everything worked out fine. The only places I knew of were Carnaby Street and Piccadilly Circus so I took a cab to Piccadilly and by the end of the day, I met some English students who put me up, and by the next night I was in their neighbor Emma's bed. Within a month I had a Triumph motorcycle, a circle of chums, a grant to study journalism at the Regent St. Polytechnic, and a smart, foxy, aristocratic girlfriend, Tisha.

As a coda to this fluke, Tisha and I came back to the U.S. and spent the Summer of Love 1967 working for Norman and Beverly Mailer in Provincetown, Massachusetts. I'd first met Norman the year before when I was a roadie for the rock band Charlie Brown's Generation, and Charlie, the lead singer, was Beverly's half-brother. When the band played in Provincetown for the summer, I briefly met Norman and Beverly, who had a house there. Norman might have said three words to me.

I took Tisha to Provincetown because in the summer, P-town is the most beautiful place on earth. We got jobs working in a souvenir shop, but Tisha hated it, so when I heard the Mailers were looking for a housekeeper, Tisha and I knocked on their door. Norman and Beverly liked Tisha, a proper aristocrat, and she went to work for them.

I used picking her up as an excuse to see Norman and one afternoon he invited me to his deck overlooking the ocean and made us gin and tonics. He told me he learned to make the perfect gin and tonic from his South African father. He put ice cubes in the glass, ran the lemon around the rim, squeezed in the lemon, added the gin, which came from the freezer, and then the tonic. He gave a short dissertation on the difference between good machines and bad machines and why electric can openers were bad machines because they sucked electricity, took a worthwhile physical exercise away and were not necessarily faster or more efficient.

One day Norman asked me if I would like to come to work for him, too. He had two young sons—Michael, three, and Stephen, about a year and a half—and a house filled with women: his wife, two daughters who were visiting for the summer, his secretary, a mother's helper or two, an occasional visiting ex-wife or two, and Tisha. He told me he wanted another man around to do heavy work and fix things when he was out of town but mostly so his sons had another male to relate to.

He suggested Tisha and I clear out the garage and turn it into a bedroom so we could move in. He'd also feed us and pay us $100 a week. He asked if I boxed. I didn't. Would I be interested in learning and becoming his sparring partner? You bet. We were a decent match boxing. I was twenty and he was forty-four. I was taller and he was broader. He was skilled and I was optimistic.

So I spent the Summer of Love living with my English girlfriend in Norman Mailer's garage, fixing things, shopping for food, (sometimes cinematically by boat across the Provincetown harbor) chauffeuring him and guests to the airport either in his Corvette or Beverly's larger Citroen, listening to "Light My Fire" and "Lucy in the Sky with Diamonds," smoking pot (never with or in front of the Mailers), and putting on the gloves in the afternoon and getting the chance to punch my boss in the face.

That fall, Tisha and I got our own place in Manhattan, got real jobs and got married. Three years later by the summer of 1970, a year after men walked on the moon, I was twenty-three. Gas was $.36 a gallon, the average income was under $10,000, a new home cost $23,000, Jimi Hendrix and Janis Joplin died, Tina Fey and Kelly Ripa were born, and after a horrible third year of marriage my smart, foxy, aristocratic wife Tisha left me and went back home to England.

I was working as a journalist in the alternative underground poorly paid press. With Tisha and her paycheck gone, I took a job selling ads in the underground papers with a company owned by Concert Hall Advertising, the hippie ad agency. Ad salesmen made more money than alternative journalists and I was tired of being poor.

One day I was at Apple Records, the Beatles' company, trying to sell them ads. The Beatles had split up and all were doing solo projects, and Apple had signed Mary Hopkins, James Taylor, and Badfinger and was making a run at being an actual record company.

Allan Steckler, the creative director I was pitching asked, "Do you know any good advertising agencies? We just fired ours this morning." I mentioned that the company that owned the ad sales company I worked for was Concert Hall. He smiled, took a long pause and said, "Okay, Concert Hall is now the agency for Apple Records." Overnight, I became the account executive for our new client, Apple Records. "I am the eggman/they are the eggmen/I work for Apple/Goo goo ga joob."

After months of placing ads and begging for some creative work, I got my first assignment: the trade and consumer ads for the simultaneous release of John Lennon's "Imagine" album and Yoko Ono's "Fly." While waiting for the art directors at my ad agency to work with me, I sat there doodling silly project-related stuff. I couldn't draw, paint, or design, and at that moment if you had asked me what kind of artistic ability I had, I'd have said about seven on a scale of a hundred. I knew I could write ad copy, but art was an incomprehensible enigma to me.

The art directors didn't much like my copy ideas. "Too simple," was their response. They asked me to add more copy. I didn't think it was necessary, but these were the pros, and my superiors, so I added more copy.

The art department came up with five nifty ideas that they translated into beautiful comps (comprehensive presentations), all mounted nicely on stiff cardboard with pretty tissue cover sheets. They looked professional.

I walked into Apple the next day to see Steckler, completely confident about my first creative presentation. Steckler looked at each beautiful, professionally packaged comp and said, "Boring! Boring! Boring! Boring! Boring!"

I had nothing to lose, so I pulled out my little doodle, unwrinkled the tiny piece of paper, and handed it to him. He laughed in an indecipherable way that was either, "My God, what a pathetic asshole you are!" or "Hey, this is really amusing!"

I had been poking around in an art closet at Apple the day of the assignment and saw a striking photo of John Lennon wearing a white suit, playing a white piano in a white room. I loved it. It was so strong that I wanted to use the least amount of words, so I took the words "Imagine," "John Lennon," and "On Apple Records" and put them together to make a single imperative sentence. "Imagine John Lennon On Apple Records." All I did was add the period. Plus I lifted some lyrics from "Gimmie Some Truth," a Lennon song from the album, and put them in a cartoon balloon over John's head—"No short-haired, yellow-bellied son-of-Tricky Dicky's gonna Mother Hubbard soft soap me." I did the same for Yoko with "Fly Yoko Ono On Apple Records." For Yoko I used a photograph of her face and drew a stick figure of a fly on it so it would make you want to cringe. Steckler said, "This is great! Let's see what John thinks."

I didn't sleep much that night waiting for John Lennon to decide my fate. Next morning, early, thank God, Steckler called me and said John loved the doodles and sent a note back saying, "I like this. Let's have this guy do all our ads from now on."

Overnight I became the media designer for Apple Records. There had been some problem with billing through the agency I worked for, and Apple wanted me, not Concert Hall, and would help me set up my own little agency.

Because Apple Records was run by Allen Klein who had first managed The Rolling Stones, my little one-man ad agency would occasionally inherit work for the Stones including lots of ads, a radio commercial and even the album cover, "Hot Rocks." My little one-man band company also did the album for the cult film, "El Topo," and John Lennon's "Sometime In New York City." (For all three albums, which were far above my design ability, I hired my friend Michael Gross, who was then design director for *National Lampoon.*)

The net takeaway of these stories is: (1) I can speed off with direction but without a destination and (2) good flukes sometimes visit me.

10

The hooker, her husband, her sugar daddy, her lovers and me

Six o'clock on a Friday night in June 1980

It's around sixty-five degrees with clear sky, sun shining and a clean slight breeze. I am waiting downstairs from Eureka at 54th and Madison. Laura walks out in jeans, sweatshirt, sneakers, and no makeup, looking exactly like a hippie and nothing like a whore. Her eyes are greener in daylight and I can smell her before we touch. She still smells like a sweet fuck even though she showered and her hair is still wet.

First thing, she gives me $85. We walk hand in hand toward the East Side. She starts talking. "I don't know how I'm going to do it but I want to be with you. We'll have to figure it out.

"I want to spend the weekend with you so I told my husband I won't be home. Sometimes I stay in the city and make extra money. It was a really good week but I'll tell my husband it was only mediocre, and I'll have to earn about $350-$400 more in tricks by Sunday."

My pace falters.

"Oh, no," she says, "Not from you, Jeffrey, but you've got to understand that sometime over the weekend I've got to hustle $400 in tricks. It won't be a problem."

Laura speaks in staccato bursts. She's coked up. "If I can reach him, I'll see my best regular, Walter and tell him the truth. And about you. He'll understand and give me the bread. We have that sort of relationship. He's married and a megabuck oil man. I always tell him the truth.

"Or, if I can't get to Walter, I'll call some other johns I know. I've got a list. Guys give me their numbers. It's against the rules, but sometimes I take them. Plus one of my Eureka girlfriends turns tricks and she'll include me in a double or turn some business over to me. Anyway, it won't be a hassle. I just want you to know what's going on."

I don't know what's going on. I hope she's being straight with me. I think she is and I'll follow her lead.

We continue toward my flat hand in hand, like children whose mother told them to hold hands the whole way and only cross with the lights. Even in the real world her hand is warm to the touch. Laura is hungry; the day's drugs are wearing off. She doesn't want to eat out. Not tonight. Maybe tomorrow we could go for sushi, she suggests. She sometimes eats "animal flesh," mainly fish, but most days she eats fruits and vegetables and avoids supermarkets, which she calls "straight stores."

We stop at one of the five million Korean groceries in Manhattan. She buys salad veggies and fresh bread and tofu. She says iceberg lettuce is the vegetable equivalent of junk food and buys greens I don't recognize. She finds some ginseng pop for me and holds the bottle up close to her face in a TV commercial parody and says in a low, slow, male voice, "Ginseng. It's a man's drink."

Far out, she does shtick. This is a good sign. I know so little about her that every minute reveals something. I buy several more ginseng pops, figuring I can use all the help I can get. As we walk we chit chat about nothing in particular. She doesn't watch much TV. She likes to read. She points out good-looking sexy women to make sure I won't miss them. When I ask why, she says it's not that she's that turned on by them, although she's a bit bi, it's just that they are more visually interesting than men. She tells me she's twenty-seven years old and her name is Laura Bradley. In the elevator we smile at each other with the sly anticipation of randy kids out on a first date.

Once in the flat we avoid touching each other as Laura prepares her healthy fuel. She is chopping carrots when I finally put my arms around her and nibble her neck.

Every part of her is sweet musk fragrant. The wispy soft hairs on her neck tickle my nose. We explore with our hands and our lips and our tongues. We canoodle, we rub against each other, frisson overtakes us and in jump-cut-to-the-chase fashion we are in the bedroom on the white iron and brass bed, naked, fucking.

She seems taller and leaner in bed than when she is standing. She's fit but not overly muscular. She's strong but there is nothing about her body that isn't soft and feminine. Her face is classic Anglo-Saxon beautiful, as un-Jewish as any face ever in my bed. She has a high, wide forehead, a fine, long, aristocratic nose and bright hazel-green eyes, more jade than emerald and an eye color, maybe even a color, I never saw before.

Her ass is a bit warmer than the rest of her, maybe because it carries the only fat on her body other than her tits. She's twenty-seven so everything is still where it belongs. Her breasts are the minimum requirement for a B-cup, but her nipples, Jesus, her nipples are huge, they protrude, they belong to a woman with much larger breasts; maybe there was an accidental nipple switch in the hospital when she was in the nursery. Or maybe they belong to a female of another species, maybe another genus.

"One of my favorite things was to have my nipples played with," Laura remembers. "But for hours, I mean, *days*. And I wouldn't want him to stop playing with them. So he wouldn't stop. Sometimes Jeffrey played with my nipples to help me fall asleep when I was coked up."

When I touch her giant nipples she whimpers and leans into me. I get a little firmer with them and she gets hotter. I squeeze them just a little too hard and she says, "Thank you."

She is dripping wet as I go inside her. Maybe it's from the other men at the whorehouse. I ask her and she says no, she showered and douched before she left. "That's just the way I am. Aren't all girls like that?" If only.

She comes more easily than any woman I ever met. Sometimes her orgasms blend together for minutes. And she comes again with me every time I climax.

> "The most amount of orgasms I ever had with Jeffrey was thirty-four in one day!" Laura grins. "That was definitely the most I ever had. I think that's the exact number—thirty-four. It's probably not that accurate. Lots of times we would fuck twenty-four hours a day. When you get into that space, you kind of lose it. I remember it was hard to tell the difference between twenty-four and twenty-five—they kind of blended together. But it was at least thirty-four; though it might have been forty-three!"

My orgasms are different with her. Not just different, but new. They are very strong but that's not the most significant quality. They're more primitive. They start down deeper.

She looks up at me when I fuck her in some spaced-out overwhelmed simple way, the way women looked at men 50,000 years ago when they got fucked by someone they weren't afraid of being killed and eaten by. Or maybe just how they looked when they got fucked. Something vestigial is going on. We are sexual anachronisms. I hear myself making noises I never made before, primordial yawps to accompany my ur-orgasms.

Around midnight we finally take a break and eat salad and bread. I get my first taste of arugula—which I like and think tastes vaguely like meat. I also discover Boston Bibb lettuce, which is as delicate and as soft as her skin.

Saturday morning we sleep late after making love once during the night. We sleep close. She loves being held tight, which is my natural instinct. That morning is the first time I ever see Laura straight. I like it. She is less scattered, looks younger, healthier and prettier. There is a relaxation to her face that drugs steal.

When she pees she doesn't sit on the toilet but rather squats on it with her feet on the toilet seat. She's like a Stone Age aborigine who doesn't know how to use it.

> "Squatting is the way a lot of people sit and go to the bathroom. I lived in a van for so long with Sandy—for so many years we camped and lived in a van—squatting to go to the bathroom was just the way. I still do," Laura smiles. "I'd rather go behind a tree than go into the house and use the bathroom."

I want to know what happened the last time we were together when it went from love to hustle. I don't ask right away but curiosity gets the best of me while we're drinking coffee and eating bagels, so I ask.

She explains how she ran back to the dressing room where all the ladies hang out between sessions. As they always did, one of them asked how much of a tip Laura got. She told them how excited she was to see me, how she loved to fuck me, and that she paid for the session. They all razzed her and got on her case, especially Tanya, an ex-street whore I'd fucked many happy times who said, "Sure, Jeffrey can fuck. I even like to fuck him and I don't like fucking many johns. But business is business, honey and he ain't your man. You stoned, baby. Don't get lost. Jeffrey is just playing you. Go get the money." Laura caved in.

> "They were right," Laura confesses, "I loved fucking Jeffrey right away, but it couldn't interfere with my money goal. There's nothing wrong with doing business with friends. I am a sucker for an amazing kiss and Jeffrey was an amazing kisser but I was still paying back a big debt and fucking was my job. But by this point my body didn't care about the

money anymore. Now I begged Jeffrey to love me, to *do me*, to *manipulate* me *into him*..."

She says she's sorry. I forgive her. We move on.

She tries to get in touch with Walter, but can't reach him. After a few more calls, she sets up some tricks. We nap until 2:00 p.m. When we wake, she goes into the bathroom, climbs up on the sink, again in a primitive squat, and moves close to the mirror to put on lipstick. As she leaves, she says she'll be back before dark.

Laura returns around 7:00 p.m., $600 richer and carrying three men's shirts in my size. She also gives me a gram of coke she got from Mark, her boyfriend who is a dealer. She said she fucked Mark and two tricks, one of whom was a shirt manufacturer. This is a lot of information to process.

We do two lines and get back between the sheets. I pin her arms down, forming gentle cuffs with my thumb and index finger around her delicate wrists, allowing them to move but restraining her hands from sliding through. She goes wild enjoying the struggle.

Laura moans, "Use me. Please use me. Tell me what you want. I'll do anything for you." She opens her eyes and looks straight into mine, "I want you to own me, all of me. My pussy is yours. My tits, my mouth. They're yours. I want to be yours. I want to be your banquet of pleasure."

When she says it, it's poetry. Her submissive eloquence makes me come.

She dances from one paragraph to the next. Every move she makes is graceful. I am not graceful and look upon hers with respect and envy. When her "banquet of pleasure," metaphor pops out, it touches me as unrehearsed. Her speech is a little hippie-dippy-groovy, but also lyrical, like a songwriter or poet who never stops working.

My instinct declares this is more than skin passion. This is something thick and soulful and complicated. Her scent ignites my testosterone and I feel more macho than ever before. This is love I never knew. It's a quantum shift, a difference of kind, not just of degree. I had been living in black and white—and was happy—and now I discovered color. She is a movie. She is the star of every scene.

The downside is Laura does too much cocaine.

I never loved coke. I felt it was overrated weak speed. As they say, it's God's way of letting you know you're making too much money. If offered, I'd do a little, and stop. But Laura loves it. And she loves giving it to me in small doses, not enough to make me lose my hard-on, but enough to keep me awake all night fucking her. I begin to re-examine my prejudice against the drug.

Laura is sweet and polite in a way that signals she grew up with family warmth. During intermissions between fucks she gives me her life history. The Readers Digest version goes like this: She grew up in Idaho in an upper middle class family. She was a borderline acid-casualty hippie during high school, then a teenage runaway vagabond who hitchhiked to San Francisco. Her dad is VP of a national company and she's the middle one of three sisters. She speaks of her family with genuine love. She sees them once or twice a year and it's always a great Norman Rockwell-style reunion. She became a drug-free West-coast Sufi fruitarian, way to the right of a simple vegetarian. Her diet was so restrictive she developed TB, which you can only do if you work at dietary deficiency hard enough.

She met a guy, Sandy, and they became best friends, but with no benefits. They began making silver jewelry and selling it at Renaissance fairs and arts and crafts festivals. Their cottage industry thrived.

She didn't fancy Sandy sexually, but they did share a deep spiritual bond and they were on a spiritual quest. She loved travelling to the festivals to hear, in her opinion, what the most enlightened people in America had to say. She lived to chant, become one with God and Earth, eat healthy and purify herself. She'd been a vegetarian for ten years.

Pressured by his family to give his father joy on his deathbed, she married Sandy. They were monogamous, fucking only three or four times a year, sometimes less. After five years, whatever sex drive Laura had was repressed.

They decided to move from Marin, outside San Francisco, to artisan-friendly New Hope, Pennsylvania. Then, in a blinding storm of chance during a vacation in Reno she discovered he had a gambling problem. Then Laura discovered Sandy was fucking other women. This infidelity changed their odd and mostly sexless but semi-workable marriage. Sandy slid right into the joy of sex and Laura slid into focusing on her work. Their spiritual quest, made even more holy by their abstemiousness, was now shattered. Without both Laura and Sandy paying the right attention, their business suffered.

During this crisis, Laura got back into drugs. Psychedelics were her thing. Then she became friends with Lindsey, a top fashion model, who introduced her to cocaine, alcohol, uppers, and downers. Laura jumped in with flagrant disregard for her well-being. She tried everything that was offered; cocaine and Quaaludes became her favorites. With Lindsey came her flock of admiring men, and many said Laura was at least as pretty as Lindsey.

> "I was really very inhibited," Laura laughs, "except when I had cocaine and Quaaludes, which released me. Absolutely. Definitely—particularly the Quaaludes. The whole thing was so new, and such a different experience—and the drugs definitely heightened my desire for intensity. I just wanted more—more of everything! *Everything, just more intense!*"

She enjoyed her reputation as an available party girl in her local town, kissing guys and girls and on the dance floor and giving head in parking lots. Sex & drugs became a united event. She started getting high almost every day.

Her first day at Eureka, she met a client, Mark, a handsome coke dealer she went home with. He tied her up and fucked her. This was new to her. She liked it. She started staying with him some weekdays, returning home to Bucks County on weekends.

Another of her tricks at Eureka was big fat tough brilliant Walter, a rich Texas oilman. She started to see him on the outside, too. He liked coke, fucking and fantasy sex, and became a kind of sugar daddy. Then she met me.

We fuck, do coke, fuck, do coke, talk, fuck, and do coke until mid-Sunday afternoon when I beg for sleep. I am careful to limit my coke intake so that it doesn't interfere with my ability to get hard. I just keep doing less and less every time.

"Let me do something for you," she said. "I'm too coked up to sleep. You can have absolutely anything you want. Can I rub you?"

"Yes, that would be lovely."

"Can I lick your asshole? Please?"

Wow.

Laura licks and sucks until I just can't stay awake for another moment of pleasure.

It was the first of many of the most peaceful sleeps I've ever known, her warm tongue kissing me good night at both ends.

I sleep without interruption. I awake early Monday. The sun is half up. She is in my arms. I smell her deliciousness before I know my own name. I remember the circumstances of how I went to sleep. I smile and think there must not be any better way to start a day.

She has a swimmer's body. She has almost no fat, except, as I said, and it's worth repeating, on her plush bum. No cellulite. Smooth skin still warmer than it should be. She is a heat pump. She is winter pussy without the plumpness. I wonder what it will be like to fuck her in the hot summer. Well, that's what air conditioning is for. If wild fucking and sucking my asshole are the only two things Laura does, if she is a Bimbo Savant, these two great skills are enough to cover at least the first decade.

Sleep has replenished my hormones and I am hard again. I must have come six or seven, maybe eight times since Friday. I wonder how long this can last, if I'll simply run out of my allotment of hard-ons.

Laura is curled between my arms and legs. We are a Turkish puzzle ring. I maneuver inside her. Her body dances with me before she is awake. She murmurs, "Please use me. Thank you for using me." Maybe I am still sleeping. Or maybe this is a dream come true.

When I was thirteen, I made a wish at my Bar Mitzvah that I wanted God to send me a high fashion model, or at least a female who looked like one. Send me a tall, thin, preferably blonde shiksa with cheekbones, just like the girls on the Clairol hair color boxes. And I wanted her to be a "nymphomaniac," which was the second big word I learned after "delicatessen."

When I found out later in college that clinical nymphomaniacs didn't attain orgasm and were generally frustrated, hostile, and man-hating, I revised my still unfulfilled but unforgotten wish to "very, very oversexed female."

God must have had an enormous amount of paperwork and my request got lost in the shuffle, but finally, twenty years after my Bar Mitzvah my wish was finally granted and I was sent this gorgeous, sweet, sexually avaricious libidomaniac.

I decide to tie her up. She likes Mark doing it so I better get on the bandwagon. The few times I'd done it with other women had been fun. I went to my closet and pulled out five or six of my least favorite ties. Bondage before breakfast.

"Lie face up," I order with flat affect. I'm not going to lose her. She wants to be my slave and I will hold up my end. You give a submissive woman what she needs—or she'll get it someplace else. But at that moment I'm not analyzing anything. I'm just enjoying the power of domination.

My ties never looked better than around Laura's hands. I take each wrist and tie it to the bed frame. I tell her to spread her legs wide and I enter her, pulling her tightly against her bonds, spreading and bending her legs to suit the deepest entry, driving her through half a dozen screaming orgasms. I feel invincible. Maybe only Muhammad Ali or Genghis Khan ever felt this strong!

I tie her ankles to her wrists. She is folded in half, open in the middle. Her vagina tilts toward me surrounded by sparse wispy soft down. I can smell its invitation. I pull her hips until her ass is lifted off the bed. I fuck her hard. She comes before me and then with me.

"Yes. Yes. This is what I want in my life," she cheers me on as I spill into her. Her green eyes get bluer and look up with need like a puppy.

I pull my wet dick out. It's hard, demanding more! I need to own this woman. But how can I own a woman who fucks five or six or more other men everyday, some better looking, some with bigger cocks?

I must be the only man branded into her soul, scorched into her libido, burnt into her heart. I want her to be at work fucking and thinking what a second-rate fuck she is having compared to me, Jeffrey, with the fuck no one else can provide.

I slide my hands over her. She flexes, stretches, moans and mews like a cat. I control an atavistic cannibal urge to take a bite from her flesh. I am crazed, balancing on the edge of sex madness. A million years ago after stealing and raping a woman maybe you ate her if you were hungry. Maybe one smells and tastes so wonderful you decide not to eat her, but to hunt and feed the both of you so you can keep on fucking her. The one in my bed is this one. This one lives.

I loosen the neckties and command her to get on her hands and knees. She complies. I pause. After a moment she begins to shift side to side like a bored, caged cat. I leave the room—to raise her tension—and lower mine. I need a break from her pheromones.

I stand in front of my living room window and look down twenty-four floors to the beginning of the day. There should be an audience looking up at me like they do at jumpers. How can the outside world walk by unaware of the energy I am creating? It's the ultimate solipsistic blindness of ego: how could the universe dare not know how powerful I am? With one wrong move, atoms will collide, fuse beyond critical mass and destroy everything.

Being away from her calms me. My breath slows and I walk back into the bedroom. She is still on all fours, still swaying, waiting for the next act's curtain to rise.

11
The 'test spank' and beyond

One moment later

Many women want to be spanked. Some like it hard. Some like it gentle. Some don't like it. But most do not dislike it. At least not the ones in my survey.

I had a girlfriend who enjoyed it, as long as it was playful and very light. She was particularly fond of it when I took her over my knee and made believe she had been naughty and was being punished. Sometimes she would ask for it. I think it was a way of resolving her ambiguous sexual feelings for her stepfather who was good looking and just a few years older than me.

To submissives, the metaphor and the scenario are as important as the act. To non-submissives, the spank just gets jumbled in with all the other good feelings and heightens the intensity in some minor form of crossed-wire synesthesia.

If you want to go in this direction you need to start with a Test Spank. The proper Test Spank is two medium-firm, open-handed love taps to the fleshiest part of the bottom, preferably while you are fucking doggie style so your partner is already excited and doesn't see it coming.

The responses vary:

(1) A jerky turning around with a "Yo! What the fuck do you

think you're doing, asshole?!"

(2) A civil, "No thank you, I'm not into that."

(3) A grunted, but definitely negative, "Uh uh."

Or if you've pre-qualified your partner correctly:

(4) A pleasurable moan.

(5) A polite "Thank-you."

(6) A pleading "Harder," or "More."

(7) Or my all-time favorite from a lovely pixie and divorced mother of three who took a long, deep breath, turned and said, "Oh, thank you. I've waited twenty years for someone to do that."

> "I don't think that I ever asked Jeffrey to spank me the first time," Laura recalls, "I'm not graphic like that. He *just knew*. He intuited it. He probably gave me a little and then I wanted more. I definitely liked the real thing. It had to be *real*. It couldn't be just patting—a patty-pat. I definitely wanted it hard."

I come back into the bedroom and administer the Test Spank. Laura turns to me and says, "Thank you. Please hit me again. Harder."

I hit her harder, then firmer yet, driven by her encouragement. Then she says the words that change my life, if not forever, for many years: "Hurt me."

I stop and put my mouth right next to her ear and whisper, "You want me to hurt you? Tell me about it." I slap her hard, half a dozen times.

"I need you to hurt me. I want it. I need to show you how much I want you to own me."

God did I want her. I wanted to own her. How could I not?

"I need to give you my pain. Please take pain from me. I want you to take pain from me."

I slap her bottom a dozen times, each harder than the last, to make her already reddening ass the color of Pantone Matching System color 32, nearly the red on a pack of Marlboros.

I'd heard a lot of naughty slutisms come out of women's mouths.

I'd heard women say, "Hurt me with it," to spur me on to fuck them harder, but no one ever asked me outright to hurt them.

I get behind her and push my cock inside her, reaching around to pinch her nipples. She pleads, "Harder. Please, harder." I squeeze her nipples harder. She starts to come and begs, "More."

I pull out, tell her not to move an inch, and tie her hands and feet with the neckties, one to each corner of the bed frame. I spank her till my hand is sore. Laura just asks for more. I pause. I am on the precipice of weighing the ethics of right and wrong but I am interrupted by another request: "Please use your belt on me."

Fuck right and wrong. Being reluctant is over. I reach to the floor for my pants and yank off my belt. I fold it in half the way my father did before he punished me and for the first time in my life I whip a woman. In retrospect, spanking is sometimes spanking and sometimes it's S&M gateway sex.

I start light and gain momentum until I know that if she were hitting me I'd be crying. Laura moans in appreciation. Each smack ignites a vocal response that is the opposite of what I expect. She moans with pleasure. She says, "Thank you for hurting me."

I'd like to say I didn't enjoy it as much as I did, but I fucking loved it. Immediately.

Whatever internal discussion starts in my ethics forum gets shelved in committee. I whip her and I am King of the Universe.

I look at the welts on her beautiful behind. The leather makes contact hard enough to emboss the intricate bas-relief design of the belt onto her flesh. She never asks me to stop. She just makes deep small noises. I listen closely and only hear pleasure. I am freaked out. I am afraid of really hurting her and decide to stop hitting her.

I mount her. Molten lava pours through my veins and I breathe fire. For a sex junkie this is the ultimate fix. I am at the edge, about to soar to some new place. I don't care about the danger or if there is no way back. If this is what she wants, I will do it.

I fuck her and massage my thumb into her smaller as of yet unused hole. "Yes," she begs, "yes!" I spread her ass with two fingers and nestle my wet cock head just inside her. Lubricating with my spit I push inside her. Then I plunge inside.

She falls onto the bed shouting "Oh, my God! Take Me!" The heat of her welts warms my belly. I fuck her through three minutes of her seamless orgasms. It's time for me. I cannonball my load up into her. I am spent. This would be an okay place to die.

She is the dirtiest female I ever met. She has no bounds. I am frightened. I am excited. I'm lying there and Pink Floyd is in my head: "Ooooo, I need a dirty woman. Ooooo, I need a dirty girl. Will some woman in this desert land make me feel like a real man?"

I untie her and without speaking we curl up and fall asleep.

I wake to hear Laura on the phone apologizing to Liz that she'll be late for work. For three one-hundredths of a second I can't figure out why my right hand aches so much. Then I wonder how Laura's bottom feels. As she speaks to Liz, she's standing in front of the full-length mirror looking at the black and blue marks on her ass. "Come here," I call after she hangs up the phone. She obeys.

I have questions about the belt scene. Did she like it? Did I hurt her? Too much? Enough?

"Jeffrey, I need what you do to me. I love it. It doesn't hurt. It just makes me feel good. Slutty. I like being your slave. I want to come home and be used by you and sleep with you every night. I'm moving out of Mark's apartment today after work. Please tell me it's okay and that you want me."

"Of course I do."

The next time she mentions anything about loving being spanked and/or whipped my insecurity rears its ugly head and I ask if it's different with me than with other guys.

"There are no other guys."

"Really? Not now or not ever?"

"Well, Mark spanked me a little but that's as far as it went, nobody else does it to me at work."

"I'm the first?"

"I guess you are just the right guy at the right time."

"Did you always want to be whipped?"

"I thought about it a lot. I masturbated thinking about it. I wanted it in a secret way."

"Why do you like it?"

She takes her time to speak, and pauses between her thoughts. "It's what I need and you are the right man to give it to me. I love it when you hurt me. It doesn't feel bad. It feels like I'm getting rid of something that it's good to be rid of. It feels right."

"When I was about twelve years old," Laura confesses, "I read this salacious story about someone getting whipped in New York—and it totally lingered in my head.

"It made such a huge impression on me, it was so decadent, and it was so *other*—because this woman was totally having pleasure in searching out these hot guys who would whip her. And I was like, 'WHAT? OH MY GOD!'

"I don't remember the name of the book or who wrote it," Laura continues, "it wasn't *The Story of O*—I just remember that this woman was searching out hot guys who would whip her. It was such an amazing thing! It was just such a foreign concept to me. And it intrigued me—so I always wanted to be in it for real. I was creating my own novel out of my experience. I would do anything to take orgasms to the extreme, and Jeffrey was doing that for me. I was in a place where being whipped felt good and I knew Jeffrey was the right guy to take me down this road. I knew being slutty and whipped was the next place I wanted sex to take me.

"I finally did read *The Story of O* when I was going out with Jeffrey," Laura explains, "and God, *The Story of O* definitely has preoccupied a huge amount of my orgasms for most of my life."

She dresses, smokes a joint, and heads off to work. I wonder what her tricks will make of her black and blue ass. Out of bed and brewing coffee, I look in the mirror. She's gone. I am not Mick Jagger or Clint Eastwood anymore. I am just this Jewish guy with love handles who finally has the woman of his dreams.

12
Whip this

That first whipping turned on a new switch inside me. I had enjoyed power and domination games, and I could get into talking all kinds of strange shit. But that was just words and didn't leave welts. I had never had an urge to whip a woman.

I met a few guys who would boast about some chick who loved to be tied up and hurt. Once, at an orgy, a black pimp smacked around the white girl he brought who not only didn't just take it, she loved it and begged for more. It was unsettling. During a break while sharing a joint he gloated about other beatings he had inflicted on other women who wanted it. He was sinister, perverted in a way that I didn't admire. I remember thinking his behavior was a weakness, not a strength. Slapping asses and snapping directions were my limit.

For some reason sadism seemed less odious in women. An orgy buddy, Janet, an ex-Playboy bunny, worked as a dominatrix. She spent her days humiliating and whipping men. Usually they were rich and powerful men who, I guess, needed a vacation from being boss. I accepted it in her. In bed with me she was a submissive pussycat.

Once I met Janet in her lobby as she was coming home from work. Inside her apartment, she opened her coat to reveal her black-leather Mistress-Janet, Goddess-of-Pain, uniform.

"I didn't get a chance to change. What do you think of me looking like this?"

"You are startling to behold." I convulsed back in a hammy theatrical cringe. These were the days before girls dressed like that to go to rock clubs, proms, or bar and bat mitzvahs.

She must have had on a dozen pieces of clothing, yet half her lovely Playboy Bunny body was exposed. Arm bands, wristlets, bra, corset, coarse fishnet stocking with garters, hip boots, crisscrossing bandoleer belts, choker necklace—all black leather—and metal studs everywhere, especially on her leather thong. "And what naughty things did you do today, little boy?" she grinned, taking what must have been an elephant whip out of her closet and posing like a postcard from Hell.

"Nothing that bad."

I took the whip out of her hand and dragged her into the bedroom and playfully threw her onto the bed. We kissed. She slipped out of her weaponized panties and turned into the gentle, affectionate Janet I knew her to be. After a few minutes, she slipped back into her business persona, rolled me over on my belly and spanked me hard and true, each crack a testament to her professionalism. I refused to ask her to stop. I got into the rhythm of the pain, but I didn't enjoy it. It was more like hazing than sex.

She finally stopped and checked to see if I was hard. I wasn't. How could I be? I was in the middle of testing my pain threshold. I did get real hard soon after and had one of the best fucks ever with Janet. But I never gave it much thought or attached any special meaning to it. And never wanted to do it again.

Nor did I give much thought to that first whipping of Laura, at the time. I certainly have since.

Maybe it was my high testosterone?

Maybe it was atavistic caveman courtship?

Maybe excessive dominance medicated my insecurity?

Maybe submission medicated her insecurity?

Maybe I chose not to think about the implications, but the line between the conscious and subconscious is not a hard frontier with armed guards. I believe that thoughts and moods slide between the obvious and the unknown. I knew I was travelling somewhere more dangerous than merely naughty—some place where metaphysics meets the road—but being a successful sadist was never my goal. It never appeared in my catalog of fantasies of rock star, football hero, movie star, or even in my occasional daydream of being a pimp.

I wanted Laura. I needed her flesh, her taste. I was willing to pay the price. I was slave to her desires. My lust for her was stronger than my morality. I was willing to go to the dark side.

13

Laura moves in

Late June 1980

"This guy, this very, very rich man," Laura confides, "had asked me if I would go to Greece with him. I was like, 'Yeah, I'll definitely go to Greece with you.'

"The guy said, 'Okay, look, I have to go to Florida, and then I'm gonna come back and I'll pick you up and then we'll head off to Greece.'

"In between that time I met Jeffrey," Laura continues, "and we just could not get out of bed. We couldn't get out of bed for days and days. We just stayed in bed. I blew off everything. Basically all we did was fuck.

"I wanted him to be in complete control. I wanted to have that feeling of him being in absolute complete control. And just completely giving myself over to him; maybe it was religious or something, it was similar in vibe.

"Like a religious fanatic.

"So the rich guy calls from Florida," Laura resumes her story, "and I was in bed with Jeffrey and the rich guy was like, 'Look, I'm coming back up. You're still definitely going to come to Greece with me?'

"And I said, 'Oh, yeah I'll go to Greece with you.'

"Jeffrey overheard this and he freaked out. When I got off the phone he said, 'You're not going to Greece with some other guy. I'll take you to Greece. I don't want you to go with him. You can't go with him.'

"So the rich guy came back to New York and I wouldn't even see him," Laura laughs, "Jeffrey wouldn't even let me out of the bed. I mean, it's not like he prevented me, I mean, I chose not to go, because the sex was so good! Yes, Jeffrey did own me at that point. His penis was the perfect size and the hardest I ever met. And it stayed hard and got hard again right away after he came. He owned me. His cock owned me. It was like I had given myself over to him. It was my choice to be owned by him."

The night finally arrives when Laura brings her stuff from Mark's apartment and moves in with me. I help carry in her two suitcases and two duffle bags. Her entire wardrobe is tie-dyed, paisley, patched denim, or well worn cotton with a splash of working girl slut clothes and a few traditional skirts and blouses in case she has to disguise herself to make an escape or in case her parents visit. While she unpacks I ask how her day went.

"Great. Mark was upset but he understood," Laura says. "I was straight with him and he's much too macho to blubber. I was very busy at work—five guys. And one of them gave me a $200 tip and all he really wanted to do was worship my body, eat me, and have me piss in his mouth. I never got one of those before. Almost all the guys at Eureka just want regular sex.

"It took a while," Laura continues, "I had just pissed before he arrived so I had to drink gallons of water and then when I had to piss it was hard to do it in a guy's mouth. Yuck, so gross! But I wanted the $200. He drank it all and said it tasted like champagne. Real weird dude... a real average Joe-looking 'suit.'

"Just before he left I had to piss again and he pulls this empty jam jar out of his coat and asks if I would fill it up for 'later.' I figured why the fuck not? So I go back to the bathroom and I'm sitting there pissing in a jar and laughing my ass off. What a strange way to make money! Altogether I made $460. Not a bad day."

"Did you come with any of them?" I ask.

"Most of them," Laura confesses, "Not with the guy I pissed on. Or the guy I gave a blowjob. But I fingered myself into coming right after the blowjob left. Is it okay with you Jeffrey? Are you upset?"

"No, just curious." Actually I do feel something. Not upset, but maybe a third of a twinge of jealousy. This is different than going to an orgy with a lover. At an orgy I'm there in the next room or on the next mattress and I'm also having a wild time. I am adjusted to having my woman fuck other men while I watch, but this isn't that.

"But Jeffrey, I thought of you all day," Laura says. "Every trick that came in, I made believe you sent him in and that I was fucking him for you."

I respond to her erotica with a dash of my jealousy and grab her and push her up against the wall. I look into her eyes, which at this moment seem more emerald than hazel or blue. It occurs to me that her eyes change color from one scene's lighting to the next. They say she adores me.

I have never been so adored. I like it. She moves her mouth to my ear and begs for me to hit her. I turn her around to face the wall. I slap her ass a dozen times.

"I want more." Her voice is halfway between begging and commanding.

I grab my belt. I make her ass red.

I unzip my Levis and release my cock. It hones in and goes inside her. I hold her hands high against the wall and fuck her from behind. She counters every thrust, coming early, coming again, and then coming again when I erupt. We go to bed and nod off. We wake up and make love again for a long slow time with much more tenderness and fondling and rubbing. Sometime in the middle of the night we finally go to sleep.

The next morning after we untangle and make love sweetly, normally, Laura tells me again how every time a trick comes into the room at work she'll make believe I am her pimp sending them in. I add that I want her to come with every man and it is her job to think of me during orgasm. "Think of me while other men's dicks make you come," I say.

Laura's eyes are wide and excited. "I'll do it for you. I swear," she says.

Laura's sex drive is as strong as mine. We are kin. Even women who are as horny as me usually can't keep up. Laura also has stamina to match mine. She is my masturbation fantasy, a drop-dead gorgeous tall, thin long-haired girl who loves to fuck, has her own drugs and money, is way out at the edge of sexy and thinks I am God's gift to her vagina.

What's not to like?

We fuck at least four or five or six or more times every day. If we are together at home we're in bed fucking. If we are anywhere and there is a bed and privacy we're fucking. If we are anywhere and there's a bed and no privacy we throw people out of the room and fuck. Sometimes, if we're anywhere with a bed and we're with people, we fuck in front of them. Sometimes we fuck in express elevators quickly; sometimes we find closets and fuck. Sometimes we go up on a roof and fuck. Sometimes we pull the car over to a rest stop or just off the road and fuck.

Every day after work Laura recounts the day's eros-for-money adventures: The black U.N. diplomat who was very gentle, the old guy with the horse-sized schlong, the little bald guy who only wanted to suck her asshole and jerk off, the young, good-looking guy who paid her $250 to fuck her in the ass and then tried coming onto her for a date, the rich guy who gave her $200 just to squeeze his balls hard while he jerked off, the two "suits" who shared her and then gave her $200 cash and nearly $500 worth of their cocaine, the Japanese guy who spoke no English and had an amazingly rigid dick, the little American guy who had a small dick and was mean to her, and the many nondescript dudes that just came in, fucked, tipped, and left.

Each little vignette ends with Laura telling me how she came for me, how she performed for me, how she was my slave, how she repeated, "This is for you, Jeffrey," in her head every time she came, how she even startled a john by saying it out loud and how he asked afterwards, "Who the fuck is Jeffrey?"

Her description of each sexual encounter is exciting foreplay to me. I am the perfect boyfriend for a call girl. I have no jealousy. I approve of her having sex with other men.

Just thinking about "my whore" pleasuring other men makes me incredibly hard. Sometimes I get so excited during the day thinking about what she is doing, I jerk off imagining her in that little room with men using her. I don't consider the morals, I don't consider the ethics, I don't consider the psychic tax. I just love it, sick fuck that I am.

Men's horniness is just about the most interesting thing in the world to me. Starting with mine. I'm not sure where polymorphous perversity ends and homosexuality begins but while I have zero desire to be fucked by a man, watching men with their genetically engineered hard-ons use my woman as I did at 300 orgies or hearing about them use Laura as I do every day satisfies some compulsion.

I am fortunate that my obsession is within the quasi-socially acceptable and quasi-legal limits of perversion. One more crossed neuron someplace else and I could have been a shoe fetishist, scat worshiper or worse yet a pederast. It's just luck that I have my set of desires rather than some more hideous.

Every day Laura reveals more of her personality.

"The first time I ever remember having an orgasm with anyone," Laura muses, "was with this actor/film director whose name I'd rather not mention. I didn't even know who he was. I'd never seen any of his movies. I was in this pub with friends and this guy started talking to me. My friends had to tell me who he was.

"I must have had an orgasm before knowing him," Laura laughs, "because I had so much sex, but I didn't know it was orgasm. I just didn't know the name of it or how to define it. It was just this good swelling feeling. Not that he taught me how to define it, but he—he just made it so obvious, the orgasm he gave me was just so profound, so much bigger than anything before—and with an explosion. And so never-ending, ha, ha, ha! He had a nice cock, normal size—a nice size—but it was his tongue that first got me off.

"He really knew how to eat pussy!" Laura gushes, "oh God yeah! It was amazing! He really, really did know how to make me come!

"And you know what his technique was? He was humming as he was going down on me, ha, ha, ha! There're so few men who know how to fucking have sex. It's really frustrating. When I talk to other women, they all say the amount of men who actually know how to have sex is fucking pathetic!

"What he did have that was special—besides knowing how to give exquisite head—was how to live, how to go for the joy, how to get joy out of life!"

When either Laura or I buy cut flowers, she knows each flower by name. She sings along with the radio, in tune. More impressive are her piano skills. She comes along with me when I visit a client and sits down at an upright piano in his office. A secretary turns off a radio and goes to lunch. Laura starts plinking on the piano until she is playing the song we just heard on the radio, note for note. I ask her if she has perfect pitch. She doesn't know what that is, nor does she know the names of the keys on the piano. She just knows how to figure out which notes follow which.

Sherry and I had great chemistry of the "You Jane, Me Tarzan" variety; Laura and I are Prince Charming and Cinderella after they slept together. We live together weekdays, but she spends weekends in New Hope with her husband, Sandy. One weekend while she is packing up to leave for New Hope, Laura says: "Please help me get out of my marriage. I want a divorce from Sandy. Don't be scared or anything, I'm not hot to marry again, I just don't want to be married to Sandy anymore. If I'm your whore I can't be his. Sandy and I own the house together so we'll have to work that part out, but I want out. O. U. T."

She says she will tell Sandy about me and make some kind of financial deal with him. With Laura bringing in tons of money, Sandy has gotten lazy and spends most of his time with his girlfriend, Donna. He is even supporting her with Laura's hooking money. It annoys Laura. It pisses me off.

I ask Laura if Sandy would get physical. Does she want me to come up with her, take a motel room and be on standby? She says Sandy would never hurt her and that she wants to make the official announcement by herself. Before she leaves we make love and while cuddling she tells me again how much she loves the size of my penis and it's exactly the right size for her. Then she observes, "So many mean tricks are little guys with little dicks or big guys with big dicks. I think the little dicks are mad at the world for giving them a little dick and the big dicks think they're hot shit and are mad at you because they're paying for it.

"You know," Laura continues, "All the other girls at Eureka say you are nice to them and they like fucking you. That makes me proud."

"That's a good compliment."

"Have you always been nice to prostitutes?" Laura asks.

I had never heard Laura use that word and there was something raw, honest and exciting about it.

"I am grateful for hookers," I tell her. "As soon as I heard they existed I thanked God for making them. The idea that I can buy naked women and sex is heaven on earth to me. It thrilled me when I first heard about it. And it still does. I bless them all. Really."

"I was quite naïve before I started working in the whorehouse," Laura explains. "You see, before I started working there, I was talking to a really good friend of mine and I said, 'Oh, we're in debt, and Sandy thinks I should go work in a whorehouse. He thinks I should go to a whorehouse and get our money back...'

"And my friend said, 'You shouldn't say that out loud...'

"I said, 'Why? Why not?'

"He said, 'If you do it, just don't say anything about it...'

"I really didn't know how disrespected whores were, because I didn't disrespect them. I believed whores were noble creatures."

Laura calls several times over the weekend and reports on the ongoing negotiations. Each call is a little oasis in a lonely weekend. I miss Laura. I stay in New York and work on some projects that are due Monday. Laura calls Sunday night to say she made a deal with Sandy. She's staying in New Hope that night, going to work early Monday morning and she'll tell me everything when she sees me after work at what she now calls "our apartment." There are no moments in the day I don't think of her.

She comes home and tells me the deal. She'll continue paying all the mortgage and taxes on the house but contribute only half toward the bills and none of the phone. She doesn't have to turn over all the money she makes. It was a suckshit deal but it was made. I figured it was a first step and we'd renegotiate later. Anyway, Sandy now knew about me and they talked about getting a divorce so at least the ball was rolling.

I get Laura a safety deposit box to stash her extra cash. She puts away hundreds of dollars every week and it makes her feel secure and more mature.

14

Our first threesome

Summer 1980

Laura asks me if we can do something sexy like a threesome with another guy and I think of Freddy, my whoring buddy. He'd be great and he'd be grateful.

Freddy and I have often watched each other fuck the same hooker so I am comfortable with him. We work well together naturally, like a good doubles tennis team. Our egos never bump. Our cocks are about the same size. We both worship slutty women and he always smells clean.

Freddy is about 5'9" with a full head of prematurely grey curly hair. He's chunky, an ex-high school linebacker, once mostly muscle, who now shares his body with the excess calories from too much cheesecake. He drives a new Mercedes and dresses, even though he's Jewish, like a Mafia don's kid—lots of Italian knits in tasteful designs and muted tones, high-end shoes, bespoke suits and pants and when he's dressed up, a Ferragamo tie and a diamond-encrusted, solid gold Rolex President, so heavy he lists to his left.

I don't follow fashion but I can listen to him go on about his beloved wardrobe for forty-five minutes before I get bored and move him to another subject.

When I call him up, I don't tell him my plans for the evening. He thinks he's coming over just to meet Laura. He knocks and I tell Laura to open the door for him. She's wearing a black thong and a black lace teddy, and in high heels, towers over Freddy. He stares and lets out a soft involuntary "Wow!"

They trade greetings and as he follows her into the living room he's looking at her legs and ass and keeps repeating soft, "wows."

He brings coke and grass and we all dig in. Freddy is as particular about his recreational drugs as he is about his car and clothing. The three of us share a joint of hybrid Indica from Hawaii crossed with a feminized Afghani seed and do two hits each of Peruvian flake from the northern side of Machu Picchu. Then I tell Freddy I want him to fuck Laura right there on the big cushy couch.

He looks into her face. She grins her approval.

> "Freddy was just always ready," Laura laughs, "He was like, "Yeah, I'll do that! Sure, let's do that!!" Freddy was always willing—and grateful—and very kind when the fucking became, uh, very delicate, like in my ass, ha, ha, ha!"

He wastes no time and kisses her. He gets up and stands in front of her. He slips off his mocha and tan fully-leather-lined Bally slip-ons and takes off his long-sleeve ecru silk shirt already open at the neck two full buttons revealing the oversize gold rope chain that held the dangling matching detachable coke spoon recently in use. Before he can do it himself, she unbuckles his Gucci analine leather belt with 14k gold horse bit buckle, pulls down his tan Italian wool lightweight gabardine flat-front trousers and his Parisian silk bikini briefs better suited to his former figure. She catches his tool in her mouth as it springs out. I move in like a camera for the close-up.

Laura puts her hands on his ass and with his hard penis in her mouth gargles that Freddy has the smoothest skin she ever felt on a man. I feel his back as he is grooving in and out of her mouth. I had never thought about it before but she is right—he has baby skin.

"His skin was softer," Laura explains, "than you would ever think a man's skin could be."

He pushes her back and she lies on the couch. He crouches between her legs and returns the oral favor. She purrs and groans and looks straight into my eyes.

He is vein-bulging hard. He kneels and enters her. He moves in and out, slow, metered, each penetration deeper. Laura acknowledges each push.

I get down near the fuck and stare at the copulation point. It is an erotic organic sculpture, half oil rig-mechanical and half porn. I touch it where it meets, not enough to startle, just enough to feel his contact with her. My her. The woman I love. The woman I need. The woman who heats my blood. She who is to die for.

I suggest we all go in the bedroom so I can join in. On the bed I put my cock in her mouth while Freddy re-establishes his fucking. When we switch positions I watch close up his cock go in and out of her mouth. Her eyes are glued to mine.

We are eye to eye and she is sucking another man's cock, what in some cultures is the world upside down and grounds for justifiable homicide, but to us it's just what Swingers call "The Lifestyle." Laura is lost on the path to orgasms. She has one, then a second runs in behind it and pushes out.

I am fucking her and she comes again. She takes Freddy's cock out of her mouth and kisses me. The sex fire burns so hot the usual rules of heterosexual engagement are suspended. It doesn't make me cringe. In unison Laura and I say we love each other.

"Right at this moment I love you both," says Freddy.

Freddy fucks her until he comes. I stick two fingers up her ass and feel him throb as he pumps his juice in her and I feel her convulsions as she comes again. I tap Freddy to slide out pronto and before her writhing subsides I go into her wet just-fucked pussy. Laura and I have an entire wordless conversation of wonder, surprise and pleasure as her face muscles go slack and her tongue falls out of her mouth.

I come and she joins again.

Laura Bradley is as high as it goes. She is being here now, breathing, alive, at the leading edge of experience. Her primitive eyes smile large and stretch her face with love. She is complete with everything good the universe has to offer. She is right now and she is 20,000 years old. Only Laura goes to where it all began.

We lay there, Freddy on one side and me on the other. Laura is the Nookie Queen. Freddy looks at me with an admiring grin and says, "Don't lose this one."

I don't feel an ounce of self-conscious depravity.

Outlaws? Yes.

Morally corrupt? No.

I feel like the Eskimo who shares his wife on a cold night. It is ur-holy and animal good.

We share another joint, this time deep rich brown Jamaican Lambs Bread. We do two more spoons of coke each. I do little spoons; they do large. Laura plays with my penis and in ten minutes I get hard again. We fuck and Freddy puts his soft cock in her mouth, and it doesn't stay soft for long.

I lie on my back and she sits down on me facing away, reverse cowgirl, and slow and easy works my cock up into her ass. Her long back and narrow waist and waving hair go up and down on me. She crouches on the soles of her feet and on each up stroke her only connection to me is her asshole.

I lean her back and invite Freddy to use her pussy.

He pushes into her. Laura goes wild. We've hit the Big Top: This is "DP," Double Penetration, The Flying Wallendas of Porn.

"I remember Freddy's cock in me," Laura recalls, "as Jeffrey was lying on his back taking my ass. Freddy and Jeffrey were really tuned in to each other and both of them adored me. And the rhythm worked when they both fucked me at the same time. They both switched holes a couple of times."

I'd been on the high wire a few times before. It's usually performed with a guy lying on his back, penis in vagina of the girl on her knees straddling him and her rear entered by another guy behind her who does something between straddling and crouching. It takes balance, two very hard cocks and one sex-crazed limber adventurous female.

It's weird for guys because no matter what entrance you take, you feel the other guy's cock in the other tunnel. But it's so horny and women go so crazy that once again the normal rules of heterosexual engagement are suspended. You need penises that are at least slightly bigger than average and they must be bones. Anything squishy pops out.

Finding the right rhythm is necessary for the dance to move smoothly with everybody getting what they came for and nothing popping out or bending at an unfortunate angle.

You've got to move the way a watch works. As horologists say, it's a "complication," this one flesh and blood, with each part dancing with the others.

> "The trick to keeping two dicks in you at the same time is very complex," Laura explains, "because of the rhythm. You have to be really tuned in together. It's best done on acid, ha, ha, ha! It depends on how sensitive the guys are to the woman—and to each other.
>
> "It's very important that the men are tuned in to each other," Laura continues, "so that the rhythm can work. If there is any kind of an ego fight between the two men, it doesn't work at all. I've had cocks popping out of me because the guys weren't in 100 percent harmony with each other—but that didn't happen with Jeffrey and Freddy!"

Laura starts to scream so loud I get scared the police might come. Freddy must have the same worry and gently cups his hand over her mouth. The machine speeds up as we all come. Me first, then Laura, then Freddy, followed by another little one of hers, all within maybe half a minute; the moans, groans, grunts, orgasmic sighs and callings to "God" melding into music.

Our three-part crescendo fades until all I hear is breathing. Once again she is between us.

"I never did that." Laura says flatly. "I want it again. Right away."

"Easy for you to say," says I.

I am spent. So is Freddy. I get on my knees on the floor and beg, "No More! Please No More!" Freddy seconds the motion and we all laugh.

(This is about one month before Roberto Duran in his second fight with Sugar Ray Leonard cries, "No Mas! No Mas!"—No More! No More!—and quits at the beginning of the eighth round and makes the plea for surrender, in Spanish, famous in the headlines. He was getting beat up. I was getting fucked out. We both knew the meaning of no more.)

Laura says, "I guess I need four guys."

Maybe she does.

An hour after Freddy leaves I get renewal and make love with Laura again while she talks and replays the scenes, taking a long time when she gets to the double penetration.

15

What lives in the slime on a porn booth floor?

Late summer 1980

My relationship with Laura is now several months old. We get along well, the sex still steams and the S&M part is still frosting and not the cake. I find myself wanting her to stop working at the whorehouse. Health concerns are not a giant part of my reasons why. This is the era before AIDS. This is the era before the herpes scare. I just had enough.

Periodically she has to work double shifts, some weeks she works nights and occasionally she works weekends including Saturday or Sunday night. Whorehouses are easy marks for robbers, especially at night and on weekends. Sometimes they get held up, sometimes the girls are raped, and sometimes girls and their clients get shot and killed. It happens. Plus, Laura doesn't have any control over whom she fucks. If she doesn't want a particular dude she has to fuck and suck him anyway. She doesn't mind it too much but I don't like that.

She occasionally does tricks on the outside. She likes these better because she can choose her johns and she makes more money per fuck than at the whorehouse. When she does them in our apartment I go for a walk with Necort or I go to the movies. I'm sure she'd be able to make enough money on her own with her regulars.

Another thing I want changed is her turning over the bulk of her money to her husband. She keeps some, but she is supporting Sandy and his girlfriend. My inner pimp asks what Silky and Iceberg Slim would think of a pathetic white boy Jew living with a whore who turns over most of her money to another man.

I decide Laura and I need to talk. One Saturday afternoon of an early autumn weekend at my cabin I tell her that I want her to quit the whorehouse and to stop paying Sandy so much of her hard-earned money. Splitting the cost of a house she doesn't live in is way more than enough. I tell her I make enough money to support both of us and she can keep all her "trick" money. She says she doesn't want to quit Eureka because it isn't just the money. She loves being a whore; she loves having sex with one strange man after another and then coming home to make love to me. And what about the money for Sandy and her house, she asks. Could I handle all that too?

"No, I can't. I don't want to. Why should either one of us pay the entire mortgage and taxes and insurance and half the bills on a house you don't live in?"

"But I told Sandy I'd pay all the mortgage and taxes and insurance."

"I don't care. You'll renegotiate"

"I can't."

"Yes you can."

Our voices rise to shouting. We are having our First Fight.

We argue. My rationality exhausted, I play my trump card and threaten to split up. I hold my breath. She cries and begs me not to leave. Through my bravado I know I am full of shit and would crumble the first moment my bluff is called. I know, if not in words, that even if she fancies herself my slave and gets off on me owning her and using her that I am the real slave. I can't be without her.

We talk more and strike a deal. Laura will leave the whorehouse. She'll tell Sandy she'll pay half the mortgage, taxes, and insurance and only the bills that she runs up. She'll turn occasional tricks from her black book. She'll resume making silver rings and pendants and hustle her art as well as her body. We'll go to orgies together so she can have her fill of men. It'll be my job to take her on sexual adventures.

I entice her with promises of promiscuity. We'll pick up guys in bars for threesomes; go to S&M clubs, orgies, adult bookstores, on-premise swing clubs. The works.

She says, "I've got years of not having enough sex to make up for. I love the days when four or five customers come and they all use me hard. I love doing that and coming home and you fucking me for hours. I just can't get enough sex. But I want to try."

She is dying to turn a trick in front of me. I am dying to watch. It's a fair deal. We have our first make-up sex. There is no S&M. It's just, as Henry Miller calls it, "a good old-fashioned fuck."

She is a hippie-whore after my own heart. She is the flip side of me. I understand her. She's a very yangish yin. If I were a woman I would be her. (And God willing, if this transmogrification happened, I'd pray to be blessed with her stunning good looks.)

That night after a dinner out to celebrate our new deal we are driving back to the cabin when Laura, tipsy and stoned says, "Let's go find adventure now! I'm feeling really horny!"

> "I would fuck anyone Jeffrey told me to," Laura explains, "oh, absolutely! He would tell me who to fuck and who not to fuck. I would have sex with anybody he wanted me to have sex with. I trusted him. I knew he always was taking my fantasies and painting them with sex."

I suggest the adult bookstore.

Located in a dull building on a drab, downtown street, the adult bookstore is a magnet for swinger couples, gays, and regular horny guys. This is before VCRs and videotape; if you want to see porn films you have to go to a bookstore booth with a roll of quarters.

The films are on 8mm loops and what they lack in production values they make up for by existing.

I'd gone to adult bookstores for years, alone and with a few different girls and we'd fuck while watching a porn flick. Sometimes we'd pick up another couple or a single guy and go back to their place. Most often I went to a bookstore by myself.

The front of the store sells books and movies and is well lit. The back of the store is dark, with about a dozen small cubicles for watching films. Some booths have no holes though the shared wall, some have small holes just big enough for a dick, some have two small holes, one on each side for, I guess, the real gay party boys, and some have bigger holes, maybe four inches in diameter that a cock and balls could fit through or an ass could press up against.

Most times I'd choose a booth with no hole and just jerk off, preferably to a large-breasted blonde being gangbanged by several black men or a skinny hot young girl sucking off an older man.

Sometimes, I must admit, I'd go into a cubicle with a hole in the wall and wait for the sign: fingers sticking through the hole beckoning my pecker to have a good time. I'd stick my cock, or if the hole was big enough, my cock and balls, through the "glory hole" and enjoy. If I were in a booth next to a couple, I'd hope it was the woman giving me head, but I never really had a prohibition against letting a guy suck my dick. Gay guys give great head. They are obsessive about it and are technically proficient in a way that few women can match. And they love to swallow and continue sucking once you've shot your load.

When I was in second grade, Susie, a girl my age asked if I wanted to play naked games with her. We danced naked. We touched each other's bodies everywhere. We spent a lot of time spreading each other's asscheeks and looking at each other's assholes and laughing. Assholes were funny. We'd kiss (without tongues) and watch each other pee. I would touch her slit and she would touch my miniature boner. I don't remember it ever being soft around her. One time she started kissing my penis and soon she was sucking it. I liked it immediately. Since I had no reference, I thought she invented it. She was toothy and I had to keep reminding her not to hurt me but it was definitely a great thing. I also knew it was a bad thing and that we shouldn't be doing it, but I didn't care so I knew I would go to hell.

A few years later, when I was nine or ten, but still before I knew what sex was, an older boy, David—maybe thirteen or fourteen— seduced me into letting him play with my little penis. It felt terrific. I loved his warm mouth and gentle hands playing with my favorite places to touch. He made me swear not to tell and I never did. Until now. He never asked me to touch him and I wasn't curious about it, so it never came up. So to speak. All I knew was that he sucked my penis better than Susie and maybe it was something other people did and Susie hadn't invented it. And since I was already going to hell, what could it matter.

Laura and I get to the bookstore just before midnight. There's another couple and about a dozen lone men roaming around, eying each other, cruising. Most appear gay, some I suppose are bisexual, and some like me consider themselves heterosexual—but are so horny they let anyone suck their cocks.

Laura and I are casually dressed for warm weather. I am wearing shorts and a T-shirt; she is wearing a short skirt and a tube top that lets her big nipples speak directly to the public. Her beauty and skimpy clothes catch every eye in the store. The straight guys want to fuck her and the gay guys want to be her. We cause a murmuring stir, but walk around unhassled.

After getting five dollars in quarters I choose a booth with one hole. Laura and I squeeze into the narrow stall and start kissing standing up. Our shoes make squishy noises.

I feed some quarters into the slot. To my delight an attractive blonde on her knees stretching her mouth to suck two big black cocks at the same time appears on the white cardboard on the back of the door that serves as a screen. Ah! The perfect ambient visual!

I feel something poke my leg and look down to see a large cock sliding through the wall. I put Laura's hand on it. Her eyes smile. I sit down on the little bench at the rear of the booth and by the flickering light of the movie watch Laura hunch down like a primitive cave woman on the soles of her shoes.

She watches my eyes watching hers, her head on the other side of the cock between us. She ever so slowly puts out her long tongue and licks it. The cock responds with a wiggle and a stretch and Laura moves around in front of it, facing it, and slowly works it all the way into her mouth. God! She is hotter than any porn movie I've ever seen! And she is live! And mine!

I unzip and start playing with myself and drop more quarters so I can watch Laura by the light of the porn. She holds onto the guest cock with one hand, moves toward me and buries her face in my lap. She goes back and forth between cocks until she sucks the mystery dick to completion as muffled moans of joy seep through the plywood wall. Laura turns, opens her mouth to show me her viscous trophy, exaggerates the motions of swirling it around, and finally, with an audible gulp, swallows it. "Thank you, Jeffrey," she says, hugging me.

Laura stands up. She slides out of her panties and lifting her miniskirt sits on my stiffness. As she rides up and down we hear sounds from next door: The mystery dick leaves and another is getting ready to take its place. I tell Laura how to invite the new one in by wiggling her fingers through the hole and soon another cock, smaller and already standing at attention awaits her review.

She bends down to suck it and I move her off me so she can concentrate on the little soldier. She asks me to finger her while she sucks. Soon she displays a new mouthful of spunk.

More noise from the changing of the guards and, seconds later, a monster, semi-hard and already half the size of a kosher salami, lumbers through the wall. Laura rubs the horsedick back and forth and stretches it out till it grows harder and longer, ten inches of massive dick, as big as any I've ever seen live. I ask her if she wants to fuck it.

She bends over with her ass facing the cock and works it into her pussy. I love it. She is an animal and she is mine! I tell her to pull away. She obeys without hesitation and I turn her around to face the cock now bobbing blindly.

I squeeze behind her in the narrow booth and lift her up. I tell her to climb the wall with her feet as I hold her, till her shoes are above our heads and her back is nearly parallel to the floor. She is light, I am adrenaline strong and the booth is so narrow I am pressed against the wall. I guide her pussy back to the big cock, and she uses her hands to push the thing back in. I hold her up as she fucks, rocking her back and forth. I look down between her legs and watch the cock fuck my baby's pussy.

Laura says she feels the cock starting to come. She stretches her head up to kiss me and cries softly, "For you Jeffrey, I swear this is for you," and climaxes in response to the pulsing pumping of the huge dick.

I move her harder until her moans and the ones from the horsedick's booth die down. I am exhausted. Laura's pussy is flat against the hole in the wall and the huge cock is still pushed inside her. She presses against the wall just enough to give her space to pet the penis and slowly move in and out on it.

> *"Glory holes!"* Laura gushes, "oh my God, *I loved it!* I thought that was really, really, really incredibly exciting! Cocks coming through the wall! So wonderful. So decadent! I still think about it a lot. It was a ton of fun! It was just so out there!! *It's a girl's dream come true!"*

She pushes her feet against the wall, pulls back and slides off the cock. It drools come and hangs there limp. I balance her as she puts her feet on the floor. The cock withdraws and disappears.

"Jeffrey, I love you, baby," she smiles as she sticks her hand in her pussy and tastes the big dick's delivery, "what do you want me to do for you? Thank you for taking me here and letting me fuck another cock in front of you. You proved your love for me, Jeffrey; I'll do anything you want. You own me. Let me give you my tits," she whimpers as she lifts her top and pinches her huge nipples so hard she winces.

"Give them to me," I order. She bends down putting her nipples in my hands. I squeeze hard, digging in my nails. She kisses me murmuring, "Thank you. Thank you for wanting me. Now please fuck my pussy."

My whole body is a hard-on. I stand up, lean back against the bench, point her toward the door, bend her over, guide myself in and slide into her wetness. I move with the determination and single purpose of a drill press, pumping away until I add my juice to her collection, alive—live, breathing, actually here—in the middle of the hottest, dirtiest porn film ever.

We put on our clothes. I hear men shoving each other outside the booth next-door, jockeying for the hole position.

"Tell me what to do next. Tell me to do things for you." Laura seems more stoned than before, as if decadence itself is a drug. We are about to leave and I'm almost out of quarters when another mystery dick juts through the hole waving up and down, begging like a dog.

She looks at me, smiles, and reaches down and starts jerking it off while we kiss. When she feels it start to come she bends down to suck it and just before it shoots—she pulls back and it squirts all over her face. The film is running through the credits so the light is bright and like a strobe. I see the come shoot out and appear frozen in midair on the way to her face. Next flicker a second later and it is on her face. Next good light, after a patch of darkness her face is lathered with come. I never in my life saw anyone come that much.

She stands up with spunk all over her face. I wipe it off with my shirt and kiss her. I love her. We are two sides of the same coin.

As we leave there is a line of single guys still waiting outside the booth next to ours. There is even a couple, and Laura asks me if I want to play peephole with them. I tell her I don't, though they are a rare lucky find. The girl is short, skinny-sexy, definitely wasted and has that trampy country shiksa look I adore. The guy, a biker wearing the colors of the toughest local gang, wants to trade and fingers his slut under her short skirt as a sales pitch; I can see she's without proper undergarments. He also exposes her small breasts as a way of beckoning me to take her for a test ride, but I am fixed on

Laura. I want to go home and fuck her in a bed. I tell them we have to go. I apologize to the couple sincerely in case I am ever single again in my life, still living in the country and still going to adult bookstores.

Three guys say, "Thank you," as they escort us toward the front of the store. Just as we exit, the back room breaks out in whistles and applause.

> "What was nice about doing it in adult bookstores," Laura remembers, "was that Jeffrey always made sure that I wanted to do it. And of course, I always did, ha, ha, ha!"

We go home, fuck and do drugs all night. I make her talk about what she had done over and over again and draw new erotic energy with each new detail. She is my three dimensional porn star.

16

Soft-core and hard-core masturbators

Here's the difference between *Hard-core* and *Soft-core* Masturbators:

Some men, given a choice between jerking off to a hot beautiful naked girl in a soft-core magazine like *Playboy, Penthouse,* or *Hustler,* and a hard-core, full-penetration shoot with an equally sexy girl plus a man or two or five, will choose to jerk off to the single girl. These men are the Soft-core Masturbators. They don't like the intrusion of another man. Soft-core Masturbators buy what are called Single-Girl videos and Two-Girl videos and shy away from Boy/Girl and Group. These guys need to fantasize about themselves as the central character with the girl/or girls. Another man in the picture is a threat or at the very least distracting.

The type of man uncomfortable with hard core usually doesn't go to orgies because he couldn't stand seeing his wife or girlfriend in carnal pursuits.

On the other hand, we Hard-core Masturbators (who can, I suppose, under duress, jerk off to a Single Girl if that is what we are stuck with) prefer to see another man in the picture because we are not the center of the fantasy. The girl is.

We watch Boy/Girl, Group, and Gangbang. In most instances,

each of these videos begins with or skips foreplay, immediately goes to oral, then fucking, then anal, then the cum shot. We like to see the girl getting fucked, preferably by more than one man at a time.

We Hard-core guys appear to be more mystified by the other gender, more curious, more driven than the Soft-core Masturbator.

What sets Laura and a few others like Erika the Cum Junky apart from the rest of the women in the world is more than just their pre-qualifying overactive libido. These are the women we super horny Hard-core Masturbator men fantasize about, whom we dream of meeting, and more important: They are the women we driven men think we would be if we were women.

In a strange testosteronic way, although they are ultimate female icons, they are in fact masculinized in their sex attitudes and we men identify with them on a subconscious level.

The mystery dick bookstore experience was sex at its most primitive. The fundament. No names. No faces. Just disenfranchised cocks. Men in their essence, performing their only necessary evolutionary function. Having Laura pleasure isolated penises of unknown horny men was my erotic noblesse oblige and cut to the quick of my erotic psyche. It was dirtier than porn. I couldn't wait to do it again.

17

Laura quits the whorehouse, shaves her legs, and becomes a model

Autumn 1980

Back in New York City on Monday after the bookstore sex, Laura quits the whorehouse. Liz calls me, happy that Laura and I have fallen in love, pissed I've taken away one of her best girls. Liz says that if Laura ever wants her job back she's welcome to it. As a going-away gift Liz gives Laura the answering service number of two of Laura's biggest fans, rich men always good for $200 tips.

"As I said, I thought there was a certain nobility in being a whore," Laura explains, "but other people didn't. And after being at the whorehouse for a few months, the *disrespect* started showing up. Most johns don't respect whores, *nobody* respects whores.

"I don't know why. Maybe because it's illegal, I don't know...

"I mean, most johns were polite to me—but they didn't talk to me like a woman; they talked to me like a commodity.

"Oftentimes they'd say, "Why is a beautiful, capable woman like you *here?*

"I'd say, 'Why wouldn't I be *here?'*

"They'd say, 'Because this is a *horrible job!'*

"I grew up so naïve. I found out it is *not* a noble profession. And as it wore on, everything had to be secret all the time—it got really tiring. So once I had that $10,000 paid off, I quit the whorehouse when Jeffrey suggested it.

"I didn't stop having sex with lots of men after I left," Laura laughs, "I had *more and more* sex, but I stopped getting money for a lot of it. I had as much sex as possible. That's what I wanted. That's why I was with Jeffrey. I wanted as much sex as I could get and I never met a man more sexual than Jeffrey. He could fuck a lot, he let me fuck clients and he'd get me lots of other men to fuck. It was perfect. Most of the fucking I did for free but I still got money for some of it because I kept a bunch of clients and they would refer me to other clients. I loved it all. Paid or free, sex is sex. I just wanted as much sex as possible."

Over the next few weeks, as the season changes to fall, Laura and I are no different from thousands of happy couples in the early '80s. We settle into a routine of Tuesday through Friday in the Big Apple and long weekends in the country. Laura continues to do too much cocaine.

I am completely in love with Laura. Just getting up from the sofa she moves as smooth as jazz ballet. She is a star in every room she enters and at any party if I look for the largest crowd she's in the center. When she talks it is melodic poetry that bathes me in images and metaphors. She doesn't just want to garden, she wants to plant a "storybook garden." She never just cooks a meal, every dish is something special. Even when she throws together what looks like a random selection from her hippie wardrobe of jeans and frilly shirts, she looks like a professional stylist dresses her.

Being thin and 5'8" helps but it's more than that. She walks with confidence. She is a tall beautiful brunette princess with a flower power smile and heart full of peace and love. Even though Laura is beyond sexy, she's so sweet that women, contrary to the way their impulses and prejudices often move them, are not threatened by her. In a movie she could play the lead romantic role or the funky best friend.

When she dances she moves like her bones are liquid, and her grace is just shy of being misconstrued as a religious ceremony or Asian calisthenics.

Her home base is being happy and her default facial expression is a smile and people return the favor because when she talks to them it makes them feel better.

I arrange my business meetings with Laura present so I have a better chance of closing. When I walk into a room to meet male clients and I am accompanied by a tall gorgeous woman, it's a leg up. I am the Indian brave with many scalps on my belt. Female clients might resent my arm candy, but men are pigs and respect a man who sports hot pussy. Men assume I am rich or have a huge penis or both, which in my case are two misconceptions that work in my favor.

All Laura has to do is smile, feign interest and look at me with adoration. She doesn't even have to talk except to say hello and goodbye. When she opens her mouth and constructive, creative concepts come out, she rises so many notches above bimbo that even female clients can't dismiss her or dis me. And to men, I am below Japanese emperor status but above that of an unemployed TV action hero from a long running but now cancelled series.

Laura is terrific at drawing storyboards, critiquing my designs and coming up with her own creative concepts, some preferable to mine. At video shoots she styles the sets, wrangles the actors and outshines the other production assistants. No one suspects she is a whore. An arty hippie? Yes. A beautiful girlfriend? Yes. A whore? No way. She is the last person you would cast as a prostitute unless you were casting against type.

In October, Laura goes to her friend Lindsey's wedding. A well-known fashion model, Lindsey is marrying an up-and-coming actor. Neither Lindsey nor any of the Bucks County crowd know of Laura's demimonde life. At the reception, the owner of Lindsey's modeling agency walks up to Laura and says, "My, you're pretty. Who are you with?"

"I'm with Jeffrey but he's not here," says Laura.

"No. I mean what modeling agency are you with?"

"Modeling agency? None."

"Well, now you're with us. Come see me Monday morning and I'll get you started."

To get ready for Monday, and with Lindsey on her honeymoon, Laura goes to see another one of her friends, a girly girl, who helps Laura shave her legs for the first time in ten years. She also gives Laura a remedial lesson in make up, and sends her out with a shopping list of cosmetics. Up to this point Laura's make-up kit is some mascara and two shades of lipstick.

Monday, in New York City, the head of the agency sets up Laura with photographers so Laura can build a portfolio. The camera sees her halfway between Botticelli and Giacometti.

High fashion models, she learns, need to be beautiful and symmetrical but also bland so the clothes don't have to fight for the spotlight. I guess that clothing designers want a face that looks like it stopped developing somewhere in the first or second trimester, as if ontogeny, facially anyway, didn't fully recapitulate phylogeny. They want girls who look like embryos.

Laura isn't just pretty, she's sexy and full of character and it limits her value, at least at a high fashion agency. However, within a few weeks and twenty-five go-sees, she gets her first paying job modeling lingerie, which appears to be the only kind of job available to her. It's the kind of modeling that best suits her personality as well as her face.

Laura asks me to come by and pick her up at the shoot. When I get there, they're running late. I'm told to wait in the kitchen of the huge photo studio and help myself to coffee and snacks. The place is buzzing with models, dressers, photo assistants, hair and makeup people, a caterer and lots of young people with clipboards and/or duct tape. I don't see Laura anywhere.

A giant glamour goddess with huge teased hair walks toward me. She looks familiar but I can't place her. Maybe she's famous. She kisses me on the cheek and says that she'll be ready to go soon. For three one hundredths of a second I don't recognize that this giant is Laura in dramatic make-up and heels.

Usually a few inches shorter than me, she now stands a few inches taller. In addition to the theatrical makeup, she has something else I never saw on her—a hairdo. Her natural wavy hair is now wild and huge and looks like she just stuck her finger in an electrical socket.

"I'm taking all this stuff off and I'll be ready in fifteen minutes," she says.

"Please don't take it off," I beg. "I love it. I want to make love to you this way." It's the first time I ever say "make love" instead of "fuck" to her.

"Sure," she smiles with a small rise of one of her lush eyebrows.

Since the shoes are props we buy her a pair of high heels on the way home. We care less about what they look like than how much taller than me they make her. We make love and/or fuck, with her shoes on, till nearly all her makeup is on the sheets or me.

There's something about her made-up self she likes. Most of her life she was an orthodox hippie. Now she starts to wear a little makeup when we go out at night and when she turns tricks. Only one of her johns asks her to take it off. His wife is an Italian from the Big Hair State of New Jersey who always wears too much makeup and sleazy lingerie. He likes to put his penis in the unpainted hippie chick nature girl who just took off her plain white cotton panties.

In addition to an occasional modeling gig Laura turns about six $100-$300 tricks a week, which covers what she needs to cover with some extra. She deals small amounts of coke on the side and there is always some around.

After six weeks, Laura decides she's been a model long enough.

She doesn't like being so intimately involved with her looks. She said it's changed her relationship with herself, and she doesn't like that every time she looks in the mirror, it's work. Also, she's not getting that many jobs, the go-sees take too much time and she makes more per hour hooking than modeling.

With no slight to me, she says she misses getting fucked by three or more tricks every day. "I love having sex with lots of men every day. I never get tired of it. And I promise to always give you whatever you want. You could never want too much. I mean if you were a woman wouldn't you want to get gangbanged every day?" I see her point.

Laura needs to feel like she is "my whore," so every so often she buys me something with her "pussy biz" money, a necessary homage to her pimp. My wardrobe grows. She also buys whips.

I pay for my country cabin, the NYC apartment, our cars and the NYC garage which at $140 a month is only $5 a month less than my country cabin mortgage. Laura pays for all our food, drugs and entertainment.

It's a great easy time. Mystical magic greets me each morning. It's my birthday every day. She is my dirtiest fantasy come to life.

"Jeffrey liked to get really high-paying guys to fuck me," Laura laughs. "He would take me to the Waldorf Astoria— he'd get me all dressed up and we'd go there and I loved it!

"Oh my God; it was so much fun to just fucking blow men's minds! I was really into getting men off, and I didn't ever want to be just another 'off!' I wanted to get men really fucking crazed! That's the way I would want to be treated!

"We'd go and we'd find these lonely guys sitting there on a business trip and Jeffrey would say, 'Why don't we go up to your room and you have sex with my wife?'

"They'd be like, 'What?'

"Jeffrey would do the business. He explained that I was his wife and that I wanted to make believe I was a whore and if the guy would pay me and he could watch then the guy could use me for sex. Some guys were afraid but many could see we were good souls and take us up on the deal."

Laura laughs, "Whatever Jeffrey would do, he would do for fun. He was definitely not doing it for the money, but he liked to see how much he could get for me. Sometimes it was a lot. Sometimes $200 but sometimes $500 or more. I think he got me $1,000 a few times. He made sure I always got the money and put it in my bank account. It was important to him that he remained a sex maniac, that I got all the money and that he wasn't a real pimp.

"He didn't want to lose his amateur standing, ha ha ha..."

18

Autumn almanac

October–November 1980

Our unusual erotic avocation and Laura's vocation of fucking men for money and her knack of dealing just enough to keep us in coke is balanced by measuring out our life in coffee spoons, more often than coke spoons. We spend our days planning dinner, going to movies, reading, cleaning and shopping. Friends visit us in the city. We go to her house in Bucks County when Sandy isn't there and spend time with her New Hope buddies. My friends visit us at my cabin on the river. We take walks with Necort the dog and play with Angel, the cat, and her new kittens.

We are still in our honeymoon period. At my urging Laura finally agrees to rein back on coke to only on weekends and holidays and sometimes when she turns tricks because so many of her tricks did coke. Among a certain class of alpha men in the big cities, fucking hookers and snorting coke competes with baseball as America's Favorite Pastime. This is the period when lots of people—middle class people with kids and good jobs—are becoming cokeheads. In some circles it is as common as alcohol or German cars.

My work takes new directions. I want to learn how to make TV commercials and I can afford to take a part-time job for $75 or $100 a day as a production assistant, a fancy term for grunt and gofer.

I see the back end of film and video. I watch directors coax brilliant performances from union pros and non-union amateurs. I see directors' egos fuck up scenes and drive productions into overtime. I find out what a gaffer is and why there are always gaffer tape (duct tape), gloves, pliers and clothespins hanging from his belt. I watch gaffers light up scenes using these tools. I learn the names of lights, their wattage and how they are used. I find out that a grip carries cameras and camera stuff and that the best boy, who also always wears gaffer tape, gloves, pliers and clothes-pins, works for the gaffer. I learn lighting jargon: Roscoes (color filters), silks (material to either bounce or diffuse light), butterflies (frames that hold silks), cookies (cut-outs that cast shadows), and tweenies, blondes, and redheads (different kinds of lights).

The men's magazine business is still part of my life. I am still on call to answer questions, attend editorial meetings and produce some porn shoots with photographers who prefer working with me. I also continue to be *Puritan's* figurehead spokesman and go to conventions where I am well known. When Laura comes into the picture, she joins me on assignments.

From 1975 until 1978, at the end of my twenties and the beginning of my thirties, I'd been the co-founder of *Puritan*, a pioneering men's magazine and the first to combine literate writing and explicit, beautifully produced hard-core photography. My co-founder was the brilliant and courageous John Krasner, a self-made wealthy Pennsylvania porn store chain owner. I was the mother who gave creative birth and John was the father who put up the money, came up with the name and offered lots of great ideas and let me run the show and have my way.

We both had strong work ethics and both put in sixty-hour weeks, he sometimes more. I made a deal with him whereby he had to tolerate one major dislike and two minor peeves per issue without interfering with my authority. He did get to tell me everything he thought and through the years I don't remember him ever substantially disliking any of the stories or photo shoots we published.

On February 7, 1978, John Krasner age fifty-three, was gunned down during a robbery in Ft. Lauderdale, Florida. At first everyone thought it might be organized crime-related but it was a simple robbery. John was tough as nails and I don't think he took kindly to someone rummaging through his car for loose change and then putting a gun in his face. John went for the gun and during the struggle the gun fired, and John was mortally wounded just above the eye and died within a few minutes. The man was captured and sentenced to life without parole.

After John died his kids took over the magazine and in gratitude for a peaceful transition, I was paid a very decent stipend for three years for a part-time job that didn't interfere with my freelance work. John's two sons liked me, which was a blessing because they were two of the physically toughest men I ever met and both were on my Top-Ten List Of Men I Don't Want Mad At Me.

I gave a copy of every *Puritan* issue to my friend Norman Mailer, who was generous in his critiques. He liked some of the photos and said that I elevated the production values of porn while retaining all the heat.

Norman's girlfriend and the mother of their two-year-old son, John Buffalo, is Barbara Jean Norris Church Mailer, a whip-smart gorgeous Wilhelmina model, painter, actress and playwright with a disarming Arkansas accent. Although Norman and Norris know Laura is a hooker, they are well mannered and do not question her about it. Laura and Norris get on well.

The first time we all go out for dinner we meet at P.J. Clarke's on Third Avenue. After drinks at the bar, Norman leads us to the back and into the dining room. Heads turn. Like synchronized swimmers, everybody looks at Norman because they recognize him. They look at the two stunning women, both taller than he, and then they glance at me for about a second and conclude I'm not worth looking at. I'm just some guy. I may be the guy with two hot babes and Norman Mailer but I have little to offer a celeb gawker. I walk the emotional tightrope between pride and humiliation.

At another meal we all share at Elaine's, Norris moves into the category of awesome when she takes a maraschino cherry stem into her mouth, makes more contortions than I ever saw a gorgeous face make and then with her gorgeous face back on, sticks her tongue out and with childlike pride presents us with the stem tied in a knot.

On November 11, 1980, Laura and I are among the few guests at Norman and Norris' impromptu wedding. José Torres, Patricia Kennedy Lawford and Doris Goodwin are there and maybe four more non-Mailers. The invitation is so sudden it's like they eloped except they get married at home. Norris tells us she agreed to marry Norman not just because they have a child together, but because he is such a great lay.

There is a fat cloud of soberness in the room when Norman and Noris repeat their vows in front of a dual ministry of a priest and a rabbi. Norman speaks his vows with great theatrical diction and when he gets to the part about "fidelity" he drops half an octave lower, drawls the word with precision and looks Norris in the eye with conviction bordering on a glare. Not a threatening glare but a drop-dead serious I-swear-to-God, strike-me-dead glare. This is Norman's sixth time at the plate and he has yet to hit a home run. He has seven children with five previous wives so he sure got on base, even got a few extra base hits, but the long ball has eluded him.

Getting this wedding together involved a whirlwind of legal manipulations. Norman wanted his daughter, Maggie to be his full-blooded lawful daughter and since he'd never married her mother, Carol, they quickly married one day and divorced the next. I don't remember exactly how Norman did it but I do remember mayor Ed Koch and the mayor's deputy, Ed Fancher, had something to do with the marital acrobatics because they both crashed Norman and Norris's wedding after the ceremony.

Afterward, the bride and groom flew to London, where Norman had been asked by director Milos Forman to play the part of architect and womanizer Sanford White in the movie, *Ragtime*. Norris sat next to him in a huge fancy dress in the scene where White is assassinated by Harry K. Thaw, the crazed jealous millionaire husband of Evelyn Nesbit. Norman acted with such vigor that he slammed his head on an ice bucket on the way to the floor and hurt himself. When Norman and Norris returned from

London I asked Norris what sights she saw in London. "Mostly the ceiling of my hotel room," she laughed.

Shortly after the Mailers' wedding, my mother calls and urges me to bring my new girlfriend when I come down to Florida to our ancestral condominium for Thanksgiving. Definitely. I know Laura will love my parents and I'm sure they will love her, and when they all meet, they do.

Around my folks Laura is sober, bright and bouncy. Her All-American Gentile Beauty, uncommon not only in my parents' home but also in their gated country club complex and the larger community of Boynton Beach is a special treat for them. She amuses them by knowing the name of every flower in their garden, and by shopping for exotic ingredients to prepare the type of salads they enjoy in restaurants but never make at home.

In the clear light of a drugless day with just a bit of makeup and one of her flowing cotton dresses, Laura is full of poetry and art and possesses one of the finest of Mother Nature's smiles. She is a sweet, very beautiful Flower Child, the kind of girl whose beautiful face you could put on a breakfast cereal box—if the Grateful Dead had their own brand of granola.

Around the Thanksgiving table with my parents, aunts, uncles and my brother The Lawyer we seem like any American family with a moderately successful hippie kid and his fashion model girlfriend. You can't tell anything about our perverted idiosyncrasies after we take a bath—and after Laura's black and blue marks go away.

19

John, Yoko, and the washing machine repairman

December 8, 1980

It is Monday morning, December 8, 1980, three days after my thirty-fourth birthday, one day after the thirty-ninth anniversary of the bombing of Pearl Harbor. I call my brother The Lawyer in Miami, and mutter the least accurate statement of my life. In my best approximation of FDR, I joke, "Today is December 8th, a day that will *not* live in infamy."

That evening, Laura and I are in bed in our apartment in New York, watching television, when whatever we are watching is interrupted by a news flash. John Lennon has been shot. A few minutes later it's announced he's dead. I call Allan Steckler, my main man at Apple Records and a good friend of John's. Allan is sleeping and perturbed that I called. I tell him that John Lennon is dead. We spend the next ten minutes wordlessly crying into the phone.

That night into morning, my phone rings a dozen times as friends call and we all cry. Laura and I sit in bed holding each other for hours, crying past the point of tears.

A Beatle is dead. The poet warrior, the man with the biggest set of balls in rock & roll has been slain. It is the end of something, but

I don't know exactly what.

The assassinations of JFK and Bobby and Martin Luther King were horrible enough, but John's death cuts deeper. Many of us loved and revered those three political leaders, but we never went around humming their music. What kind of society assassinates artists?

What died that day in the public collective consciousness, and unconsciousness, was the tail end of flower-power innocence. It was quoted repeatedly on TV that night in the man's own words: "The dream is over."

This loss of idealism was a significant factor in the drift to greed and selfishness, soon to be the fashionable religion for hippie-turned-yuppie Boomers during the remainder of the 1980s. We might have already been heading in that direction, but the Lennon assassination fueled our worst tendencies. That December day a new cynicism was born.

This was the "More popular than Jesus," "Woman Is the Nigger of the World," "God is a concept by which we measure our pain," "Imagine there's no Heaven" idol smasher, public blasphemer, wit, and hero of the sexual revolution. In some small way Laura and I owed our liberated sexuality to the movement that started with the Beatles. Even the Rolling Stones owed their success, in part, to this man who co-wrote their first chart single, "I Wanna Be Your Man."

John Lennon was the godfather of hippies and of modern-day long hair, and the mass culture of hipness. The Beatniks were an influence on many people but they didn't have mass appeal like the Beatles. Beatnik music didn't dominate the top ten. Teenyboppers didn't hound Jack Kerouac and Allen Ginsberg when they got off airplanes. The Beatles influenced us in a much larger and more direct way, a real way that changed how we lived, dressed and wore our hair. John was the cultural center of the Beatles and now he wasn't breathing any more.

For those who had never lost an immediate family member or a best friend, it was their first salty taste of real grief, of crying on and off for days till numbness set in. On the streets nearly everybody had red eyes or was walking around crying. Strangers half-nodded with sad smiles. The impact was universal and probably strongest in New York where we all felt grief mixed with shame that it happened here.

The news channels were filled with talking heads who knew Lennon well. Friends called me and asked what Lennon was really like. I was as close as they could get to John. What did I feel? What were my favorite memories of him?

The first time I met John I'd been working with Apple for about a year and only dealing with Apple's creative director Allan Steckler. While I had heard Steckler's end of a phone conversation with John or George or Ringo, or even Paul (who had already split from day-to-day Apple and was being represented by his lawyer father-in-law), which was thrilling enough, I hadn't yet met a Beatle. That was okay; I was thrilled to be making a living just in their periphery.

It was early summer, 1971, business was slow, and I decided to take two weeks off and hitchhike around New England with my then girlfriend, Andrea, to visit family and friends. (In 1971 hitchhiking was still a popular mode of transportation with little risk.)

I asked Steckler's permission and he said okay as long as I left my itinerary with his secretary. Itinerary? No one had ever asked for my itinerary before. I was flattered. I left the phone numbers of my friends and family and approximate dates of arrivals and departures and we took off, by thumb, for Vermont.

A week into our trip while staying at my parent's house in Boston, I get a call from Steckler on a Monday morning. He's in L.A. where it's 7:00 a.m. and he's just gotten an urgent call from John who wants me to help put an ad together immediately to promote his and Yoko's interview in *Crawdaddy*, the rock magazine.

Me? Wow!

Steckler asks me to meet him at the Apple office the next morning and go with him to the Pierre, where John and Yoko are camping out. (This was just before their move to Bank Street and several years before the Dakota.)

The conversation with Steckler:

"I'm hitchhiking."

"We'll pay for a plane."

"My girlfriend's with me."

"We'll pay for her ticket too."

"I'll be there."

"Good."

I make reservations and run to the airport—because John Lennon needs me.

Far fucking out, John Lennon needs me.

The next morning I'm ten minutes early and wired. Steckler arrives and we head to the Pierre. I ask if there are some bowing and scraping and/or always-walk-away-from-them-backwards-with-your-eyes-down protocols to follow and Steck says no, just be normal. Normal?

I'm going to meet John and Yoko and I should just be normal?

At the elegant Pierre we are escorted by security to John and Yoko's suite and are greeted by the ever lovely May Pang, John and Yoko's assistant (who becomes even more prominent in John's life later.) May is a buddy I know from the Apple office. She's twenty-one; smart, slinky, tall and I have a moderate crush on her. She lessens my anxiety a notch with her smile.

Steckler and I walk in and John and Yoko are sitting on the floor with a blank piece of paper the size of a *New York Times* page. I think to myself, "Holy Shit! That's actually John and Yoko!"

A few other people are milling around the suite, which is the most magnificent hotel room I've ever seen. Huge. Really high ceilings. Opulent lighting, opulence everywhere.

John and Yoko are working furiously and never look up to greet us. Steckler motions with his head for me to get involved and I move in closer and concentrate on the design developing on the blank page in front of me as John and Yoko arrange various cut up pieces of type and photos and the *Crawdaddy* cover with them on it. After five minutes John sits back and says, "There! That's right. It's all done." Steckler pokes me in the ribs. He wants my opinion and without a second thought I spew, "No. You're wrong."

The room goes silent.

Before I can even contemplate whether one of the huge windows would break and allow me to defenestrate myself, John smiles, looks at me, and says, "Really? Show me."

Steckler, who I hear snickering jabs me again to keep going. I get down on the floor and rearrange the pieces and cut up bigger pieces of type and in about ten minutes I put together a better, more dynamic design. I hope.

Yoko says nothing, gets up and walks over to talk with Steckler. John is still on the floor next to me, watching. I've suspended breathing. John turns to me and, sounding just like a Beatle from Liverpool, says, "You're right. That's morch betta."

He then sticks out his hand and with an easy casualness, and just in case I was the one person in the western hemisphere who happened to not know who he was, says, "I'm John, I'm glad to finally meet you. I loved the ads you did for 'Imagine' and 'Fly.'" He points and says, "This is my wife Yoko." We nod at each other.

This is too hallucinogenic for me. It would be more likely for me to awake from this dream sequence than not. This is what pinching yourself was invented for.

I introduce myself and take just a moment too long to stop shaking his hand. John gets up and asks if I want anything to drink; looking up from the floor I ask for a Coke.

Then John Lennon is standing right there next to me as Steckler comes over to chat with him and look at what we've created. John Lennon is standing next to me. John Lennon is wearing moccasins. John Lennon's feet are only inches away from mine. My dormant Beatlemania grabs hold of my central nervous system and it occurs to me—that's a Beatle Foot! And there are two of them. REAL ACTUAL BEATLE FEET!!

May, smiling at me knowing I'd get more of a thrill if John Lennon hands me the Coke than if she does, gives him both cans and he hands me one. I don't know if I should open it or keep it as a souvenir. Thirst rules. I vow to take the empty home, but in the scramble to complete the ad, the can gets left behind.

John Lennon sits down on the floor again right next to me. ("God," I'm thinking, "I hope I'm not sweating!") Yoko, who is sweeter than I expect, joins us on the floor. The three of us edit the quotes they want to use from the *Crawdaddy* article, and make a few fine-detail design decisions together. I become self-conscious when I look at John eye-to-eye and make sure to turn away quickly to avoid staring. When we're done, I'm off and running with another handshake with John Lennon—two in one day!—and a quick goodbye.

These were the days before computers and Quark and Illustrator, back when you had cold-type galleys, rubber cement, Photostats and Exacto knives. What would take one person two hours to do on a computer today took six people in three separate businesses at least two days, with lots of drop-offs and deliveries by me or messengers.

But John wants it submitted to the *New York Times* that afternoon. Steckler gives me permission to spend whatever is needed to complete the task. It's amazing what the twin engines of "JOHN-&-YOKO-NEED-IT" and "MONEY-IS-NO-OBJECT" can accomplish. In only five hours I produce finished artwork ready for reproduction. I never stop moving and two messengers don't either. I submit the ad to the *Times*. They want the money up front because, Apple or not, they don't have an account and any new business is COD.

The on-the-spot payment is arranged with Apple's bookkeeping, which means I also get paid my commission that same day. What a package deal!

That evening Andrea and I went to the usual kind of social gathering we attended during the early 1970s—an orgy. The next day when a friend asks how I am doing, I tell him that yesterday was one of the best days of my life. I got to meet and work with John Lennon, I went to a great orgy and I made and collected money. (I made $669, which was 7.5 percent of the cost of the ad, which was $8,920.)

The next time that combination of events came up I just told my friend, "John Lennon/Orgy/Money" and to this day, I still think of truly great days, even those without John Lennon or an orgy, or even money, as John Lennon/Orgy/Money days.

Although I was flattered to be needed so much in the middle of my first vacation while at Apple, it was less exciting being called back the second time; and by the third time my vacation was interrupted, it was a pain in the ass. In the little over three and a half years I serviced Apple, I never had a single uninterrupted vacation.

On the plus side of the balance sheet was Beatle Dope. I never smoked with John, and he never gave me a joint directly but through others who had more intimate contact with him and his stash, I ended up with bits and samples of whatever he was smoking. I had my first ever hair-straightening top-of-your-head-comes-off hash oil, and grass that was the best available in the world at that moment. Who on earth is going to sell or give second-grade weed to a Beatle?

Another plus was that John Lennon was funny. Laugh out loud funny. He did shtick, with lots of voices and accents, especially various American accents including Southerners and middle-aged Jewish women from Queens. And although he had his tantrum moments—one of which I watched but since it wasn't my fuck-up, I wasn't the focus of his bite—he was generally kind and thoughtful and at least he remembered my name.

Unlike Yoko.

Yoko had worked with me maybe four or five times but never remembered my name. These people were my bread and butter but Yoko's forgetfulness annoyed me. I never mentioned it until one day I felt so humiliated that I either had to say something to her or swallow a foul taste so rancid I knew I was one step closer to kissing cancer on the asshole.

The Ono-Lennons were then living on Bank Street in the West Village only a few blocks from where Andrea and I lived on Tenth Street. Walking over to their big basement flat I used to think, "Can you imagine? Having to go to John Lennon's apartment!" Like it's work and I have no choice! I was amused by the irony dealt to me by fate.

One brilliant spring day I was on my way to their flat just dying to run into someone I knew. No such luck.

I got to their place and May Pang let me in. I sat down at the kitchen table and waited. Waiting was another annoying regularity. After fifteen minutes John walked by and said, "Hello, Jeffrey.

Would you like some granola?"

"Yes, I'd love some."

"Help yourself," he said as he took out a bowl, milk and a box of granola for me.

John had offered me granola as soon as he saw me ever since our second meeting when he gave me some of his specially made granola and I glommed down two bowls of it. It was the best granola I ever had and I told him (and I was straight, for I would never go to their place or Apple's office stoned—this was business). Even once when we ran into each other on the street he asked me if I wanted some granola.

John grabbed a chocolate brownie and a chunk of chocolate. He was a fiend for anything chocolate and was working his way though a giant five-pound Hershey bar. He headed back to the bedroom and said he and Yoko would be out in a minute. We were meeting to go over the artwork for the ad campaign for David Peel's "The Pope Smokes Dope," an album John was producing.

I was eating granola when Yoko came running out annoyed and excited, pointed to me and asked, "Are you the washing machine repairman?"

"No. Sorry, Yoko."

She zipped back into the bedroom.

John and Yoko came out about thirty minutes later. During our meeting the real washing machine repairman showed up. I was focused on the work and Yoko's insult was fading. Then John quickly stood up to answer the phone. It hit me. I had to say something.

"Yoko, I love working for you and John and you people are not only my heroes, but how I make much of my living and you are great clients and I only have one request."

"Yes," she said, trailing the ending of the word the way people do to show mild disbelief or disgust.

"Yoko, you never remember my name or who I am. I'm Jeffrey Michelson and I'm not the washing machine repairman. I do your advertising and I don't mean to be disrespectful, but it hurts that you don't remember me."

"Well. John and I are so busy and meet so many people."

"John remembers my name."

"Well. Okay, I'll try."

"Thanks, Yoko. That's all I ask. It's Jeffrey Michelson."

She repeated it. I'd never heard it said with a Japanese accent.

* * *

A few weeks later I was leaving the Hammock Store on Bleeker Street where an informal gathering of local arty types including writers and painters and Warhol superstar Holly Woodlawn would come stoned and hang out on many a late afternoon. We lounged in a variety of Yucatan hammocks and had, if not the most insightful and clever salon in the West Village, then surely the most comfortable.

As I stepped out the door, I saw John and Yoko across the street. Our eyes met. I waved, John waved and Yoko looked puzzled but I could tell she was trying to remember. I yelled out. "That's okay, Yoko. It's me, the washing machine repairman."

I don't know whether John said something to her or she remembered, but finally she said, "Hello, Jeffrey," and I smiled.

My strongest recollections about John Lennon are not the often overly long advertising and design meetings but the breaks for bathroom and food. More than once John picked up his guitar and went into the opening riff of "Day Tripper," which he loved to play. Once he picked up his guitar and did a great flashy loud Elvis imitation—voice, wiggling pelvis, throbbing leg, and all. May Pang, Yoko, a few other assistants and I were rolling in laughter as he exaggerated each move, each note, each Elvisy gesture.

Another favorite memory was the night Steckler invited me to the Record Factory recording studio to see John, Yoko and Phil Spector mix "Happy Christmas (War is Over)." Andrea came with me and to our surprise when we got there we were escorted into a big studio with lots of other people, old, young, black and white. We were going to be the chorus. We practiced until we all had the melody and timing and then we all sang several takes for the final recording. If you listen closely you can hear me singing "War is over if you want it."

My relationships with the other Beatles were limited. I never met Paul and in three and a half years my entire connection with him was earning $18.75 for changing the catalog number on an ad for him.

I met Ringo a few times and he was as charming and happy-faced as you might imagine. The first time was at Apple's office on the forty-first floor at 53rd and Broadway. I walked into a meeting room to give something to Allan Steckler, and Apple staffer Paul Mozian, who hung out with Ringo, introduced us. They were all eating lunch and Ringo, a vegetarian, without prompting, offered me half his cheese submarine sandwich.

George I had a bit more to do with and we met enough times that he remembered my name. I learned two life-altering lessons from George.

I was sitting in Steckler's office listening to acetates of the final mix of George's new solo album, *All Things Must Pass*. Tears had come to my eyes on side one during "My Sweet Lord." Most songs blew me away, especially "Wah Wah," "Isn't It a Pity," "What Is Life," and his cover of "If Not for You." I was listening to song one side four, "I Dig Love," and George walked in. It's a heavy lightweight song with one of Ringo's best performances. The arrangement is simple, sparse and stunning, my favorite kind. George said hello and asked me, as if my opinion mattered, what I thought of the album. I told him it was brilliant. He asked, "Really?"

"Yes George, it's bloody brill," I replied parodying English slang. I asked, "Don't you know it's great? It's great. Not like I think it's great, like I know it's great."

"Thanks, Jeffrey. That means much to me."

Steckler walked in and I left while they did some business. George left and I went back into Steck's office. He lit up a Pall Mall and I lit up a Marlboro. It seems alien now but that was what people did then.

"George is really insecure today," said Allan. "Beyond normal pre-album release jitters. George feels bad because he had to hire someone to write out the charts so he could copyright the music and the sheet music. He feels bad because he doesn't know how to read or write music."

Two things hit me. If George Harrison, one of the top earners in the music industry was insecure, then there was no hope for me. And probably not for you either. Fuck, he was a Beatle! How much more approval did someone need? Second, if he was that great and still insecure, then insecurity just doesn't matter. It won't stop you from being great, so just keep moving forward no matter how scared you are. I can't say I never had any more insecurity. I have it right now as I'm writing this book. But it doesn't matter.

What does matter is putting your best effort into whatever you're doing. It doesn't insure greatness but it's almost always a prerequisite. That was the lesson I learned at Apple. Everybody, Bob Gruen, May Pang, Paul Mozian, and the people I introduced to Apple, Michael Gross, Tina Rossner and Toby Mamis, all gave all they had every day. We left it all on the field and took nothing back to the locker room.

In addition to charging $15 an hour for design and making 7.5 percent of the ad budget, I would do odd chores for John, Yoko and Allan. I'd research photos, pick up something and courier it if that was the most expedient method and because I lived right around the corner from John and Yoko, I'd be asked to make Xerox copies (nobody had a machine at home in 1971) or find three dozen red balloons or whatever else inspired John and/or Yoko that moment. Allan asked me how much I would charge for doing these odd jobs, figuring it would be less than my design fee. I told him $15 an hour because there were sixty minutes in every hour I worked for him no matter what I did. He laughed and agreed.

Allan Steckler, who at one point in his life was the Creative Director for the Beatles and the Stones at the same time, set the bar high. One day Allan gave me the assignment to listen to all the tapes kids sent to Apple Records so the Beatles could sign them. There were hundreds of tapes and no one had listened to any of them in years. Allan said it wasn't right to just throw them out without them being heard. He told me that if I thought the tape was good, he didn't care about it. If it was GREAT, he still didn't care about it. If it knocked me out, he'd listen to it for ten seconds. Out of hundreds only three knocked me out and none knocked Allan out.

My favorite John Lennon/Orgy/Money story of them all happened when John and Yoko appeared on the Dick Cavett Show to plug their new single, "Woman Is the Nigger of the World," that had created an uproar in both the black and white communities.

California Congressman Ron Dellums, who is black, wrote a defense of John's language, "*If you define 'niggers' as someone whose lifestyle is defined by others, whose opportunities are defined by others, whose role in society are defined by others, then Good News! You don't have to be black to be a 'nigger' in this society. Most of the people in America are 'niggers'.*"

I was asked to create a response ad to John's critics using Dellum's quote. I set the quote in the largest type possible and covered the entire page with a small attribution at the very bottom.

That night, I was at a giant orgy on 57th Street with about twenty couples. At 11:30 p.m., I left the designated wall-to-wall mattress orgy room and went into the living room to turn on the TV to the Dick Cavett show. John and Yoko were performing the song with Elephant's Memory, their back-up band. They'd asked Allan Steckler to be there to mix the sound and I wanted to watch and hear them. With Steckler at the knobs, it was the best live TV sound I ever heard.

I sat on the carpet real close to the TV and didn't have the sound up very high. Two naked girls came over during the performance to watch. I was smack in the middle so one sat on one side and one on the other. One of them was lanky with long, wavy reddish brown soft hair. I'd already had her earlier in the evening and really enjoyed myself. She was a moaner with a beautiful melody.

The other was tiny and adorable, the smallest girl I'd ever seen at an orgy, well under five feet, perfectly proportioned with an ass I could definitely hold in one hand. She might have been a tall midget because she had perfect proportion but I think she was just a small person. I don't know where the line is drawn.

She was bubbly, had a high-pitched but not unattractive voice and although I hadn't yet had her, she'd been a popular attraction. I'd watched her fuck and suck and desired her for the obvious erotic and perverted reasons. Her name was Noreen and the reason I remember was when she first introduced herself I thought she said fluorine and I wondered why anyone would name their baby girl for the ninth element on the Periodic Chart.

Both said they were Beatles fans and were excited to see John and Yoko on television. After the end of the song during the commercial I told them John and Yoko were my clients. They were very impressed. The little one started stroking my balls.

After the break, John and Yoko joined Dick Cavett to talk about the controversy. John held up my ad with Congressman Dellums' quote, the camera pushed in really tight, and John read it word for word. My ad was full-frame on the tube being seen by millions of people. I screamed, "That's my ad!" Anyone who wasn't in the middle of sex came out to the living room, including the guy who lived there to make sure we weren't getting cum stains on the carpet. I repeated, "That's my ad that John's holding up!"

Andrea came in and proudly confirmed to everyone that I really did do John and Yoko's advertising and everyone congratulated me. Noreen, who had been fondling me dove into my lap and started sucking away and I had the first inkling of what having sex with an underage groupie must be like.

When the show segment ended, I turned off the TV and with lanky-girl on one arm and cute-tiny on the other, I took my now hardened prong into the authorized orgy room. The adorable little girl, with matching tight small vagina, was a wiggly screamer and looked into my eyes with groupie adoration. Just to make sure that this was going to be fantasy perversion instead of felony perversion I asked her age. To my surprise she said twenty-six, older than me.

Noreen was so small that it was hard to get my penis all the way inside and I don't think I could have if I'd been any larger. We couldn't easily kiss and fuck at the same time. What the fuck lacked in choreography it made up for in visuals. Lanky-girl rubbed me and played with my balls as I came. If I could have been arrested for my thoughts I would have been. Like so many times before or since.

I was a kind of mini-celeb, on par with a particularly handsome man with a huge cock. Several other girls were now more interested in me than they were before, and I obliged. My cock was absolutely hard and seemed to me to be at least two inches bigger than the one I came to the party with. Ego! What a drug!

And a tip of the hat to John Lennon. He might have affected many people in many different ways, but I'm sure I'm on the short list of those whose penis got bigger because of him. Brian Epstein not withstanding.

20

Puritan interview with Norman Mailer

December 28, 1980

Our John Lennon Assassination Funk doesn't substantially dissipate till ten days later when Laura and I start prepping for our interview with Norman Mailer for *Puritan* magazine.

After negotiating for a year, Norman comes to an agreement with one of John Krasner's sons, now the publisher. Norman will take two weeks to prepare for the interview, give the interview and then spend his and his secretary's time editing the transcripts of the tapes. He will be paid $10,000, which is a huge amount for the publisher of a porn magazine to part with, and less than Norman usually makes for the same amount of time.

Having Mailer in *Puritan* will be bragging rights to influence other interviewees, a strengthening of a legal defense in case we are ever busted, and good publicity. The first and third reasons work out well, and we never had to test the second.

To prepare for the interview, Laura and I work with *Puritan* editor Stanley Bernstein four days a week for six or seven hours a day for two weeks. We take it seriously. We want it to be great. We read more than thirty previous Mailer interviews and cut down a list of 200 or so questions to a manageable list of less than fifty.

Laura and I interview Norman in the dining room of his home in Brooklyn Heights on December 28, 1980. Norman's apartment, (a maisonette, as the English would call it because it is the largest apartment in the building and has two or more floors), is the top three floors of an elegant Brownstone overlooking the water just south of the Brooklyn Bridge.

The space has a nautical motif and the second floor is accessible only by climbing a ship's ladder and the very top floor has a room that can only be reached by walking a plank. A few different times in my life I lived in his apartment, sometimes for a few months, most notably in the summer of 1969 after Tisha left me.

Norman had just published *The Executioner's Song* and *Of Women and Their Elegance* about Marilyn Monroe. Being interviewed in a hard-core sex magazine between photos, even lovely ones, of fucking and sucking, with his recent high visibility was particularly bold and against much advice from his personal and business circle.

Norman said this interview was one of his three or four best out of 500 or more. He chose it for re-publication in *Pieces and Pontifications*. Here are some of my favorite excerpts from the interview, with remembrances from Laura:

JEFFREY MICHELSON: What do you think makes for great sex?

NORMAN MAILER: Great sex is apocalyptic. There is no such thing as great sex unless you have an apocalyptic moment. William Burroughs once changed the course of American literature with one sentence. He said, "I see God in my asshole in the flashbulb of orgasm." Now that was one incredible sentence because it came at the end of the Eisenhower period, printed around 1959 in *Big Table* in Chicago. I remember reading it and thinking, I can't believe I just read those words. I can't tell you the number of taboos it violated. First of all, you weren't supposed to connect God with sex. Second of all, you never spoke of the asshole, certainly not in relation to sex. If you did, you were the lowest form of pervert. Third of all, there was obvious homosexuality in the remark. In those days nobody was accustomed to seeing that in print. And fourth, there was an ugly technological edge—why'd he have to bring in flashbulbs? Was that the nature of his orgasm? It was the first time anybody had ever spoken about the inner nature of the orgasm.

> "The day of the Norman Mailer interview was my twenty-eighth birthday," Laura remembers, "and Jeffrey and I had rolled around in passionate sex too long that morning, as usual—and then it was a rush to curl my hair, put on my makeup and get ready. We were in Manhattan and had to get to Brooklyn Heights, I think it was snowing—so we had to rush to get there on time.
>
> "I was excited about doing the Norman Mailer interview," Laura recalls, "I mean, I'd met him already, a couple of times, and I liked Norman a lot. He made me feel sexy. He always gave me this dirty little grin that just made me feel like he would be good in bed..."

JM: When does a graphic representation of a sexual act become art, and when, smut? Can you suggest any criteria on which to base a judgment?

NM: Let me ask you: what would be your idea of smut?

JM: Things that are particularly degrading to either sex.

NM: Get specific.

JM: I guess it's stuff that turns me on in a way I think I shouldn't be turned on.

NM: Excellent.

LAURA BRADLEY: I feel the difference is if it's commercially and sloppily done just to get another page in the book, then the insult is to the art. Where it's a true and honest representation of feeling, then no matter what it represents, it's got to be respected.

NM: Mmm, that's very well put too. You would be saying in effect then, Laura, that smut is the equivalent of a sexual act that's casual, what we call sordid, no love, no real pleasure in it, a cohabitation with a rancid smell to it. So a lack of respect for the seriousness of the occasion when a photographer takes a picture of a woman in a pornographic position makes for smut. Jeffrey is saying, as I gather, that there are certain acts that tend toward the bestial, the fecal (I assume these are the sort of things you're thinking of) that may be arousing, but you find that your moral nature disapproves.

JM: I'm wondering: Is smut to pornography, to good pornography, as trashy romance novels are to good literature? Is it just the lower end of the genre?

NM: It's certainly complicated. Take Laura's criteria, pictures that are transparently cynical. The model's worn out, the photographer's worn out, disgusting. Yet that can be arousing in a funny way. For instance, in *Hustler*, often I find that the most interesting section is those cheap Polaroid pictures that untalented photographers send of women who are not models.

JM: The reality turns you on?

NM: The sordid reality. My sexuality, I expect, is aroused by knowledge. The moment I know more than I knew before, I'm excited. Those gritty Polaroid shots in *Hustler* are often more interesting. They communicate. You know, the picture of some waitress who lives in Sioux Falls. I know more at that moment about Sioux Falls, about waitresses—even if they're lying, even if she isn't a waitress, there's something about the very manifest of the lie that's fascinating. It arouses your curiosity. Whereas superb pictures of models can get boring. There tends to be a sameness in them. Aren't enough flaws present? The very question of the sordid is . . . tricky.

"You know, talking about sex is always kind of sexy," Laura laughs, "so I wanted to fuck Norman. Absolutely. I was

sitting there during the interview thinking about having
sex with Norman. Was I fantasizing about sucking his cock?
Maybe, probably, knowing me, ha, ha, ha!"

LB: Have you been sexually pursued by literary groupies? What's it like being fucked as an image rather than a person?

NM: Well, I've usually been drawn to women who aren't necessarily that interested in my work. My present wife had read one book of mine before we met. She hardly knew anything about me. It's probably analogous to the poor rich girl, who wants to be loved for herself and not her money, remember all those movies?

"Norman was very loving toward me," Laura remembers
fondly. "He always looked me in the eyes and made me
feel like what I had to say was important. I felt beautiful
and sexy around him, not slutty, even though I was in my
slutty period of life. He had this intense serious side that
was so present surrounded by his smiles and chuckles.
He was stocky, like a hobbit. It felt like he was from the
center of the Earth or from the center of the universe. The
things he said usually surprised me. I expected him to say
big profound things and instead, he would say very basic
simple things that were immediately obvious, even though
I may have never thought of it before."

LB: In Woody Allen's movie Annie Hall, he's on the street and he walks up to this little old lady and says to her something like, "Why are relationships so difficult?" And she says, "Love fades..." As a man who's had six marriages, what is your reaction to this dialogue? Do you think that love fades and do you feel that sex fades?

NM: I don't think that sex fades in marriage necessarily. Without talking about my personal life, I'd say that compatibility is nearer to the problem than sex. What I mean is people can have marvelous sex and not be terribly compatible. That sets up a great edginess in marriage. Some people, in fact, can only have good sex with people who are essentially incompatible with them. I might have been in that category for years, I don't know. If you're terribly combative, then you're drawn toward mates who are not too compatible. Anyone who has a violent or ugly or combative edge is not going to be comfortable with someone who is really sweet and submissive. They want something more abrasive in their daily life. Otherwise they are likely to lose their good opinion of themselves.

There's nothing worse than being brutal to somebody who's good to you. Whereas if you're living with someone whose ideas irritate the living shit out of you, and you fight with them every day and feel justified about it, that can be healthier than living with a soul whose ideas are compatible to yours. All the same, if you do choose this fundamental incompatibility, there will come a point where it ceases to be fun and turns into its opposite. Faults in the mate that were half-charming suddenly become unendurable.

Every one of us who has been in love knows how fragile—what's a good word for skin?—how fragile is the membrane of love. It has to be mended every day and nurtured. We have to anticipate all the places where it's getting a little weak and go there and breathe on it, shape it again. In a combative relationship, obviously, that's difficult. You have to have a great animal vigor between combative people or they just can't make it for long.

JM: What about love fading?

NM: Well, I don't think love fades; I don't think there's anything automatic about it. I think most of us aren't good enough for love. I think self-pity is probably the most rewarding single emotion in the world for masturbators, which is one of the reasons, I suppose, I'm opposed to masturbation, because it encourages other vices to collect around you. Self-pity is one of the first. You lie in bed, pull off, and say to yourself, I have such wonderful, beautiful, tender, sweet, deep, romantic, exciting and sensual emotions, why is it that no woman can appreciate how absolutely fabulous I am? Why can't

I offer these emotions to someone else? Self-pity comes rolling in, and cuts us off from recognizing that love is a reward. Love is not something that is going to come up and solve your problems. Love is something you get after you've solved enough of your problems so that something in Providence itself takes pity on you. I always believed that whoever or whatever it is, some angel, some sour sort of our angel, finally says, "Look at these poor motherfuckers. He and she have been working so hard for so many years. Let's throw him or her a bone." So they meet and find love. Then they have to know what to do with it.

JM: Love is a function of having paid your dues?

NM: Truman Capote has got this book he's writing, *Answered Prayers*. I gather from something he said once that its theme is that the worst thing that befalls people is that their prayers are answered. Which is not a cheap idea. Love is the perfect example. Everybody prays for love, but once they get love, they have to be worthy of it. Love is the most perishable of human emotions. It never fades. That's my answer to the question. There is absolutely no reason why people can't love each other more every day of their lives for eighty years. I absolutely believe that. Without that, I have no faith in love whatsoever. I think it would be a diabolical universe if you're introduced to all these wonderful sentiments that illumine your existence but something is put into the very nature of it that will make it fade. That's the sentiment of a person who is full of self-pity: Love fades. That old woman was full of self-pity.

> "Norman loved to make himself laugh," Laura recalls. "He seemed to have such a good time inside himself. And I specifically remember how Norman would take a long time to think about the questions before he answered. Then, sometimes he would get so serious and those eyes would pierce into mine, he would hold his chin and I felt like I had to listen very carefully because now it was very important for me to totally understand what he was saying."

JM: Norman, I'd like to discuss the nature of inhibition, something that interests me. To put it bluntly, why is it that some women like to get fucked in the ass and some women find it distasteful? Some women like to suck cocks, some women don't. It surely is not purely physical.

NM: You can't talk about it generally, you just can't. Everything we do sexually is as characteristic of us as our features. The question you ask is truly bottomless. You could say to me, why do some people have noses with an overhang, and why do some tilt up? Why do we respond to these noses in different ways? I could give an answer; I mean, a nose that tilts up often suggests optimism, confidence about the future, fearlessness, but a nose that turns over suggests a certain pessimism about the very shape of things, an attachment to sentiment of doom. You have to ask next: What is the nature of form? Why do curves do these things to us? But in sexuality, you also have to ask which period of one's life are we talking about? Anyone who's lived with a woman for a few years learns that a woman's tastes can change as much as a man's. There are women who detest being fucked in the ass, as you put it—you see, I refuse to use those words myself... The woman who wants nothing to do with a phallus in her crack one year is turned on immensely by it another year. I will make one general observation: It's very dangerous to stick it up a woman's ass. It tends to make them more promiscuous. I'll leave that with your readers. They can think about it from their own experience. They can test it out. Those who are scientifically inclined can immediately approach their mate and tool her, if they're able. Then they can observe what happens, watch her at parties, get a private detective, and check up on her.

So I guess I answered your question: a woman doesn't want it up the ass because she's doing her best to be faithful to that dull pup she's got for a man, and she knows if it blasts into the center of her stubbornness, that's the end of it. She won't be able to hold onto fidelity any longer. That's one explanation. It doesn't have to be true. But you might ponder it.

"I remember being in Maine with Norman that next summer," Laura continues. "He was so adoring and protective of his children. He and Norris had a very young boy, John Buffalo that Norris had just given birth to a year before. Norman would stare at John Buffalo and smile this big internal smile. He was engaged, yet detached, as if he were observing a different species.

"Yeah," Laura laughs, "I felt like that sometimes when he looked at me; like he wanted to figure me out, like I was an alien. I probably was to him. Actually, I was an alien to myself then."

"But I definitely would have had sex with Norman if he wanted to have sex with me. But he never asked me. And I was also *so* into Jeffrey that it didn't seem practical. Besides, Norman was with Norris, and she was *so* nice—he had just married Norris at the time of the interview. I was always under the impression that Norris was going to be the last woman Norman ever fucked. And it wasn't like *I* was going to get in the way.

"It really seemed like true love."

21

My first orgy

Flashback to May 1, 1971

It might seem like a huge emotional transition from being a normal regular Joe boyfriend to being the boyfriend of someone who spends her days fucking one strange man after another for money, but I had some training that prequalified me.

I started out like any other possessive red-blooded American boy. At age nineteen I struggled with the fact that my then-girlfriend had been with other men before me. The image of her being, what was to me, violated by other men, haunted and hurt me. The thought of a guy putting his penis inside her made me cringe. I got past most of that but I was still possessive and jealous, to a lesser degree.

What prepped me to be the boyfriend of a whore happened at my second orgy in late May of 1971, nine years before I met Laura.

But first, let's visit my first orgy.

It's May 1, 1971. In Washington, DC, 500,000 march in protest against the Vietnam War and 7,000 are arrested. Charles Manson and the Manson Family are sentenced to the gas chamber. The Ed Sullivan Show goes off the air. Movies cost $1.50. Miniskirts are everywhere.

I'm living in New York City. I've been divorced from my English wife Tisha for about a year. I'm dating, but there is no one special.

No girl I ever get to put my penis in do I ever consider higher than a six out of ten, and most are fives and that's being generous to both them and me. None of them look good in a miniskirt. I am one of the horniest men I've ever met, heard of, or read about. I am getting laid on occasion, but the frequency is best described by the fact that I am probably jerking off twenty times for every fuck.

It might even be fifty.

My luck is about to change. I finally wrangle my first invitation to an orgy from an acquaintance, George Kaye, "The Party King." George goes to parties every night of the week: gallery openings, discos, press parties for the music and movie biz, book launches, private parties, and corporate shindigs. In his nightly travels he finds his way into a crowd who were the pioneers of the middle class New York Orgy.

Before that, most orgies were thrown by outsiders: flappers, beboppers, beatniks, hippies, artists and musicians, and they hadn't really caught on much with 1950s Ozzie-and-Harriet types. In earlier times, orgies were sprinkled throughout history, usually among the privileged. To me orgies were just a wonderful promise in history books, a perq of the rulers of the Roman Empire. As soon as George tells me about his first orgy, I want in. It's the first one I ever hear about first-hand.

The problem is to get in, I need a girl partner. I call every girl I've ever dated and endure hang-ups, and worse, name-calling, like "pervert" and "sicko" and "depraved animal," that I know are all true. After dozens of dead-end phone calls I start visiting girls I know on the Lower East Side who do not have telephones. Five addresses later I talk one of my more adventurous semi-occasional fucks into going. I've got my ticket to the circus!

Saturday night and my date—very sweet, somewhat pretty, and a little plump—whose name I no longer remember, takes forever to get ready, gets cold feet and backs out while putting on her make-up. I am destroyed.

I sell it to her like I've never sold before. I tell her that if she doesn't like the party we'll leave immediately. I beg, I plead, I offer her $20. She says it's not about money, she just doesn't feel right about it. I offer her fifty. That makes her feel right about it. We are an hour late.

We catch a cab, go uptown and arrive at a doorman building on Riverside Drive. Now we are an hour and a half late and I worry if we'll be let in. The doorman calls to announce us. I am relieved we are to be admitted.

We take the elevator up to a high floor and stand in front of 22B. I smell sex seeping out the crack under the door. We knock and I say, "George sent me." The door opens and I see sex.

George stands there wearing just a tie and a naked girl on each arm like a heaven-on-earth vision of an aptly named Saint Peter.

We enter a room full of naked people; maybe thirty of them. Some of them are having sex right there in the open in clusters, some in twos, some in threes, and some in larger piles on mattresses on the floor. We walk around silent and peer into other rooms also filled with naked people talking and fucking and laughing and sucking. In one corner there are four couples all sixty-nining, like sardines. Mouths and cocks and tits and pussies are everywhere! Holy Shit! I'm scared. I'm thrilled.

Red alert—lights on the screens in my hormone control room flash. Valves open. Potent molecules stored inside me for just such an occasion rush into my bloodstream. My adrenal gland operators pump catecholamines to raise epinephrine, norepinephrine, dopamine, phenylalanine, and tyrosine to battle-ready levels. My parasympathetic nervous system shuts off my entire digestive tract so more blood can flow to my penis. All systems are go. It's T-minus sixty seconds.

My date is led off into another room by two guys. "Good luck" I wish her. I never see her again. Not just that night. Never. I'm standing there talking to George and watching the best-ever porn movie "live" when a stark-naked skinny little blonde takes my hand and says, "I'm Barb, George tells me this is your first party. Let me be your initiation." Far fucking out, free sex!

I follow her to one of three mattresses on the floor in an otherwise normal French Provincial style middle-class living room. Barb unbuttons and unzips me. I am still my mother's son, even at my first orgy and although there are clothes strewn everywhere, I neatly fold mine on top of my shoes in a corner so they won't be disturbed. What about my wallet? Where could I hide it? Fuck it.

I inhale a symphony of healthy young bodies. Their soaps, shampoos, perfumes, baby powders, and aftershaves blend together with harmony. I kiss Barbara, because I guess I start the same way here as in real life.

After a few minutes of hot kissing and touching, this willing lovely creature guides me to lie down on my back. She kneels between my legs and gives me great head with unprecedented eagerness. Then she eases me into sixty-nine by straddling me and facing away from me and squatting down on my face.

She tastes sweet and salty. She's very wet, and I hope she's the kind of girl who needs to wash and douche after every fuck but it doesn't matter because she has my cock bouncing off her tonsils. I think, "Fuck it. Some other guy's jism won't kill me. Girls swallow come all the time and never get sick." Besides I've tasted my own.

I'm making Barb moan and squirm and I must pass muster because she rewards me by pausing to talk to an attractive brunette with major boobs sitting at the edge of the mattress smoking a cigarette and talking to guys about the Mets. "Gina," she says, "this is Jeffrey and it's his first party. Come join in."

"Wow. Two at once! Now that's something I've always dreamed of," I blurt.

"You never had two at once?" says my tour guide.

"No," I say, "I've only seen it in porn films. I never thought it would happen to me."

"Well, lie back and enjoy this," says Gina who puts out her cigarette. She's got great jugs, not too big, round and firm, original equipment, for this was 1971 and several years before every third girl had store-bought tits. Gina gets down with Barb as each of them straddles one of my legs. I've got four tits in front of me!

I lean up on my elbows. I've got to watch these two lovely faces giving me head so I can record the image to jerk off to when I'm alone and horny. Probably tomorrow.

It's my first Major League sexual stimulus overload. It's a

masturbation fantasy I've wanked off to hundreds of times. I'd always hoped that someday before I died I'd have enough money to hire two hookers at the same time so I could have this. And here it is. For real. And for free!

Right then and there I have a revelation, my "First Theorem of Sexual Relativity." It is only anecdotal but equal to that apple falling on Isaac Newton's head: Two mouths and four hands are three times better than one mouth and two hands.

After ten minutes of Barb and Gina, the dual-action pleasure pump, I want to fuck. I enter Barb as Gina plays with my balls. It strikes me that having a harem must be as good as I always suspected.

Barb kisses great with a large searching tongue, and she purrs. Gina is making me totally nuts by playing with my balls and I explode with my first of that gifted species of orgasm that can only occur with two or more people.

One wonderful new experience leads to another. After two more orgasms with a variety (can you imagine?) of skins and nipples and vaginas and aromas and firm tushies, I take a break and go to the kitchen for a drink and a snack, wondering how many orgasms I've got left.

At a table with chips, dips, candies and pastry, I am eating a carrot stick when this naked slinky girl with slightly almond eyes and long, light brown straight hair says hello. She's wearing glasses and also munching a carrot stick.

"I'm George's," she opens.

"I'm George's too. Or at least I'm in his debt."

"I know. He told me to make sure I fucked you. I'm Andrea."

How come other men don't send me women to fuck? George, who was already high up on my list of favorite people, just moved up another notch.

"This is a fantasy to me," I say, finishing my carrot. "I've always wanted to go to an orgy. Speaking of fantasies, if you could be any woman in the world about to get fucked, who would you be?"

"Lady Brett."

Far out. She likes Hemingway and *The Sun Also Rises,* one of my favorite books. I go for the coup de grace—and pray that she gets it. I quote the last line of the book: "Isn't it pretty to think so."

She laughs. She gets it! We smile a secret handshake. Just then, "Jumpin' Jack Flash" comes on the stereo and at the exact same time we both say, "Great! I love the Stones!"

We laugh more. She walks in front of me and I love the shape of her shoulders. Her ass is cute. We lie down. We kiss. Without a prompt, she sucks my cock. She gives World-class Head. She's got soft skin and squeals like a trapped rabbit when she fucks. It takes me a while to come because it's an uphill climb after a fourth orgasm.

I'm into new territory here. I don't think I ever did five before, but then I never had this much stimulus. This is Chinese Emperor, Arab Sheik concubines and harem land.

Hemingway, The Stones, our natural chemistry and our mutual love of sex makes Andrea and me instant friends. And we're already lovers. This is so much better than dating.

I'd gone out with women I liked and fucked for two months and hadn't gotten this close. Andrea tells me she is not really George's girlfriend, they don't fuck much, she's just his ticket to orgies. She gives me her number, which, because I am naked, I have to memorize.

We part and I continue on my pilgrimage. I have no belief that I might ever be so lucky again. I save nothing. Whatever energy I have gets spent that night. I swear this is true: I have my penis inside twelve different women and come eight times. It is the first time in my life that I ever had more than enough.

I call Andrea few days later and we start dating. The sex is terrific. Better yet, she is the first girl I ever met who never says "No."

My ex-wife Tisha had said "No" maybe twenty times for every "Yes." Even girls who liked me a lot said "No" sometimes and often said, "That's enough" or "I'm too tired to do it again." Andrea's anytime attitude is unknown to me and very much appreciated.

Andrea is more than just a pretty fuck. We have a lot in common: movies, art, music and books. And she's smart. She works for the New York Public Library as a reference assistant, answering people's questions about anything. She's proto-Google.

She stops seeing George, who begrudgingly gives us his blessing. My friends like her and are extra interested in her when I tell them how we met. Two weeks later we are a true couple. With six shopping bags, four boxes of books and a sewing machine she moves into my $135 a month West Village studio.

We don't fight at all and it's not just because we are in the honeymoon period. We just get along. It's my first relationship that doesn't take lots of work. Every night we make love and I tell her that as long as I can get into bed with her every night and make love to her whatever happened during that day doesn't matter even if I have to dig ditches.

We sleep tight and comfortable on a twin mattress on the floor because it's all I have at the time, which is emblematic of how little sex I was previously getting. We spend every free moment we have together and it never seems enough.

Andrea, like me, falls in love with the West Village. In the early '70s it feels like the most socially and intellectually liberated neighborhood on earth. Many inhabitants are artists, writers, musicians, photographers, actors, gays, producers, directors, dancers, dope dealers, carpenters, loonies, crazies, yippies, hippies, and bartenders and our collective liberal vibe rules.

Sometimes Dylan passes us on the street. We give a tiny nod. Sometimes, the ultimate reward, he nods back. We spend hours pondering, arguing and drinking at the Limelight or the Buffalo Road House with an informal salon of writers, artists, and the occasional rock star.

Three weeks after my first orgy George calls and invites us to another. I suspect it's because he wants to fuck Andrea again and also to show us he's a good sport. I'm perplexed. I want to go to another orgy, but Andrea isn't just a ticket. She is now my girlfriend! What do I do?

I decide to go and risk a psychotic episode.

22

My second orgy

Three weeks later in May 1971

My second orgy happens in late May 1971. Andrea and I arrive at an East Side walk-up in the lower 80s. The apartment is smaller and more intimate than my first orgy and there are fewer people. This time we are on time and everybody is still dressed and lighting up joints and kibitzing like any group of dope-smoking New York City couples in their early twenties.

I'm blind-sided and hugged by Barb, the treat from my first orgy, and we start talking. Having been that intimate doesn't make us lovers or good friends, but it certainly makes us more than mere acquaintances. I notice that Andrea is missing. People are losing their clothes and filtering toward what I guess is a bedroom. Barb takes my arm and I walk around the corner and there in the tiny hall is Andrea, naked, on her knees, busy with another man's cock. I stop dead in my tracks. My heart stops.

I am not programmed to look at my woman with another man's machinery in her mouth as a good thing. I am enraged. Fifty thousand years of possessive hormonal programming take over. I am flushing with fight or flight. I want to kill him. I want to kill her.

Barb, still on my arm, senses all is not well.

"Are you all right?"

I say nothing, but think, "NO! I AM NOT ALL RIGHT."

Barb starts rubbing my back and a cosmic wave flows over me leaving me an epiphany. First, it would definitely be wrong to kill him. It also would probably be wrong to kill her. And if I kill either of them, I will have to spend at least that night in jail, so I won't get to fuck Barb, whom I definitely want to fuck again. Plus even if I don't kill them—and I have pretty much decided I won't—if I don't psycho-cybernetically reprogram myself right then and there, and change my head, I won't get a hard-on, I won't be able to fuck Barb and I won't be able to go to more orgies with Andrea.

I hear the guy Andrea's blowing making noises as he starts to come in her mouth. Fuck it! I definitely want to kill him and I take a baby step forward to do just that. Then one of those miracle moments occurs.

Well, maybe it's not a miracle. Maybe it's some kind of Hormonal Big Bang or maybe it's on a much more pragmatic level, like a "sit down" between the Young Turk Capos Who Run The Orgasm Machine, and just love this whole new orgy thing I'm into—and the Old Bosses Who Run The Progeny Protection Racket, the original crew I inherited from both The Bible and Darwin.

The Young Turks must have won because all of a sudden instead of wanting to kill that unfaithful bitch and the cuckolding stranger, I'm now enjoying what I'm seeing! I never switched sides so fast in my whole life before or since but right there inside me a sea change happens. Infidelity is the new sacrament. Watching the woman I love having sex with another guy goes from being the worst thing in the world to the hottest porn ever. Maybe some of it is just rationalization to allow my access to all that sweet pussy that goes to orgies, or maybe there is a tectonic shift, a cosmic warp, a subspace power transformation, but whatever it is, it's now a new ball game and I could watch my lover/girlfriend/wife get gang-banged and it's horny, not horrible.

At that moment I see Andrea differently. She is no longer a cheating girlfriend who needs to be strangled; now she is my teammate! And if she's doing great so am I. She is "Superpussy," and I am "Supercock." Instead of anger I'm filled with pride. "That's my girl taking that load. Atta girl Andrea!! Way to go!"

I'm proud she gives such great head. Like a Jewish grandmother watching her granddaughter graduate from college, I'm filled with naches. I'm kvelling.

I continue to enjoy, more and more, watching Andrea fuck and suck her way, and the men she pleasures, to ecstasy. Andrea and I spend the next three years going to maybe 300 orgies without jealousy.

The seismic change I experienced with Andrea at my second orgy was the exact moment of change that allowed me to love Laura fucking and sucking and coming with three, four, five, or more men every working day. I did not just tolerate or become inured to this seeming perversity, I relished it.

I knew other guys who went through this so I didn't feel completely peculiar. When Andrea and I were knee deep in orgies, it wasn't uncommon for some respectable middle class wives and girlfriends to become high-class call girls or work in posh brothels. It just made sense. They were going to several orgies a week, loved fucking strangers, most could make more money fucking than at their day job, and their husbands and boyfriends were already guys who enjoyed that other men pounded their lady.

I do not expect everyone to accept this behavior and morality as normal. However, really horny guys and most swingers can empathize. As a really horny guy who became a swinger that's the way it happened to me. It was only a short jump from enjoying watching other men pound my lady to being the whore's boyfriend.

23

A history of the New York orgy

1971–81

Laura asks me if I can arrange for three cocks at once, or better yet if we can we go to an orgy where a whole herd of men can satisfy her. She wants to know what it's like to have "too much sex." For weeks she quizzes me almost every day about orgies. Are all orgies the same? Are there rules? What kinds of people go to orgies? Laura wants to know every single detail.

In response, my oral history of orgies goes on for days and days. My monologues are not foreplay. We don't end up fucking. It's like giving an oral defense for a doctorate.

In the late 1960s and early 1970s, group sex in the U.S. came out of the closet, gained popularity and touched, or groped, mainstream culture for the first time. Before this proletarian and bourgeois entry into group sex, orgies were mostly an upper class event. At last, in the second half of the twentieth century, orgies became egalitarian. Because of the triad of the pill, the critical mass of baby boomer hormone production, and the flexing of sexual freedom and expression, sex expanded in every direction: reality, movies, art, music, print, gay, straight, younger and older. Sexuality got as much press and chatter as sports, politics or the stock market. It was the medium of the moment. Women were discussing their orgasms at the hairdresser.

In the early '70s Andrea and I migrated from the small circle we knew from the few parties we attended to newly discovered clans to larger developing tribes. The orgy scene grew out of small private networks, and by the early '70s, there were public gathering places such as Captain Kidd's, an ordinary neighborhood bar at 23rd Street and Third Avenue where, on Friday nights, a larger, cross-cultural collection of like-minded people called "swingers" could cruise and choose. No sex happened at Captain Kidd's, just talking, dancing, exchanging of phone numbers and party invitations, most for that night and most in Manhattan but some for a later date and some farther out in the burbs. This was before this kind of casual hooking up was called "the lifestyle," and just after "swingers" still meant cool people who hung out with Frank Sinatra.

The Captain Kidd's crowd was predominantly thirty-something middle-class married couples, which seemed old to twenty-three-year-olds like Andrea and myself. There were a few blacks, a handful of hippies, a smattering of tall thin patricians and lots of Jews and Italians from Lorng Oyland and the New Joisey suburbs who had converted their spare bedrooms and dens into specially designed flocked wallpapered orgy rooms carpeted with mattresses. Then they would send the kids away for the night or weekend.

Andrea and I got invited to lots of parties. Her slinky body, pretty face and almond eyes opened the door, and her great ass, great skin, and her love of sex got us invited back. I had value because of my lust and stamina, and as a couple, we would still be up for more sex late into the morning when lesser specimens had fallen asleep. For all these reasons we were on many swingers' "A" lists. We went to one or two or three orgies a week for the next three years before we moved out to the country where our swinger life slowed way down.

The first twenty-two women in my life I had sex with one at a time. This represents a success rate of about one per 1,400 attempts. When I started going to orgies I continued to count but I stopped at 1,000, which is like two weekends for Wilt Chamberlain.

While swingers shared psychographics (personality, values, attitudes, interests, or lifestyles) more than demographics, the parties we went to did reflect the hosts' socio-economics. It wasn't until the late '70s that the scene grew to include on-premises swing palaces like Plato's Retreat and Trapeze, where masses of kindred spirits could do it right there on the spot.

MIDDLE CLASS SUBURBAN COUPLES

These people, who otherwise were regular folk; car salesmen, insurance agents, firemen, social workers, nurses and teachers, could be counted on for excellent dirty sex. They believed, nay, loved, the fact that what they were doing was "baaad!" This was in contrast to us hippies, to whom shamelessness was second nature. We saw orgies as "the way it should be."

While I was shameless, I adored sex with women who thought it was shameful. Lapsed Catholic residual guilt is one of world's strongest strains of shame and was well represented. The fact that they were doing something dirty made me the dirty guy. I liked being the dirty guy, which being shameless, was not so easy to achieve.

Middle-class couples always served tons of food, usually great deli, but if they were white, the music was usually lame. Have you ever tried getting an erection to Tom Jones, Mantovani, or Engelbert Humperdinck? It's do-able, but in spite of, not because of.

The hottest thing about these parties, for me, was that the women had hairdos. The arty hippie women I hung out with never had hairdos, at least not like these suburban women had, the kind you have to assemble and erect.

Along with hairdos, these women wore too much make-up. I love too much make-up as long as the pancake isn't caked. Unlike hippie girls, these painted women wore lipstick, eyeliner and eye shadow (and rouge on their cheeks to accentuate their lack of cheekbones) and if you fucked them long and hard enough it would all melt. If you were a twenty-three-year-old horny hippie like me, fucking attractive women with runny make-up and destroyed hairdos was a wet dream come true.

ARTISTS & WRITERS CROWD

At first I was happy to be invited into this clique; I thought I would be able to party with My Own Kind. But they proved a big disappointment to me, really the only disappointment of the entire orgy oeuvre.

Tina, who brought me into this fold, was compact, foxy, clever, sexy, and the best graphic designer I knew. I had hired her more than once when a project I landed was too big for me alone. She was a terrific eager fuck, wore the most wonderfully inventive clothes, was great fun at orgies and had the loveliest habit of enhancing my sex experience by squeezing my balls and playing with my asshole while I was fucking another girl. Now there's a buddy.

I thought I would meet a room full of sexy Tina-esque arty types. There were a few Beautiful People but very few. On the average, this group had the least attractive people, no hairdos and, worse yet, the most fraught, self-conscious sex of the lot. These people were too intellectual for their own good. They were watching themselves having an orgy instead of having an orgy.

The conversations were way too heavy, often about sexual politics. This was that horrible period when some women felt compelled to discuss with every man they encountered Women's Lib and the roles of the sexes, the burning of bras and the structural dynamics and general semantics of Feminism as contextualized within American society. This was lousy foreplay. This was during the infancy of Political Correctness. Instead of just having a grand old sexfest these people were determined to justify their lust with its socio-political implications. All I wanted to do was fuck.

Half of these "arty" orgies I went to were hosted by a woman artist. She was lovely, warm and very political. Her paintings and drawings were skillfully rendered life studies of copulations and masturbations, mostly females, with brilliantly executed anatomies, yet some of her faces looked as if they were in pain. If you just saw the faces and not the rest of the paintings you would have thought they were created by a survivor of South American prison torture.

In just a few parties I was exposed to all kinds of dogma, some institutionalized like "Mandatory Male Bisexuality Tonight" (Andrea and I left early) and "This Room For Lesbians Only." Plus, there were personality boobytraps you could step on, like the buxom poet who declared to me, "I don't allow men to be on top." I got a hard-off immediately with that one. And the one who said, "No sex. I'm just into mutual masturbation." Right, just what I came here for, a pack of rules.

There was also too much cigarette smoking. The passing of lit cigarettes in a room full of naked people is as dangerous, non-carcinogenically, as in an oil refinery. Every once in a while a flesh-searing mistake would happen. It happened to me once, thankfully only to a leg, but my cigarette radar went up from that moment on and I would stop whatever I was doing, no matter how involved I was, to point out to the person with a cigarette near me that they were a hazard and a schmuck or a shmuckess.

Often, this crowd served only vegetarian slop of the lowest order and their music was too often weird avant-garde jazz in bizarre hard to follow time signatures, with only a smattering of rock or R&B.

To be fair, fun things did happen. I saw my first arty hard-core film when filmmaker Ed Seeman (a.k.a Edwardo Cimano, to protect his career in children's cartoon animation) came one night with a 16mm sound projector and screened his latest work, *Millie's Homecoming*. It launched the genre of One Day Wonders; feature length porn movies, all hand held, shot on film, totally improvised, with at least six hard core sex scenes and shot in one day. With Cassavetes cinéma vérité immediacy, close-up heat and raw blue humor, it established Ed as one of porn's great pioneers. Another night a celebrated hairstylist with scissors gave each girl a pubic hairstyle. Also, I got to meet an assortment of famous people, showbiz notables, horny presidential speechwriters and the man who will always be connected with the Pentagon Papers.

My favorite thing about these parties was that a frequent guest, a famous black badass film director, always showed up with a tasty date, and since he had a thing for Andrea, I always began the party by tasting his date.

I wanted to be accepted by my peers. After all, I was "creative" and all the other swingers I knew had normal jobs and careers and here was a gathering of designers, art directors, painters, writers, film makers, poets and artists.

But I didn't last long. They threw me out for being, ironically, an "anarchist" for not following some rules I can't even remember and mostly for asking two women arguing with a man about women's lib who were next to me while I was fucking to please take their fucking conversation to another room and away from those who actually enjoyed sex.

NOUVEAU RICHE

Au courant and tres chic! Ultra hip with big flashy Upper East Side arriviste apartments with spectacular views that always looked like they were styled by color-blind interior decorators who got off mocking people with too much money. These stockbrokers, entrepreneurs, surgeons and big deal lawyers always kept the majority of their jewelry on when naked. I never before saw a room full of nude folk still wearing diamonds, pearls, and expensive watches. There were more complications on their wrists than even in their personalities.

On more than one night, Marcus, one of the more fashion-conscious participants would take me on a guided tour of accessories on the bodies or on the floor. He pointed out Rolex Presidents, Movado Museum Pieces or Blue Lizard Summer Watches (in season), Cartier Tanks, Patek Philippe Calatravas, Miss Pasha Cartiers and an assortment from Breitling, Tag Heuer and even a few from Tiffany for those he considered horologically uninspired.

On the sidelines the shoe festival included Geppetto, Gucci,

Casadei, Bally, Chanel and Aigner for women, and Cole Haan, Florsheim, Gucci, Bally, Nunn Bush, French Shriner and Edmunds for men. Marcus, metrosexual before that classification was coined, was married to a purse collector and knew his brands. He pointed out Gucci, Coach, Dooney & Bourke and his wife's Judith Leiber.

They were, it must be said, mostly a good-looking group. At least the women. The men were all over the handsome map and were there because of their guile, cunning, talent and facilities. The women were there because they were trophies. They were the best pussy that money could buy. Where the fuck in the whole world could I go and fuck not just one but half a dozen trophy wives on the same night?

This group liked sex, but the men were not, it seemed, into sex as much as money. They cared too much about what you thought of the artwork on their walls, and the quality of their grass and coke and lavish catering. To their credit, they usually had high-end nouvelle cuisine that Andrea and I could never afford in our real lives. The sex was usually vanilla but the women were eager. Here was their one chance to fuck men other than the rich troll they married and not fall victim to their pre-nup.

SLUMMING BRAHMINS

These old money people owned enormous brownstones and penthouses, some with indoor pools and saunas. The sex, to my surprise, was terrific and the food was lousy. Lots of tall thin Protestants who delighted in being kinky with a flair for the visually dramatic; a bit of gangbanging here and there, a double penetration or two and guys jerking off on their friends' wives faces. They were not motivated by guilt but by the privilege of their class. They were sort of like us hippies but with more attitude, less innocence, better drugs, more stuff, and chauffeurs.

Early on I got tired of the Lipton onion dip. The Kinky Blue Bloods, I think, saw their evenings as either sex or food and never saw, as Jews and Blacks and Italians did, that both could coexist.

RICH BLACK DRUG DEALERS AND/OR PIMPS

These were the very cream of the scene. Black players always had, at least to my tastes, the best parties. These orgies had the hottest women—all shades but mostly white—including some working girls; call girls, not street hookers, who, pro bono, would come and go in gently changing shifts. This was a thrill in itself, like getting the keys to the candy store.

There were lots of black tough guys, a smattering of some wise guy business associates with a taste for "melanzane" (for some reason Italians either love blacks or hate them; I don't think they can be neutral) and those like Andrea and I, the invited.

I got invited to my first orgy with this group because a female friend of mine, a doe-eyed vixen of a Jewish girl, a bit pushy but quite sexy, was the girlfriend and top call girl of Bob—pimp, dealer, and party-giver. Bob liked fucking Andrea who especially liked fucking him, so we were always re-invited.

Black outlaw parties, and I went to at least seventy-five, mostly in Brooklyn's Park Slope, featured the wildest sex, including a little bondage and mild PG13 S&M. Most of the girls at these parties liked bad boys and girls that like bad boys are usually submissive.

More intense than the joy of hippie innocence, stronger than the erotic edge derived from shame and guilt, more powerful than the power of class privilege, is the gusto of pure, knowing, shove-it-in-your-face hedonism of those who live outside the law.

These bacchanals were incredible feasts. Not the gourmand-inspired huge deli trays of the middle-class, but spectacular gastronomic festivals of lobster, shrimp, crudités, homemade fried chicken Southern-style cooked in bacon grease, prime rib, expensive nouvelle cuisine every bit as good as the nouveau riche served, plus take-out Northern and Southern Italian from the best restaurants in Little Italy when wise guys dropped by. We were routinely indulged with delicate sauces, gorgeous presentations, the finest china, crystal, silver, and even goldware.

Not one piece of goldware was ever missing I'm sure. There's a sign in a martial arts store in Soho, London, that says, "We Dare

You To Shoplift." No such unsubtle reminder was needed here.

Sometimes, if fewer than the normal thirty people were invited and there was enough room around the dining table, we ate together before the orgy and had a chance to show off our clothes and wit. More often we ate in shifts. Couples and groups would gravitate between fuckings toward the dining room and the food.

The conversations, clothed or unclothed, were no different from any group of hip twenty-somethings having a private dinner in the back room of a restaurant; sports, movies, books, TV, or something that you read about in the papers. Rarely something sexual. Lots of laughing and lightness.

Naturally, drug-dealer orgies always featured vast supplies of the best-quality pot and occasionally small amounts of cocaine. Cocaine didn't hit the big time till the late '70s and too much of it, even a smidgeon too much, can make men lose their erections so it was never that popular with orgy crowds.

Marijuana is a homeopathic dose of schizophrenia. It complements an overabundance of sex with strangers. It also enhances all your senses and appetites, which is why it has medical applications. It's the perfect orgy drug.

Bob often peppered his parties with delightfully sleazy, swinging Eurotrash he and his Jewish girlfriend would meet during their frequent two-week binges blowing money in Europe. I'd get to fuck fast-talking, dark-haired, skinny Italian girls who would shout in melodic Italian when they came, and tall Scandinavians, the kind that darker Jewish boys are genetically encoded to lust after, the girls of Aryan propaganda, the kind Hitler wanted for breeding stock. At one of Bob's parties I once fucked a ravishing Czechoslovakian TV star who was so wild that while coming she bit the foot of the girl next to her, who just happened to be Andrea.

Blacks, as they liked to be called then, who were into orgies always had the right music. At that time I loved the Rolling Stones, Led Zeppelin, the Kinks, Jeff Beck and ZZ Top, and you can fuck to these white boys, especially if you are into quickies, but they just don't work at an all-night orgy when slow and long is the name of the game.

Black-sponsored orgies always had the right groove for sex. No music befits humping sweaty carnality like Isaac Hayes, Sly and the Family Stone, James Brown, Otis Redding, Harold Melvin and the Blue Notes, Curtis Mayfield, Barry White, Brook Benton, The Spinners, Lou Rawls, Eddie Kendricks, David Ruffin, and the Godfather of Orgy Music—Marvin Gaye, whose "What's Going On," "Mercy Mercy Me," and "Inner City Blues (Make Me Wanna Holler)," so permeated my brain after hearing them during several hundred fucks with a hundred different women that even today, decades later, every time I hear these Marvin Gaye songs, they set off an electro-biochemical chain reaction way back in my dorsal cerebellum where an entire wing of retired neurons and worn-out dendrites line up to create synapses and I feel the ghost of hard-ons past.

GATHERING OF THE TRIBES

Tribes would sometimes meet for interdenominational councils. I attended a huge multiple clan swing night at a Holiday Inn in New Jersey. The banquet hall had a hundred mattresses on the floor, private security and live bands. You entered blindfolded through a gauntlet of mouths and hands and feathers and whipped cream.

Andrea and I went to non-stop weekend bashes at resorts where I learned, at twenty-four, that a sixty-three-year-old woman can be a hot babe. We went to dude ranches with 300 couples of every color, age, and perversion. I was summoned into a room to service a woman, who was on her knees blindfolded, begging for another "gangbang mystery fuck," who called me "Number 31." By Sunday afternoon I ran out of sperm and then the blood pressure necessary to raise the beast.

ORGYMETRICS

The equalizer at orgies is stamina, which was my strong suit. Toward the end of the evening there were always more willing women than men. It's a simple physical reality that men need to be willing and able and women merely need to be willing. Late night is when guys like me who could get it up over and over and over and over earn their stripes.

For example: It's the tail end of an orgy that started at 9:00 p.m. with fourteen couples and it's now 2:30 a.m. and only five couples are left. Three of the guys are sleeping or at least have a sleeping penis which leaves five active women and two guys, and I am usually one of them. All of a sudden my stock goes up five points.

There are at least two women playing with each willing man and maybe I am the lucky guy with three. Plus, think about it. What kind of woman is still hungry for sex at the end of an orgy after getting fucked maybe six, seven, eight, nine times already? A very horny, highly sexed animalistic fucky one that would be pumping out the super-pheromones that a penis needs at that hour when a man's reputation is made. I was the Reggie Jackson, the Mr. October, of Orgies.

Another measurable attribute of orgies was the access it gave to certain kinds of women, high-class very beautiful ones, particularly, that I could not score on my own.

One anecdote explains it all. It is a Friday afternoon on Fifth Avenue near Central Park and I want to call Andrea to make plans for dinner. I notice that my watch has stopped. This absolutely gorgeous tall lady with Fur Coat And Lots Of Diamonds walks by and I ask her for the time. She doesn't acknowledge me and keeps on walking.

The very next night, Saturday, Andrea and I are at an orgy in a very posh apartment on Gramercy Park North done in stucco and stone, the entrance of which was made to look like the inside of an old English castle. Shortly after my first orgasm, I am aware, astounded, that next to me is the very same Fur Coat And Diamond Beauty, with the most beautiful God-given B-cup tits I've ever seen. She is beyond luscious. Not sexy looking but just plain gorgeous. She must have been a model. If you wanted the young executive look, the girl at the country club, or the right patrician trophy wife to show off an elegant fur coat or diamond necklace, you'd hire her.

She's on top of a dude parallel to me, riding up and down and screaming. They finish and she slides off the penis she's just wilted, and into my arms. We kiss; we feel each other all over. I hope she's more versatile and doesn't need to ride me cowgirl style, which is one of my least favorite positions because it's too passive for me.

I maneuver on top and hold each of her delicate thin wrists against the mattress to see if she responds. She does with a pleased whimper, a vain cartoon struggle and a smile in her eyes that signals it's her kind of fuck. We make long, hot, sweaty love.

She kisses great. Her skin is silky. Her eyes are light blue. She is just a few inches shorter than me. She is the single most perfect woman I ever fucked. Nothing about her hair, nails, face, hands, body, bum, legs, teeth and feet could be any better.

After fifteen minutes she suggests we 69 and as we start, before she puts my cock in her mouth, she bends around and starts sucking my asshole. I have to be really in love, or inspired, to suck an asshole, and knowing this is the same Lady from Fifth Avenue is suitably inspirational. She has one of those little hairless doll anuses nestled in a cute round firm tushy. When I stick my tongue in her bum she wiggles and squeals with delight. I add a finger into the mix and can tell this is one Very Anal Lady.

She relaxes and opens rather than tightens and closes. She then asks me ever so politely to put my cock up her ass. Actually her words are "Put yours there please." She refuses to mention any of the parts by name. I slide in and I am under siege by a battalion of different emotions, perceptions and sensations, all of them terrific. I am conquering the unconquerable, and adoring the most perfect female physical form I have ever felt. Everything about her says dainty and lady and refined, and my cock is up "there." I have one of those memorable orgasms that I hope will run a bit slower than most events when my whole life passes in front of me at the moment of death.

I never mention our outside world encounter. I hold her for a few minutes afterwards and secretly say a prayer of thanks to the Magic God and/or Goddess Of Orgy who sometimes makes the unattainable fuckable. On the way out The Fur Coat And Diamond Beauty comes over to me wearing the same fur coat from the day before, kisses me slow and tender, and whispers in my ear that she hopes to run into me at another party.

Sadly, I never see her again.

The Fur Coat And Diamond Beauty was the date of a funny looking Jewish gynecologist who was one of several funny looking Jewish OB-GYNs I met on the orgy circuit. They always showed up with the most gorgeous dates. Not only were these men doctors, which is a financial and social advantage, I suspected there must have been some benefit to introducing yourself to a fashion model while you are already between her legs.

MISCELLANEOUS ORGY QUESTIONS

Laura asks many questions, like, *"What about falling in love with someone other than the wife or girlfriend you came with?"*

It happened, but it was a rare event. I met and fell in love with Andrea at an orgy—but I was with some orgy-ticket girl whose name I can't remember and Andrea wasn't George's girlfriend. People who came with "just friends" would sometimes meet other "just friends" and fall in love.

I never worried about losing Andrea to someone else, and I never fell in love with anybody else no matter how beautiful or good a fuck. My confidence came from being twenty-four and feeling invulnerable and immortal every day. My commitment came from my trust and joy in the ease and intensity of being with Andrea. We just clicked. Both of us were avid readers, enjoyed cooking, loved walking the city streets, had lots of stamina, and loved animals, trivia, music, dancing and being silly, We both had a soft spot for Dada, Surrealism and absurdist theatre and literature. We were both always horny. We were both dedicated to sexual honesty. For the first time in my life I was in a relationship where we not only loved each other, we indulged the other's desires, we were whores for each other.

I was happy to have found Andrea and didn't want to replace her. I just wanted to also be able to fuck other females. I do not remember having even a passing thought about going home with someone beside Andrea. Love was a relationship, orgies were for sport, and I never forgot who was on the home team.

From years of seeing the same couples come to orgies, it appeared that healthy relationships were not dissolved because of swinging. In fact, I think it held many otherwise insolvent marriages together. It was something else to stay together for besides the kids.

If you wanted to fuck another woman you met at an orgy, you could meet her at another party and have her. Twice or three times in a row if you wanted to. Or if you were a female and your date/boyfriend/husband liked your fuckee's date/girlfriend/wife, you could get together with them at other orgies, or the four of you could get together anytime. Andrea and I had many mini-nookie festivals with a selection of couples.

Orgies made emotional fidelity easier. That might seem oxymoronic but think about it. Being able to fuck another girl or guy you fancied took the need "to cheat" out of your life. I mean, why bother?

Also, swinging couples were more likely to be sharing hot sex with each other so they were less likely to be unhappy with their sex lives. They were having the kind of sex at home that people who would worry about losing their mate at an orgy didn't have.

There was the switch here and there and one real life divorce/remarry inter-couple swap, but these were rare. Being able to fuck nearly anyone you wanted made whatever relationship you were in more tolerable and made this small risk worth it. Relationships were more fun with the threat of monogamy removed.

Example: I met an adorable petite smart girl named Amy at an orgy who liked Andrea and loved fucking me. She asked Andrea if she could come over in the mornings to fuck me on her days off. Amy would arrive with coffee and breakfast and jump under the covers with us. Then Andrea would get dressed, kiss us both goodbye and go to work.

Sometimes we took Amy with us to orgies. An extra female was always welcome, and a guy who showed up with two girls was treated like the living Buddha. None of us ever thought of ruining the situation, and if Amy was lonely and wanted to be with me/ us she just called and came over or I would go over to her tiny apartment nearby in the West Village. It's amazing what can be accomplished with the lack of jealousy. (Note to Amy: Please call!)

These new ethics made Baby Boomer Orgiests think we were creating a new society and changing the world.

Laura asks me, *"Can a girl turn you down?"*

Of course. But remember the odd circumstances you are in: a room filled with people who have chosen to fuck many strangers one after another. Being discriminating, selective, is not the operative mood. Private parties were by invitation and the hosts/ hostesses performed triage before you got through their door.

This was less true for on-premise swingatoriums like Plato's Retreat (I must ask why they named that place after one of history's least sexy people) where I believe the rejection rate would be higher since it was an "open" rather than an "invitational."

These public places to fuck had a very low bar of admission—usually the door money and something that vaguely reminded the doorman of a woman—so one didn't benefit from prequalification. I went to Plato's and Trapeze and a few other on-premise public swing clubs, but they were like finding too much bok choy in the moo goo gai pan.

At the 300 or so private orgies I attended, with an average of five to seven couplings at each one—and roughly 1,400 chances to be rejected—I must have experienced just over a dozen rejections, which is just over one half of one percent, the standard minimum necessary for statistical significance.

While there was a statistically significant 0.8 percent chance of being rejected, that meant for the twelve times I got rejected there were 1,388 acceptances. That's an acceptance rate of 99.2 percent. Who can't live with that? Plus my first refusal didn't happen until at least the fortieth orgy and by then it was emotionally a non-event.

Probably six of the twelve were outright rejections from females who, erroneously in my opinion, found me repulsive and would rather spend the time cleaning urinals than have sex with me. Another six were just from exhaustion. Some of these women I would conjugate with at a later date, some never. Only one I ever remember saying, "Oh No! Not you!" which did sting momentarily.

I have left out the three dozen "Oh, no, not again's," and "Oh, no, not now's" I got from females that I had had before and would have again but were either ready to go home, had their momentary fill, were just beginning a rest period, or were too hungry to be thinking about sex—logistical differences, not rejections.

This is not to say that the selection process was all one-sided. There were always some females who aggressively pursued males and sometimes other females. I was asked occasionally by ladies and only twice did I beg off. One was aesthetically challenged and one, more aggressive and masculine than me, scared me.

Another question Laura asks is, *"What about guys being so close to other naked guys and do they ever touch sexually?"*

Nearly every orgy I went to was run by average Hard-core Masturbator Guys. These orgies were the living manifestations of our (The Hard-core Masturbator's) dream world and were almost as homophobic as a gang of tough Italians. Bisexuality, not just tolerated but encouraged for women, was a tacit taboo for men. Nearly every straight guy likes to watch two women have sex with each other, but guy/guy sex is a definite no-no.

I don't know the psychobabble reasons why girl/girl is okay and guy/guy stuff isn't, but since most Hard-core Masturbator Guys feel the same way, I guess it must come bundled with our original operating system. Touching a guy happened all the time and was as accepted as it would be when playing basketball or football or even when wrestling. It was impossible not to touch each other as you crawled over a clusterfuck. If you were part of a threesome or moresome, guys would balance themselves, without even an awkward grimace, by holding onto each other. But we were all butch about it.

Occasionally, some guy would be playing near or around some female orifice you were already involved with, like a husband putting a finger up the ass of a wife you were screwing, or maybe some guy eating the pussy connected to the anus you had entered and your Johnson or cahones might be sideswiped or even fondled. I never minded it as long as it felt good and didn't impede my motion or pleasure. I only ever heard a very few true homophobes complain of these Class-C Misdemeanor Bisexual Encounters.

Once or twice in the middle of a cluster I looked down to see who was sucking me and it was a guy and a girl or just a guy and I just let it continue, especially if it was a guy and girl.

At the huge orgython at the Holiday Inn in New Jersey I was fucking this lovely lady and felt my balls being sucked and played with and I thought it was my friend Tina who often did that for me. I turned around and saw a tiny Japanese man down there and it felt so good I just kept pumping. It got a bit strange, however, because he followed me to provide the same ancillary benefit to my next copulation. This time I told him, "Thank you, but no more please." I don't think he spoke English, but he understood the International Body Language for "Go away or I'll kill you."

Laura also wants to know, *"What about VD?"*

This is what we worried about before we knew enough to worry about—"YOU'LL NEVER GET RID OF IT!"—herpes and —"YOU'LL DIE OF IT!"—AIDS.

I have no idea why, but I swear in over 300 orgies I have no memory of anyone ever getting anything and I never saw one condom. The answer must be that we were a healthy disease-free group and stayed in our own circle. Or, as I like to think, we were doing God's work and were protected by Guardian Angels.

The last question Laura asks is, *"What about anal sex at orgies?"*

At orgies where you really did have license to fuck, anal sex was a privilege. Most women didn't want it. Some women only shared it with their mates. Some liked it selectively. A few liked it equally to fucking and a very few, God bless them, preferred it.

I would say that anal sex was available from less than ten percent of the women and only once in a blue moon with a blue ribbon anus like The Fur Coat And Diamond Beauty. A gentleman never pushed the issue past a little cajoling. In retrospect, the vast majority of the sex I had and saw at the hundreds of orgies I went to in the early '70s was vanilla or at the most cherry vanilla. Lots of fucking and sucking, a sprinkling of rimming and a smidgen of anal sex. I never saw a whip or even handcuffs.

We were a randy bunch, but not really eccentric, once you got past the part about having sex with strangers in groups.

24

Laura's first orgy

Early 1981

The prospect of taking Laura to an orgy raises my anxiety level. Would there be a price to pay? There already is one, just me wondering if there *would* be one. Dread pokes me in the kidneys. Here I am, about to risk my most precious love gladiator in the modern-day Roman Sex Circus. What if, even if it's an outside chance, she finds a man/dick at this orgy who jazzes her toenails more than I do?

What if? What the fuck if?

I make a few calls to people I know from the old days who might still be travelling the orgy circuit. I am only half surprised that after an absence of seven years it takes me only twenty minutes to find a party that is about to start in two hours.

Laura is excited. She's got more questions: "Can I really fuck anyone I want, Jeffrey? Is that really okay with you? Can I say 'no' to anyone? Can I ask a girl? Do you want me to ask you if it's okay with you before I fuck someone?"

I spend the cab ride to Larry's explaining Orgy Etiquette. The eavesdropping cabby nods each time I make a point—"Do what you want." (Nod.) "Don't do what you don't want to do." (Nod.) "Respect other people's wants as well as their not-wants." (Nod.)

Laura wears lots of makeup, big sexy dangly earrings, high-heel red slut pumps, a slinky, short, tight, fire-engine red leather mini-dress, sheer stockings and garter belt, and white cotton bra and panties. She's a dichotomy, a sexual ice cream sandwich, whore on the outside and virgin inside.

We arrive a bit late. Larry, tall and GQ handsome as ever, greets me. "Hello, Jeffrey, it's been so long everybody thought you were dead." After making eye contact with me for 15/16th of a second, he oogles Laura.

"My God, you're lovely!" he slimes, stifling a drool. "Jeffrey, you always do come up with great-looking women, but Laura is the top of your game."

Larry, who has not looked at me since the first 15/16th of a second, holds Laura's hand and coos, "Please come in and join the party. I can't wait to get to you later, Laura."

Laura whispers, "I don't have to fuck that creep, do I?"

"Only if I tell you that you have to," I whisper back.

Larry's apartment, filled with about two dozen nouveau riche perverts, is an overdone, flashy, big two-bedroom on Sutton Place, with formal dining room and a very large living room. The second bedroom, the main "orgy room," is done like so many others I had seen, in expensive ugly New Orleans whorehouse-style red flocked wallpaper and obligatory wall-to-wall mattresses. Naked people mill and mix with clothed people, the late arrivals or late bloomers.

Orgies were almost always couples. If you didn't take a wife, you took a girlfriend or had the decency to hire a call girl (not a street hooker) and pass her off as a friend. But if you counted heads at Larry's, you'd always come up with extra guys. Larry, a lawyer, would always sneak in a horny client/partner/friend or two. It never bothered me because Larry always had lots of very high quality pot, terrific purple sensimilla, and the women at his parties were always equal to the drugs.

Larry's crowd is flash, moneyed men, mostly youngish, well groomed and fit, and the beautiful horny women attracted to them and/or their money. Most of the men are in banking or law or Wall Street. "Suits," Laura calls them. This is before the term goes cliché.

"You can smell they are Republicans, but that's okay," she adds. "Most of my clients are Republicans and most can fuck good."

These are "straight" hypocritical motherfuckers who do drugs and fuck each other's wives on Saturday night, then vote for people who want to give drug dealers the electric chair and would like to see personal freedom redefined with great limitations. Going to orgies and stealing money from the IRS, and anyone else they can screw, are the ways these "suits" rebel against society. My pre-orgy anxiety vanishes. Laura can't possibly love any one of these dudes enough to run off with him, even if he has more money and a bigger dick than me.

But... but... but I adore fucking their women. Their women are generally the kind who think shopping should be an Olympic sport. A bit superficial for my tastes, but not for my dick's. As I've stated for the record, I love banging straight wives and girlfriends with hairdos, especially good-looking horny gold-digging sluts. They are alien creatures to me and I find them erotic the way some guys can have a "thing" for black girls, or the way some men fancy Asians.

The evening starts off with a nookie explosion. I come back from the bathroom and find Laura wearing only her white garter belt and stockings on Larry's leather sofa in the alcove study with her head bent back sucking a nice-size cock while Larry—who I guess in the mania of a group is acceptable to Laura, or she doesn't know it's him—is eating her pussy. Two other men, each with one hand fondling their dick, are groping some part of her anatomy with the other hand.

I stand there and observe. Laura's delicate olive frame is the center of energy. I feel my blood pressure rising fast, kicking in the turbine on my hormones, shifting my libido to the red line. The one-woman, many-man configuration continually changes shape. I concentrate, listening to the slurps and ahhhss, wet squishes, slippery slides, an occasional "Beautiful," "Yeah, just like that," and, "Oh my God what an ass!" The syncopated clanging of her long earrings sounds better than Larry's lame background disco music.

A cock pulls out of her lips and shoots its first squirt of come on her face and in her open mouth and then slides back into her mouth to finish. The cock pulls out and Laura makes a big deal of swallowing. Some ejaculate drips down her cheek. Laura sweeps it onto her finger and passes it to her tongue while looking right into the penis-owner's eyes. What a pro.

Laura's face is a three-act play when she's having sex. Big-eyed anticipation is Act One. Act Two is the striving lust, the intense athletic woman pushing her physical limits. Act Three is the droopy-eyed tongue-hanging slut. Her face relaxes, loses all musculature and is half begging dog, half exhausted victorious prizefighter.

Larry stops eating her and Laura turns around and elevates herself into doggy position. Larry fucks her pussy and another man takes over her mouth. In a few minutes Larry climaxes inside her, rests for a moment, pulls out, gives her ass a playful slap, which he follows with kisses to her buttocks, left cheek, then right. Now another man is fucking her. A black dude is fingering her ass while waiting for the pussyfucker to complete his mission. New cocks wait on deck for the opportunity to go to bat. Laura is in constant movement, a perpetual-motion sex machine.

When we are alone at home and I fuck her, I am aware when Laura crosses from making love to me, her man, Jeffrey—to a place where names, personalities and love evaporate. I know after she's crossed over I could pull out of her, insert just about any cock in the world, and she wouldn't miss a beat. I envy that.

I never get that mindless. I never get that uncerebral. I adore sex but never go into ecstatic coma, never achieve the perfect oneness of Zen Nookie. Laura goes blank, has dervish fits, and is One With The Orgasm. I have orgasms. She is orgasm. I am getting horny. I walk around the flat looking for a pussy to fuck. I hit on the first leggy naked blonde I see. At Larry's there are always a few.

She's smoking a cigarette, snorting cocaine, and sitting on the couch in the living room. Her body is wet with her last fuck's sweat. I sit next to her fully dressed, full of myself, look straight into her bleary hazel eyes and giant pupils and with my best Humphrey Bogart say, "I'm Jeffrey and I'm ready take you on a ride."

She welcomes my invitation with bent-lipped smile and crushes out her cigarette in the ashtray. I grab her and kiss her half tenderly, exploring her mouth with my lips. She undoes my zipper. I taste the cocaine dripping from her nose into her mouth. We stand up to go find someplace to fuck.

She is about 5'10" and since the drapes match the carpet she is a natural golden blonde. Her skin says she can't yet be twenty-one. She is model thin with small tits, not much of a waist but a lovely protruding mons pubis, the kind that feels great to bang against but leaves your own pubic bone sore after a few hours of hard fucking. But then I'm not going to fuck her for a few hours.

She has a firm ass, on the smallish side, one size down from the rest of her. She is a nice choice, a fine vacation from my olive-skinned brunette Laura. We go into the orgy room and fuck ourselves silly. She never opens her mouth to speak one word the entire time but she does moan.

Blondie is only a semi-interesting lover compared to the passionate meltdown level lunacy I share with Laura, but she has a vagina and I have a good time. Post-coitally, Blondie speaks and tells me her name is Michelle and she's come from Indianapolis to model in NYC and is having some success.

Laura rushes over, falls into my arms, smiles at Michelle and gushes, "Jeffrey, I need you to fuck me right now." We fuck while Michelle watches without joining in. Laura tells me about the line of guys who fucked her and how she lost count of them. She speaks as I fuck her, replaying the scene. I explode in her. We come in unison as usual and hug for a long, long while.

Two men lying nearby start pawing Laura and I tell her to service them in front of me. I watch as the primal sex animal inside her is unleashed, the amoral hormone-driven epicenter that knows no name, no loyalty, only faceless erotic fire. The evening continues.

It's way past 2:00 and the grinding is grinding to a halt. I fuck two other unremarkable women and Laura fucks just about every man in the room, some twice. In a room full of sexy women Laura reigns supreme, in looks, libido and physical stamina. I'm watching Laura. The guy standing next to me says, "She's amazing. How do you get a girl like that? Are you rich?"

"No," I say. "Not financially. I'm rich because I have her."

"If that's rich, what's poverty?" he asks.

"Poverty is not having a woman you love who adores your penis and takes care of you exactly how you want everyday. And it doesn't matter how much money you have."

"You might be right," he says with a smile that makes me think he's already begun to reprioritize his life.

I do have one pang of jealousy, over the smallest detail. I watch Laura fuck a pretty, fit blond boy named Steve. After they fuck she fluffs up the pillow under his head to make him more comfortable, just as she does for me, and I am more than jealous, I am injured.

Something I think is entirely mine isn't. I watch one man after another stick their private parts in her and make her shiver and scream in orgasm and I am not in the slightest green-eyed. The next moment she fluffs up a pillow and I'm emotionally raped. In the land of hard-core sex, an act of tenderness is betrayal. I wonder whether that pang will return the next time she fluffs up my pillow. (It did a few times and then it went away.)

It's around 3:00 a.m. and I'm sleeping on a mattress with my arm around a girl I may or may not have had sex with. Laura wakes me up and asks to go home. She's naked, sweaty and wearing a variety of men's colognes.

"Everything all right?" I ask. "Have you had your fill already?"

"Fucking these guys is great but it's all so vanilla. Nothing really, *really* exciting. Everybody is gentle with me. I want to go home so you can whip me and use me." The coke in her takes over and she motor-mouths, "Aren't there any orgies where I can get tied down and whipped? That would be exciting, to have you whip me in public or watch me get whipped by a strange man. Or more than one. These guys are all so regular. Do some coke and take me home. I'll do anything you want."

"I wanted fucking, sucking and whipping," Laura exclaims,
"especially the whipping—definitely as far as getting
pleasure from the pain, it was just a new sensation and it

definitely took the fucking to a different height, because it brought all my sensations to a new level.

"So when Jeffrey was whipping and fucking me, those orgasms would be at a different level—a higher level than if he was just fucking me. Whipping elevated the sensation. Absolutely. It got my entire body, that's definitely it. It had to do with the extreme, the tingling, and the heightened intensity of feeling. It magnified everything—but that's an understatement; it brought my whole body to this incredibly intense feeling place. It was so incredibly filled with sensation. Then fucking was just some icing, but the whipping made my orgasms bigger and better. It made them beyond what I ever imagined an orgasm could be. It's like orgasm times orgasm."

I go into the dining room and snort two fat lines. We hunt for our clothing. As we leave Larry begs us to come back again and thanks me personally, as if I'd just loaned him a lot of desperately needed money. We get home and I beg Laura to stop doing coke but she doesn't. She begs me to whip her and I do. I fall asleep somewhere in the middle of whipping and before we fuck.

25

Hot babe gone wrong

Flashback to 1972

Now that Laura and I have enjoyed her first orgy, let me explain my pre-carnal carnival jitters. Most of the women you meet at an orgy are sevens or above. What you don't find often is a nine point five like Laura.

If you're the man who brings a prime, hot, rare, magnificent woman, you are The Ego King. Every man nods to you. It's like being rich, handsome, and a famous quarterback all in one. You are The Sex Elvis. There are two downsides to being The Sex Elvis. One is that you will not find a woman as hot as the one you brought. The second is that you risk, as small a possibility as it is, losing The Spectacular One.

I'd brought The Über Babe to a few orgies before. She was a drop dead luscious stripper and the first girl I ever met who called herself Tiffany. (This was before people actually named their daughters Tiffany, Brittany and Ashley, and when the only girls with these names were hookers and strippers.) I didn't lose Tif to someone else and it wouldn't have been terrible if I had. Tif and I were just fuck buddies.

Taking someone visually charismatic, whom I love, like Laura, comes with an acrid whiff of fear because I had seen "The Guy Who

Brings The Spectacular One" go wrong. It happened in 1972, right in the middle of my Orgy Period with Andrea. It was at Bill Lester's regular Friday night ten-to-twelve-couple soirée on the Upper East Side. Bill's orgies were unsubtle. His apartment had a short hall leading into one large room which was carpeted with mattresses that I suppose got piled up in one corner when it wasn't Friday night. It was a no-foreplay kind of swing. You knocked on the door, walked into the apartment, quickly stripped and started fucking.

A slick but likable Jew in the electronics business arrived with his new girlfriend. Slick always came with hot babes but this time he'd outdone himself. She was a redbone light-skinned black girl with unexpected blue eyes. They were the color of a clear sky, azure but with a touch of robin's egg. The music from her Jamaican accent was a charming accessory.

She was of average height, about 5'5", with perfectly proportioned C-cup melons. (Again, remember, this was the early '70s before every other girl had an augmented rack.) She took off her red silk short-shorts worn with no panties and her tight white T-shirt worn without a bra. She was phenomenal with skin a lustrous buff color between mocha and light sepia and long straight black hair. Her pubic hair was short, trimmed for a tiny bikini.

She had a delicate yet chiseled face. Her nose and her lips were midway between black and white, and celebrated racial diversity. Her smile revealed perfect teeth that spoke of genetic luck or expensive orthodontia. Her thighs and legs were shapely and just a bit muscular. Her rosettes were only a quarter shade darker than her skin tone and her nipples already had hard-ons from her excitement—or the air conditioning—or both.

She had one of the ten best asses I ever saw live. Round, and a half-size larger than need be. And on top of all this she had those blue eyes. She was the healthiest woman I ever saw. She triggered The Prime Objective: I wanted to make a baby with her. But I would happily settle for simple non-reproductive carnality. She was the desired erotic icon, and Slick was the envy of every dick in the room. But envy is a devil vibe and has to be regulated the way a matador manipulates the bull.

The evening started off well although several of us did make fools of ourselves fawning over The Spectacular One. Me included. She said her name was Annabella and this was her first orgy. She was a bit timid and stood with her arms folded in front of her. The boldest among us, not me, led her off to a corner and in a few minutes she was screaming like an unselfconscious seasoned pro.

I was the fourth man to fuck her. At first, I thought that she was being a bit theatrical, that she was playing it too big for a small room, but being inside her and feeling her noise suspended my disbelief. She was no act. She was just that loud and wild. She was one of those demure women whom sex morphs into rational derangement. She left little nail marks on all our backs. Right after my solo, three guys started in on her together. She welcomed them all. She had stamina to match her physique.

Slick was trying to enjoy the other women in the room but never quite got into it. This was a shame because "The Guy Who Brings The Spectacular One" is regaled, feted and spoiled by the other women. They figure he must be something special. But Slick could not take his eyes off Annabella.

He didn't seem to like what was going on. He never came over to join her and the other men. He never kissed her and showered her with light jocular compliments the way "The Guy Who Brings The Spectacular One" usually does. Two hours later Slick had already wanted to leave for fifteen minutes. He asked her several times, but she didn't respond. He got dressed by the door so she'd get the hint. She was still fucking wildly. I'd seen it happen before: The timid wife or girlfriend who finally succumbs to her man's request to go to an orgy becomes the lustful sex glutton who won't go home. Usually the man is delighted by this irony, but Slick lost his cool. I think he'd been too quick to want to show Annabella off in public. Their bond was too fragile.

First he cajoled, then he politely demanded, then he begged, then he got real mad and crossed the line of abuse and called her names like "Slut" and "Tramp."

These were names we held in holy regard and bestowed only as compliments and he was using them in vain!

Blasphemy!!

She told him to "back off mon," and that she would leave when she was "bloody ready!" He wouldn't back off and repeated his demands, slow and deliberate, with only a partially veiled physical threat. For the first time that evening she slammed on the sex brakes. She got rigid. Then she dropped the atom bomb.

"You can't treat me like that, and two of these guys here fuck better than you, mon. So go fuck yourself. I don't want to ever see you again!" Slick left in a huff without Buff.

I thought her "two guys" was brilliant because it left room for each of us who had been with her to feel included. No one asked who the two guys were; it was just too easy to assume you were one of them. As soon as Slick left, she was back in the groove. After most of the guys were limp, I had another go with Annabella. She was worth the wait.

While the party was breaking up The Spectacular One answered questions about her ethnic mix. She told us she came from Calabash Bay in the South of Jamaica. Her father was descended from a blue-eyed Scotsman who married a descendant of a slave and her mother was part Swedish and part Cherokee. Annabella got dressed, thanked everyone and left. Andrea and I offered to share a cab with her downtown but she was going uptown.

Andrea was only the slightest notch jealous. One notch of jealousy wasn't rare with Swingers. I'd get one notch jealous every so often myself if a Spectacular Guy with a major league penis spent a lot of time porking Andrea. Andrea may have sulked a bit but she knew that after we got home and I had recouped some of my energy that she would be the beneficiary of my recent adventure. It was the same for me when the jealousy was reversed. I would be the beneficiary of Andrea's heightened erotic self-image. The gift to swingers and the salve that comforts the sting of small jealousies is that the orgy doesn't end when you leave.

I never saw Annabella again, which is a shame. I saw Slick again with respectable-looking women, but never such a prize as The Spectacular One.

26

The lyrics and music of sex

One of the lesser-publicized virtues of sex, especially group sex, is the audio track. I've reflected often—right in the middle of an orgy—how infrequently the various vocalizations are out of tune. Something makes the moans, groans, pouty weeps, gasps, high-pitched exhales, sighs, and even the shriekiest wails and squeals harmonize. They are never cacophonous. And the happy slaps of flesh on flesh, and the thump thump thump of furniture and mattresses, and the creaky squeek of beds are a solid rhythm section for the players to do solos over.

The lyrics are even better than the music. I enjoy every chant of "God!," "Oh my God!," "Jesus!," "Jesus Christ," "Jesus Christ Almighty," and the odd "Jesus H. Christ!" I never found out what the H stands for. Many times I heard "Jesus, Mary and Joseph," which I believe is an exclamation reserved for Catholics, usually lapsed, usually Irish, almost always women. I've also heard people shout—again usually women, and I don't know why it's women—"Jesus Fucking Christ."

These are power cheers, like shouting "D-Fence," at a football game. Sometimes they are in smooth, soothing legato and sometimes they stab the air in staccato.

I never heard "Father, Son and Holy Ghost," "Holy Moses," "Mohammed," or any U.S. President. I don't know what Unitarian Universalists scream. Maybe it's "Oh Great Possible Nothingness" or "Holy Question Mark." Maybe they revert to the standard religious responses listed above. Maybe, as in foxholes, there are no atheists in the middle of an orgasm.

One of the loudest female fucks I ever met was a hard-bitten card-carrying Madeline Murray O'Hare-following atheist, a rabid placard waving anti-school prayer protester who once screamed, "Dear God help me!" in the middle of a climax. I never called her on it because I saw no erotic upside, but I knew there was at least a moment or two when she slid into agnosticism.

27

Olympic pissing at the Hellfire Club

February 1981

Laura Erotic Progress Report: She's gone from normal horny teenage hippie to almost sexless spiritual wife to local bar slut to New York City hooker to adult bookstore anonymous sex to threesomes to orgies. None of these have allowed her to give vent to her new hobby, masochism. I say masochism in retrospect. We never use the word. She says she likes being whipped, likes being my slave and likes taking pain, but we never use any mass marketing, pop culture labels. She keeps asking me to find a place where I can tie her down and other men can whip her.

Being alien to this scene I ask around, and eventually find a place that offers just the kind of warm fuzzy home-style sordidness she is looking for: The Hellfire Club. It's in the Meat District and most nights it's a gay S&M club. My dominatrix friend says she often takes clients there for public humiliation. They paid extra to be beaten, pissed on and abused in front of a crowd. She tells me she was struck by how many people in one room preferred drinking piss to beer.

The place is named after the famous English sex club of the Victorian Era. The motto of the original Hellfire Club was *"Fais ce que tu voudras"* (Do what thou wilt), and it was a meeting place for "persons of quality" (largely nobility, royals, politicians and clergy). Members got together to share poetry, blaspheme, drink, fuck and argue politics, philosophy and religion. Lots of prostitutes, male and female, were brought in and passed around. Oddly, the club was said to be the one place in England where men and women had equal status.

I tell Laura nothing except to take some of our more bizarre sex toys—handcuffs, whips, and chains. During the cab ride down to the triangle at 14th Street and Hudson, I tell Laura that she is to do nothing except follow my orders for the rest of the night. "Yes, Master," she replies with a twinkle.

We arrive at the Hellfire Club at about 2:00 a.m. and even in the entry we smell its noxious decadence: sweat, piss, sperm, vaginal fluids, blood, beer, hormones, vomit, leather, and marijuana all elbow each other to deliver their olfactory massage. It is disgusting and compelling. This is the real goods. Vanilla is not a flavor available here. We walk into the packed barroom and the odors intensify. I imagine that a Haz-Mat crew wearing yellow suits and gas masks might raid the club before the vice squad.

Black leather is everywhere. We migrate to the back room through the smoke and overly loud disco. I hear the sound of lashes, slaps, and screams as bodies come into view. It appears they are equally divided between men and women. Some are tied to the ceiling and some are chained to the walls. This is definitely hardball. Laura draws a few glances but so far we are just day-trippers. So much is going on, little scenes are happening everywhere and I guess here you're judged only by what you do.

We walk around. A bar area is surrounded by tables and chairs, some people drinking amid sex acts of all varieties casually sprinkled about. Behind the bar is an open space with torture racks and a brick wall with metal hooks and loops. From all the choices in the erotic scenes around me, one grabs my attention.

An attractive young white girl, maybe barely twenty, is tied to a hook hanging from the ceiling, with her hands bound over her head and her tippy-toes just reaching the floor. Two black men are whipping her, one whipping her front, one whipping her back. Her body is a Jackson Pollock of welts and bruises. She obviously loves it, shouting, "More! Please!" between strokes. It sucks the eyeballs out of my head and it turns me on. I realize immediately that small visuals, complete with sound, are being processed, printed into little loops to be replayed in my head during later masturbations.

I pinch Laura's ass so hard she squirms, turns, kisses me and says, "I want to be used like that." We walk though an arched doorway into a large area in the back. In the middle is a doctor's examining table. A slender pale man tied to the table face down is being assfucked savagely by a giant penis connected to a massive hulk of a man. The little guy is screaming so loud I have no idea whether he likes it or is being tortured to death or both.

Everywhere are roaming voyeurs like us, meandering from one scene to the next. Some people are naked, some clothed, some in between. We peer into cubicles around the perimeter. Each little tableau is more bizarre than the last.

A girl, not particularly attractive, is on her knees sucking off a man while other people, mostly men, watch.

A fat man is being whipped by fatter women and begging, in childlike tones for more.

Two black-leather gay men are whipping the back of a guy who has a cucumber in his asshole.

A large-assed woman bending over a chair, supported by a beefy man and a beefy woman, is servicing a line of men who plant themselves in her asshole one after another.

An attractive middle-aged suburban housewife with a hairdo is on her knees sucking off two guys at once while a line of men wait their turn. Some of the men who can't wait jerk off on her face or bare back, which is already caked with drying sperm.

I lead Laura back out to the bar area where we encounter a red-haired, proper aristocrat in an evening gown with her hair up in a bun—a woman dressed more for the opera than hell—with two men dressed in black leather, on leashes, like giant house pets, kissing her feet.

This is Fellini, mixed with DeSade, sprinkled with a dash of Aleister Crowley.

We walk into a tiny hallway past two toilet stalls with curtains instead of doors and enter a particularly foul-smelling area with a bare toilet in the corner and two bathtubs in the center. A naked man is sitting in the first bathtub jerking off a huge hard-on chanting over and over, "Piss on me boys, piss on me." He has a huge anchor tattooed on his forearm, the one not jerking off his cock. He's bald, extremely muscled, has a goatee and looks like a cross between Bluto and Popeye.

Laura says she has to pee. We go over to the two toilets but they are occupied, each with more than one person. I suggest she use the other bathtub, the one without the man. He might not want girl piss on him.

Laura hikes up her mini dress and takes off her panties. I hold them. Eyes converge on us. Bodies mill around. Some men touch Laura. She gives me an uneasy sign so I push them back. She backs up and squats over the tub, careful not to touch God-knows-what germs festering on the rim. Just as she starts to piss, two guys at opposite ends of the tub—oblivious to each other—simultaneously dive under her to drink or bathe in her golden shower. Their heads meet with a "CRACKKKK" so loud it cuts through the disco.

My first instinct is to laugh. Then I notice that while one of them is lapping up her stream, the other is out cold. Before I have to decide whether or not to help him before Laura finishes pissing, others get him out of the tub. Within a minute he's standing up by himself moaning, "I missed the piss, I missed the piss."

Laura whispers in my ear, "Take me some place and whip me in front of people. Let's put on a show."

We leave the pissorium with our entourage and walk past the white girl suspended from the ceiling still being used by the two black men. One of them has his dick up her ass and the other is holding her legs in the air in front of her. The man fucking her ass holds her with one hand and whips her back with the other. She isn't pretty but she is so slutty and so extreme I want to fuck her. Even more I want to know her story. But I have other business to attend to.

I lead Laura to an area off to the side in the barroom and tell her to remove all her clothing except for her garter belt, stockings and high heels. I have her get on her knees on a chair. I do not tie her hands or restrain her. I want no restraint. I want her to accept whatever is about to happen.

Laura's body radiates fragrance, not perfume but her own savory scent that fuels my insane erotic desires. I take the short multi-stranded whip out of my pocket and start reddening her ass, making her beg for each new stroke. She pleads, "HARDER BABY, HIT ME HARDER!"

"Maybe I loved being whipped because I was whipped as a child," says Laura in reflection. "My father whipped all of us as a punishment. We'd have to pull our pants down and he'd whip us on our asses with a belt. It was definitely a spare the rod, spoil the child upbringing. It was his moral duty. I remember my cousin once said to me, 'They only whip you because you cry. If you act like you don't even care, they'll stop punishing you that way.' So I tried not to cry when my father whipped me the next time. And it just didn't work cause it hurt like hell. I never enjoyed it in the slightest bit when my father whipped me. It was horrible and I hated him for it. It was a huge part of my early acid trips, getting through this and forgiving my parents. I had a long conversation with them when I was about eighteen or nineteen years old, saying I really wanted to forgive them for whipping me when I was a kid. And I still have a hard time even saying it. Because to me it was so abusive and so mortifying and so horrible. And I don't think the two things are related, but I suppose a therapist would say they are."

A sizable crowd gathers around us. I move around in front of Laura's face and say, "I'm going to give a stranger the whip, and look you right in the eyes as you take the pain."

"Yes, Master, that's what I want."

"What is it that you truly want?"

"I want to be used by men," Laura cries, "I want them to have their way with me. I want to be abused hard by men I never see."

It is a variation of the sex rap scenario we painted countless times alone together in our bed with each of us trading lines to flesh out the sordid set piece. As we talk, the crowd gets edgy for action. I feel the rise in expectations. So this is why rock groups always came out on stage late.

I hand the whip to the man wearing lots of black leather closest to me. "Hit her," I say.

"Oh, I just couldn't!" he lisps and the crowd laughs. Although he looked the part, once he spoke I understood he was a festive fellow and this was not his sport.

"I'll whip her," comes from a wiry young guy reaching for my whip.

I tell him to be firm, not brutal, and count only to ten. I move close to her face and watch every detail of her perverse pleasure. The whip comes down hard on her ass as she's kneeling on the chair. She moans with each lash. "Is this what you desire?" I ask between eight and nine.

"Yes I need this. I love you, baby, "Laura answers, "You give me what I need."

"Tell me what you want now baby, I demand it."

"I want to kiss you while men spank me and fuck me and deposit come in me," Laura tells me, "then I want you to fuck me up the ass in front of everyone."

"Who wants to fuck her?" I shout out to the crowd, a pirate captain playing social director with his men after a particularly successful pillage.

I know I can't possibly provide her with enough sex to satisfy her. I want to see how much it takes to make her say, "Enough."

A small man dressed in all black leather, much older than we were, one of the first to whip Laura and one of only two I had to warn to back off a bit, compliments me on owning a Unicorn.

"A what?"

"A Unicorn," he repeats. "You must be new to the scene. Gorgeous female slaves are so rare, we call them Unicorns."

> "I was treated like royalty at Hellfire Club," Laura brags, "I was the Slave Queen. The Slut Queen. I used to always love going there. I loved all the different contraptions and being able to be whipped and put on a pummel horse; I loved getting pummeled on the pummel horse. I was able to lean over that and somebody kind of hold me while I was getting fucked in the pussy and in the ass—one after another! I never got gangbanged before I met Jeffrey, but it was the perfect thing for a sensation junkie like me. I got exactly what I wanted, non-stop gangbang while being whipped by a gang of strange men. I was living my fantasy and it felt better in reality than even in my imagination so I always wanted more."

"Line up behind her and get your meat ready," I order. I take a fistful of condoms out of my pocket and hand them out. (This was when prophylactics were not ubiquitous at orgies, or even at whorehouses, but this wasn't the orgy crowd, a friend or a middle class trick. This was an unknown demographic and I wanted to be safe.)

The pushing and shoving grows violent. A punch is thrown. Soon the natural pecking order sorts itself out. The line is about fifteen men long and curls around so the end of the line has a view of the action in front. "Only her pussy! Only her pussy! No ass fucking and that's an order!" I say in my most brutal basso.

Some men are rough, some gentle; some come quickly, some come too quickly, some take five or ten minutes, some eat her pussy from behind for a minute before fucking her. Some come loudly, some silently. One spanks her while he fucks her. Some come inside her in their rubbers, some pull out, rip their condoms off and jerk off on her ass. Two can't get it up and are shoved aside by the next in line. While waiting, some men stroke her and play with her nipples.

> "That was one of my favorite nights at the Hellfire Club," Laura remembers. "All my fantasies had to do with multiple men so somebody was whipping me and somebody else was playing with my nipples. I was just in this mind-thing where I was just *fucking ecstatic!!!*
>
> "Some of the men who were whipping me were really into it just the way I like it and had just the right pace going. You know, because if you whip too fast, it's not enough—and I had to be able to *savor the feeling* of the whip!
>
> "For me it was the smack of the whip and then savoring the pain," Laura explains, "first the whip, and then the pain. And they were whipping me exactly right."

Laura comes with nearly every one of them who fucks her long enough, moaning with each new load until her orgasms blur into one ecstatic cry.

I call for a break after a dozen men. The line is still long with many having gone back for a second turn. I walk around behind her just to see the come drip down her thighs, framed by an ass as red as any fraternity pledge's bottom on hell night. I grab a mass of come with my fingers and fling it onto the floor. I smear what's left on my hand on her ass and legs, spank her, then let the revelry continue.

I ask her after each man if she wants more and she says yes. Her eyes get drunker with each fuck. She whimpers and begs for more as soon as each cock pulls out. During the middle of some fucks, she shakes as if hit by an electric shock.

Laura never says "enough." She doesn't come anymore, but there is no way she is going to say "no mas!" After two-dozen fucks (I've run out of condoms), Laura is physically exhausted and I tell the line the game is over. Laura comes back to life and screams, "Fuck me in the ass, Master! Please fuck me in the ass."

Her beautiful ass is as hot as a heating pad.

I take off my pants. I'm not wearing underwear. I take my already hard dick, and rub it on her hot come-soaked butt. I work it into her bum using the ejaculate butter as lubricant. She is awash in it. It runs down her legs. I lean against her and move in and out and feel the fluid; some just given to her is warm at the top of her thighs and some, received earlier, is cold, all the way down to her ankles.

Someone puts a real popper (I could tell it was amyl nitrate not butyl nitrate) right under my nose, which helps spark my climax and makes the explosion more intense.

> "Of course, Jeffrey would always come in for the fuck," Laura laughs, "because I loved fucking him. That was another one of my favorite fantasies that we acted out— Jeffrey would let everyone get me all turned on—and then he would come in and insert himself inside my ass. Yeah, insert himself right into the picture, ha, ha, ha!"

We get dressed and we go home. We take a long shower together, fumigate, decontaminate, do more coke, and talk about the experience and fall asleep without realizing it.

I wake up the next day feeling her heating pad ass. I fuck her without her ever stirring or waking up. Her nose is filled with coke and she makes little snores the entire time so I know she is not dead.

28

The Norman Mailer/José Torres
Saturday Morning Boxing Club

and my war with Ryan O'Neal

Other than fucking, my other great physical passion was boxing. From 1976 to 1984, I was part of a group that boxed about twenty-five fall, winter and spring Saturday mornings a year at the Gramercy Gym on 14th Street. The regulars were me, former Light Heavyweight Champion of the World Jose´ Torres, Norman Mailer, Norman's son Michael, and Norman's nephew Peter Alson.

We were joined by a revolving group of artists, writers, actors, lawyers, TV directors, college students, stockbrokers and even a Kennedy for a while. Most had boxed before. Some came fresh to learn. We all wanted something more exciting than tennis.

I was never blessed with much physical grace or more than normal coordination. What I brought into the ring was great stamina, fair size (just under six feet and 175 pounds), a low fear of punishment, and an aggressive willingness to mix it up. At my best I could be daring in attack and stubborn in defense.

I was an awkward boxer without much poetry, which in boxing can be its own reward. Being awkward makes you harder to read sometimes, often harder to hit and less likely to telegraph your punches. Ken Norton and Joe Frazier are two famous boxers who are considered awkward in style. Mike Tyson is another obvious example. What he lacks in grace he makes up for in power and courage. And teeth.

Saturday morning boxing protocol was simple. You'd fight a round or two, or rarely three. Sometimes José, our coach, would suggest a match between two of us.

A pact between fighters would be made as to the level of contact. One might say, "Let's just practice for a round or two, I want to work on my jab," or "I want to work on my defense so come at me and I'll just defend." Or maybe we'd agree on light contact and sometimes full contact. We all wore mouthpieces and cups. Headgear was available, but I hated headgear. It interfered with my vision, was annoying to wear and the extra size made for a bigger target.

Everyone wrapped his hands with long strips of cotton fabric to protect against injuries induced by punching. Wraps make it less likely you'll hurt your thumb and reduce the risk of a fracture to one of your wrist bones. They maintain the alignment of the joints and add strength to your punch. Mostly I just loved the ceremony of wrapping before a fight. It's always a tense scene in every boxing movie. In real life you are the warrior preparing for battle. For real. Not a video game. Low tech. You against him. May the best man win.

The object of our fights wasn't to destroy our opponent, but to gain advantage. The main difference between us and most amateur or school boxers was that we hardly ever went for that fourth killer punch or combination after we had already stunned our opponent with a great two-or-three-punch attack. And we never went in for the cold-hearted fifth. Knowing you could have finished him off sufficed. He knew it. You knew it. The other boxers and friends watching knew it. That was enough. Nobody kept official score because we all knew the score. It was boxing's version of catch and release.

Maybe you'd come in with a medium tap to exploit that second opening, or rarely, a third or fourth opening, but it was bad form to come back with a haymaker. Sometimes it happened when tempers flared, but losing your temper is more likely to harm you than help you in boxing, so tempers are tempered. It's part of the Zen of Boxing.

Some trainers preach that a professional boxer needs to be having fun because boxing is a job, and nobody can do a great job if they don't like what they're doing. Losing your temper means you are not having any fun. More important, losing your temper takes you out of the fight, steals your energy, and wastes focus on emotions. Your opponent becomes a personality rather than just some force with a specific set of fighting tools trying to kill you.

Fighting is about instinct and not thinking. Once the bell rings it's best if it's all autopilot. Your game plan, based on you or your coach's perceptions of your opponent's strengths and shortcomings as matched to your tools and weaknesses, takes intellectual awareness. Stay away from his lightning quick right. He gets tired out quicker than you so make him move a lot. Work his body and wear him down before you try to take him out with a headshot. In the ring, this thinking needs to be driven into your subconscious and modified into instinct. Lose your temper and your game plan goes out the window and a different instinct, blinded by anger, takes over. Once at the gym, we were all compatriots on the same team and nobody wanted to do real damage. That was the convention.

My fights with Michael Mailer were consistently the most punishing. Norman said it was because we were too equal. Michael and I liked mixing it up not because we hated each other but because we loved each other. I had known him since he was three-and-a-half years old when we lived in the same house. I'd carry him on my shoulders sometimes and go shopping. He was curious about everything and I'd answer questions.

As boxers we had different skills and advantages. He was a teenager, faster and a more refined boxer. I was early thirties, bigger, heavier and stronger. We were equally brave so altogether it was a brutal combination. Norman had us fight less as the years progressed when the damage and the Saturday afternoon headaches got more intense. (As a post script: In the late '80s when Michael was at Harvard and had fought in Golden Gloves contests, and he was closer to me in size and strength, we boxed a round in his basement in Provincetown and I was totally outclassed. I couldn't wait for the bell to ring and refused to fight a second round.)

The overriding joy of boxing, beyond the primordial mano-a-mano triumph of winning, is that you are never more alone, never more tuned into your own body, never more self-reliant and in control of your own destiny. Sex may be more enjoyable, but boxing is more exciting.

Your vision changes when you fight. All your eyesight abilities join together to concentrate on one job in a very small area: his fists and their relationship to you and your fists and their relationship to him. That's all there is. It's like the distance/velocity screen on the inside of the Terminator's bioelectrical optics system, except without the heads-up display.

You know exactly when you are within his reach, when he is within yours. This doesn't mean you are always right or are fast enough to react but whatever you can do, you're doing. In some small way your life depends on you and ancient fight/flight programs deep inside your hard-drive are activated. It's as real as anything gets for middle-class guys, barring a mugging at gunpoint.

There is no outside world—just your feet, your hands, your wind and some other guy trying to hurt you. Maybe he makes a certain breath sound just before he throws a right. Maybe he wipes his brow with his left glove before a right hand uppercut. Maybe he telegraphs his cross with too much recoil. Maybe he bluffs a left jab too often just before he throws one. Everything means something. It's chess and Grand Theft Auto and playing football and a hockey fight.

Your head is empty except for the challenge in front of you. It's not just visual focus. It's complete focus. Time also changes. You cannot believe how long three minutes can be if you get hurt in the beginning of a round and you know he's hot and you're cold.

Every bodily system is maxed out or shut off to let other ones work harder. If you are not used to it, you'll be exhausted in under a minute. Some guys are exhausted immediately after the first time they're hit. Guys in good shape from singles tennis or running marathons would come down to the gym, try boxing and be out of breath in forty-five seconds. With a guy throwing punches trying to hurt them, their adrenalin burns up and they are quickly spent.

No activity in the world burns calories faster than boxing. I don't mean hitting the heavy bag or jumping rope, I mean being in the ring with someone else who wants to smash your fucking head in.

I could box six rounds at my best. Most of the Saturday morning civilian boxers could go three or four, maybe five. What it takes to go ten or twelve professional rounds is inconceivable. (They used to have fifteen-round fights, but they stopped them; too many injuries after round twelve.)

One of the benefits of boxing is that you must work out, you must run, and you must not smoke. There are no options. You cannot fake it. The best reason to make sure you work out and don't smoke is so you don't get beat up on Saturday. It's point-blank motivation. A sign over the door of the gym where we boxed said: CONDITION IS A STATE OF BODY NOT MIND. I loved it. I read it every single Saturday. It was dead on. It doesn't matter how psyched up you are if you are not in shape. In boxing you can't cheat life.

After boxing we were all noisy celebrating our testosterone in the locker room and at lunch we tasted the laughter of gladiators who survived. Four to ten of us would head out to a local greasy spoon, take over the back room and relive our best moments of the matches, trade filthy sexist jokes and enjoy camaraderie that you can only get from sports that are this violent. You can't get it from golf. Guys fighting a weight problem like Norman and myself enjoyed only a few gourmet meals more than we did our hamburger-dripping-with-fat, any guilt absolved by diet amnesty earned from a morning of boxing.

Boxing is a way to earn self-respect, deepen the dialogue inside, add gravitas and take yourself seriously. You walk different every moment of the day and your level of self-respect is visible to others and your vibe elicits deference.

When I was with Laura, I tested the old boxer's myth about the benefits of sexual avoidance. Also, I wanted to see how drugs would affect my game. So I boxed once after staying awake all night at an orgy. I boxed well rested without sex. I boxed once on speed, once on coke. I never boxed on pot because I could tell that was a no-no. The last thing you need is some mind-altering drug that will affect your sense of distance and time.

I surprised myself by boxing well even after a sleepless night of sex. I couldn't box as many rounds as usual but the rounds I boxed were more than decent. I felt like a warrior and fought like one. The drugs had strange effects. With speed I was more aggressive and certainly had more stamina, but I made more defensive mistakes and missed more than usual. I felt invincible. I took more of a beating because I actually wasn't more invincible. It's like the "Sign over the Door" said.

I understood why the Nazis gave speed to their fighting men. You don't need to eat, you don't need sleep and you're irritable and aggressive. But, they lost the war because the reality of war is also just like the "Sign over the Door."

Doing coke made me more defensive and less offensive. I didn't like that. It made me feel too self-conscious, which for boxers is the kiss of death. I boxed only one round and quit for the day. Boxing is about letting go, living on the edge of instincts, not intellectualizing them. You don't have time to think. Thinking about the actual fighting while you're fighting is bad. Being conscious of your game plan is like taking more than 3.8 seconds to read a billboard when you're driving. It's a message, but it's not there to distract you from your driving.

You can't process thought as fast as you can react. Boxers train hard and that's where thinking comes in. You fight a zillion practice rounds with your coach yelling stuff like "Keep your hands up," "Stop pulling back with your jab and telegraphing it," "Keep your elbows in," or "Stick and move, stick and move." Practicing is about thinking. Fighting is about being. It's the great physical existential equation. That's why many intellectuals love boxing and that's why no stupid boxers become world champions. To be great, you need to have the machine, the attitude, the brains, and the skill.

Unless you had a miserable headache, which is how many of us spent Saturday afternoons—and evenings, and sometimes Sunday— or unless you were injured, sex was definitely enhanced. This was true for me and for several fellow boxers. We talked about it. Sex or not having sex, as far as I could tell, had no effect on boxing. But, boxing does have a tremendous effect on sex.

Sex, as we contemporary American Homo sapiens interpret it, unlike boxing, is one of those activities that goes beyond the "Sign over the Door." With sex, the state of your physical plant is superseded by who you think you are. No fuck makes you feel more "man" than the fuck after boxing, headaches notwithstanding. Even losing a few rounds gives you a tough-guy edge. And winning is pure aphrodisia. Self-respect makes everything more intense.

After expending all that energy and releasing all those hormones, then taking a long shower, eating a good meal, and taking a restful nap or a leisurely walk, you're loaded for bear. You have made a prodigious offering to the God Of Manliness and in return your balls will be thrilled to pump you a special load.

I did notice one thing—in retrospect. The more I got into S&M, the more aggressive I became as a boxer and the more chances I took in the ring. My style got more frontal, more risky. I took more hits, and gave more. I used to feel bad if I hurt someone. Then I didn't feel bad. Then I liked it. Then I lived for it. I became less generous and more exacting. I felt tougher and thought I was becoming a real fighter. I enjoyed more and more the breaking of eggs for the omelet, which is the psychic bottom line.

José Torres once told me that when he was a kid he liked fighting and hurting other boys. He liked punching them in the face. Maybe being a sadist was the necessary part of being a winner in boxing. I was getting better and stronger and all the hot sex was making me feel more manly. It was only later that I realized that I was just becoming more violent. In every way. A couple of times in the ring I paid for the extra aggression.

The 1980/81 boxing season was memorable because one of my regular opponents on Saturday mornings was Ryan O'Neal, the actor, and one tough Irish son-of-a-bitch. He was in terrific shape, with lots of great natural eye/hand coordination. He played racquetball several hours every day and had great wind, which is the boxer's secret weapon. He was a little bigger than me and a whole lot meaner.

I liked boxing Ryan. He had more reach, a half-classy style and was always an uphill battle. Plus he was an Irishman I could legally hit. Don't get me wrong. I love the Irish. I love Ireland. Two of my best friends are Irish. I love how green the country is, their lighter than drizzle "grand soft days." I love Bloomsday and the complexion of Irish women. I adore Irish horses; their big boned well-muscled Thoroughbreds, Irish Draughts, and crossbred warm-blood sport horses. I can listen to U2, Thin Lizzy, Van Morrison and Irish accents all day long.

It's just that when I was a kid growing up in the Dorchester section of Boston, there were a few clans of Jews and Italians, a few blacks, and vast hoards of Irish. Most of the times I got beat up it was by some kid named O'Donnell or O'Connell or McMartin. The chance to hit an Irishman made fighting somebody better than me extra worth it.

Also fighting someone better than you is how you get better. An added bonus, and I must admit to irony if not sadism, was that it was satisfying to be able to punch someone that good-looking, like Ryan, in the face.

One Friday night a few months before I met Laura, when I was staying with Sherry, my Texas Tornado, I was stoned on some killer weed and watching TV while she was out with her friends. She'd left her nail polish on the side table. It was candy apple red metal-flake just like you'd see on a reconditioned '55 Chevy. I picked up the bottle, shook it and turned it upside down like a kaleidoscope. I opened it and took the brush out with a gob of polish on it. I looked for a place to paint it and settled on the nail of my left big toe. I painted the toe. I let it dry. I painted it again and again until it had the depth of an excellent auto paint job. I went to bed. Sherry came home drunk and randy. We had sex. I went to sleep. I woke up the next morning, went to the gym, fought, showered and got ready for lunch.

As I was coming out of the shower Ryan noticed my big toe on my right foot, pointed it out to Norman and said to me, "What the fuck is this, Jeffrey?'

I just stood there.

I paused, looked at my other unpainted nineteen nails, and then said, "Okay, I admit it. I'm five percent gay." Norman looked at me with an extra wide smile, then looked at Ryan and said, "I'd even admit to that."

During lunch I told Ryan I was going out to L.A. for a shoot that week and he offered to let me stay at his beach house in Malibu. I got to meet his sixteen-year-old daughter Tatum and one of her drop dead gorgeous 90210 girlfriends. The beach house also had the first walk-in closet-sized shower I ever saw with a dozen high-pressure heads.

Ryan once invited me to the opening of a Broadway show and at the party afterwards at Sardi's, I came over to say thanks. He was more than half in the bag. He grabbed me, set me down next to him, put his arm around me, and told his table filled mostly with fawning groupies what a great boxer I was. He said I had "a lot of heart."

Saying a boxer has "heart" or courage is beyond saying he has craft or the luck of genetics. It's about personality, not just talent. And it's not a compliment given out lightly by one boxer to another, even if one is more than half-drunk. The looks I got from those girls couldn't be bought with money. One of them found me attractive enough to take home for a one-nighter. (I don't remember her name but she was very thin, screamed so loud it hurt my ears and urinated when she came which I found mildly erotic rather than gross.)

So I liked Ryan. It's hard not to like a talented charismatic movie star who treats you well and gives you compliments in front of slinky skirts and you get to fuck one of them. My problem with Ryan was in the ring. This was because his defense wasn't nearly as good as his offense. If you were willing to risk punishment you could get inside and hurt him. Then he'd get pissed—not lose his temper, just raise his temperature—and come back and savage you. And he had the tools to do the job. It was almost as though he needed getting hurt a little to get going.

One Saturday morning Ryan brought Farrah Fawcett down to the Gramercy Gym to watch him fight. She was a little shy and wore no makeup at all but was still the ultimate teeth-and-hair babe. That day, in front of his poster-babe, he and I decided to go two rounds of medium-hard contact. The first round was lots of dancing and a few good no-damage shots both ways. He was showboating for Farrah a little and I let him get away with it. Why not? Bringing women in to watch was permitted, but it was a rarity. I should have known he might be extra brutal that day but wasn't smart enough to adjust my game plan, or smarter yet, to avoid fighting him altogether.

In the second round after a no-big-deal series of trades I hit him with a left to the body, right to the face combination that stung him. Then I saw that pissed glare in his eyes and in the split second he took to recompose himself, I saw another opening and banged him with a hard right cross to the mouth.

I had already scored against him and could have—should have—probably been more forgiving, especially in front of Farrah. He half smiled around his mouthpiece then stormed at me with a bombardment, two three-punch combos one after another. I backed up and defended without sustaining any real damage. I thought I saw an opening as he was moving back and then, "Fwapp! Fwapp!!" He hit me with two in a row, killer force, straight lefts to my head, then neck, connecting so hard I could barely breathe. I back-pedaled and fended off his blows as best I could, caught in the slow motion twilight zone of every second taking at least half a minute.

I could tell something was wrong with my neck but I didn't want to stop the fight. I hid behind my fists to protect my face and neck and took half a dozen bruising explosions to my body. Then an uppercut to my chest just between my elbows lifted me and made me wheeze. I was in pain all over. Finally the fucking bell rang.

Ryan was awesome, relentless, and I was beaten badly. I was spent. I was hurt and talking funny—like speaking through a gravel filter. If I had been alone, I would have been crying. Even in such a macho environment I couldn't hold back a few tears. It was obvious I needed medical attention. José looked scared. Ryan looked scared.

Norman looked scared. Farrah look horrified. I left, hailed a cab and went directly to the hospital. I cried all the way.

The doctor said I had a bruised larynx and a broken blood vessel in my neck that might need surgery. He said we could wait a day and see whether the swelling went down, but that he wasn't hopeful. Then, right in front of me, he made a call and booked the O.R. for Sunday. I left the hospital thinking that I was a schmuck for misjudging Ryan and for not having the sense to pull that second punch in front of his girlfriend. Lots of guys would have killed for Farrah Fawcett who weren't even sleeping with her!

When I saw the doctor the next morning he said he saw some improvement, that my injuries looked slightly more promising and that we could put off surgery for another day. God knows where the improvement was because I was puffed up, in agony, and could barely speak or swallow.

Next day felt even worse for me but I was a bit less swollen and I looked much better to the doctor. He said I was coming along nicely, and that my voice would come back to near normal even if the one injured larynx didn't heal. He said that mysteriously one larynx compensates tonally for the other and in most cases the regular voice comes back. I never knew that larynxes were such devoted and clever friends to each other.

A few days later the swelling was down fifty percent. The doctor said I'd be good as new in two to three weeks. Four weeks later I went back to boxing and the week after that Ryan came to the gym. I ventured into the ring with him for two rounds of light contact. Whether he was gentler, which I believe he was, or I was less infuriating, or because we adhered to the rules of lighter contact, it went well. We had a good time and traded some decent blows without blood or injury.

The next week I went two rounds of full contact with him, held my own pretty much and gave nearly as good as I got. I hit him really hard in the middle of the second round with a right hand lead that split his lip. A tiny trickle of blood appeared. I felt vindicated. Then scared. He licked the blood and smiled at me without that pissed-glare. He came back and hurt me with a series of body punches but didn't go head hunting. Neither of us pulled a punch, but neither of us went for a kill. I would say I lost by a close decision.

One Saturday morning five months later when I am living with Laura, I decide to bring her down to the gym to watch. She, being a peace-loving, mostly vegetarian, hippie-hooker cokehead masochist, doesn't like fighting and in her own warped jealous way, admits that she doesn't want to watch me hurt someone who isn't her.

Ryan, whom I hoped wouldn't be there, is. He flirts with Laura as he does with every pretty girl. Laura is not a big fan of his and is not too impressed. She doesn't send much back to him. It annoys him slightly. Great. Just what I need. Ryan O'Neal with a prickly edge.

"Fighting's not my cup of tea," says Laura. "I don't get it. I don't really understand why two people would want to throw punches at each other. Norman used to say, 'It's about courage. You never know what you are going to do until you're standing there and someone's throwing a punch right at your face. It gives you a certain kind of strength and courage that there's really no other way to get; you never know what you would do unless it's happening.'

"Jeffrey was always kind of macho. I don't think he ever showed any kind of fear or hesitation in any situation. He had this machismo thing, where if somebody came up against him, he would always kind of be ready to meet them more than half way. He would always be in their face with, like, 'Oh yeah?' It was an important thing for him to always show strength. Boxing was where he could prove it and his personality was looking for a place like that.

"Boxing is nauseating to me. It's so not where we are going as the human race evolves. But it fit in with Jeffrey's Chinese zodiac birth symbol, the dog. He was like an alpha dog. Alpha dogs are like right up there ready to fight if necessary. And it works in dangerous situations,

like some of the clubs we would go into could really be
quite dangerous. But it made me feel comfortable because
Jeffrey's vibe was 'Be nice and I'll be nice. Try to fucking
mess with this and you'll be sorry.' Jeffrey wasn't looking
for trouble but he wouldn't put up with any bad vibes
toward him or me."

My first round that morning is with Norman's son Michael. We
fight as we often do to a damaging dead-on draw.

Then I box a practice round with José Torres. Boxing with José
is a blessing. He is so good he nails your every opening with a little
signal tap. He never hurts you. He never hurts anyone on Saturday
morning. He just points out your vulnerability and then tells you
how to correct it. You can come after him with all your heat because
it is impossible to touch him. It's like racing across the Atlantic, me
in a single engine prop plane and him at Mach 2 in the Concorde.
He hadn't fought in the ring in two decades but still is in possession
of all the reasons he was World Champion. Boxing with José is
better than slow-motion videotape and computer-enhanced training
devices. He is a genial litmus test for everything you do wrong.

After sparring with The Master, I stupidly accept Ryan's
challenge of two rounds of medium contact. Right away I can tell we
have two different ideas of medium contact. Ryan is throwing really
hard stuff and rather than wuss out in front of Laura and ask him to
back off, I crank up the volume. He comes at me. I move in on him.
We are both on fire. It is full contact. I know after one minute into
the first round that this will be a real chore. That is okay. I'm up for
it.

Next, I'm looking up at the ceiling. I never see the punch. I never
feel the fall but I am on my back. I lose a moment in time. Jose´ tells
me to relax and breathe. I didn't get knocked out but I sure did get
knocked down for the first time in my life. It's just like the scene
in movies with the circle of people over you and the light in the
middle. I notice how filthy the ceiling is. Laura is crying. Ryan looks
down with real concern. José is half-laughing, the proud rodeo dad

smiling over his kid who just got bucked off his first Brahma bull. I start to get up and Jose laughs and says, "Stay down. This isn't fighting for money."

Ryan O'Neal, my nemesis, had struck again!

I get up glad knowing I don't need to fight him another round. I feel fine. No pain. No swelling. He just hit some knock-down button on me I never knew I had. José says that it's often the punch you don't see that shuts out your lights.

Laura stops crying when she sees I'm all right. We go back to our apartment. I take a shower and then a nap. I awake, eat, and without any S&M weirdness Laura and I make love. She is very tender, submissive as usual. I am the wounded gladiator being cared for by his loving slave girl. In boxing, even coming up short in front of your woman has its own charm.

* * *

In 2009 just after I started the rewrite and edit for this book, Mike Lennon, Norman's friend, archivist and now biographer told me about a piece Norman wrote for *Esquire* magazine in 1993 that I didn't know existed. It's an account of my battle with Ryan O'Neal, the one witnessed by Laura. As Norman recounted:

"Getting in the ring with Ryan O'Neal became not only the focus of each Saturday but the point to what some of us had been half looking to do for years, that is, get extended a little in the ring. Ryan could be mean as cat piss. Even when he was carrying a man, he would punish him, and when he had dislikes, he liked to take them out on the opponent. In spite of every love affair in his private life, public fodder for more than a decade to the gossip columns, Ryan had his dry spot—the Puritanism of the Irish. He took a secret dislike to the bearded editor of the porny magazine.

"The editor was awkward in the ring, so it was not hard to play tricks on him. He had surprising stamina, however. Until Ryan came along, the pornographer had, in fact, the most notable stamina of any of us. Maybe Ryan equated that ability to sexual prowess and disapproved of its

presence in so unworthy a vessel, maybe he just disliked hirsute New York lumpen intelligentsia, but in any case, he all but disemboweled the man, throwing a cruel left hook until the editor collapsed, still conscious, in the middle of the second round, wholly unable to go on. What made it worse was that the pornographer's ladylove, a good-looking girl who worked in a massage parlor, was witnessing it all at ringside.

"I happened to be next in the ring with Ryan, which proved to be my good luck. After every discharge of mean feelings, Ryan would turn angelic. A little ashamed, I expect, of what he had just done to the pornographer, he was not now boxing like a movie star—he certainly did not protect his face. Since the man he had hurt happened to be a sweet guy, extraordinarily optimistic about life (which is probably how he had gotten into pornography in the first place), I liked the editor. When I saw him take this beating, I recognized that I saw him as a friend. If this seems something of a digression, let me say that it helps to carry the auctorial voice around the embarrassment of declaring that I boxed better on that day than I ever did before, or since. I was in a rare mean mood myself, mean enough not to be afraid of Ryan, and—it is very hard to do any kind of good boxing against a superior without some premise to carry you—I was feeling like an avenger. And here was Ryan boxing with his face. It was hard not to hit him straight rights, and he reacted with all the happiness of seeing a beloved senior relative get up from a sickbed. In our first clinch, he whispered, 'You punch sharper than anyone here.'

"'Go fuck yourself,' I told him."

I fought Ryan several times after that, but always with more defenses, more respect. I haven't seen him in years but every time I see Ryan in a movie and he's in a fight scene, even if he's the good guy, I always root for the guy hitting him.

29
Sex slavery at Club 0

March 1981

One Thursday night in early March 1981, Laura suggests we visit another S&M club that one of her tricks told her about. She says it sounds less hard core and much more heterosexual than the Hellfire Club. I'm game. I'm a bit tired but I never want to disappoint Laura. Also I like to think of Laura and me as more M&S, Master and Slave, than S&M, Sadist and Masochist and this place sounds more M&S.

I want to see what similarly bent couples are up to. I want to watch, probably participate a little, and then take Laura home and no doubt fuck the piss out of her while we replay the adventure. She suggests sarcastically, but with a smile, that if I am too tired, the least I could do, for the sake of our relationship, is watch another man whip her. We both do too many lines of coke and leave.

It is a little after midnight when we arrive at Club O. Laura is wearing her all black "fuck me" ensemble that sometimes greets me as I open our apartment door: very high heels, black seamed stockings held up by garters on her tight lace Teddy with built-in push-up bra, a thong that rides high on her hips barely covering her wispy pubic hair and totally exposing her delicious backside, elbow-length fine lace fingerless gloves (that look great playing with my dick, or I'm sure anybody's dick), and gold slave bands that wrap around her upper arm like a snake. Around her neck she wears a studded black leather slave collar I recently gave her. As we walk out the door she hands me a chain dog leash I never saw on Necort.

I, in homage to the scene, wear black jeans and a black shirt.

It is a chilly autumn night and in the cab Laura hides underneath her warm full-length lavender down coat. She wears her makeup in the severest manner I've ever seen on her and has wild teased hair. She is glamorous, totally divorced from her inner hippie. I can't tell what is going on in her head but she is ready.

We enter a ratty elevator in an unremarkable West-twenties commercial loft building. Laura pleads with me not to look at her saying, "Fluorescent elevator lighting is the last thing you want to be seen in tarted up like a slut on the way to a sex club."

"Imagine how disgusting people will look on the way down after a few hours of sweat and runny makeup," I add.

We go up to the eighth floor and the elevator door opens. A huge, fat, leather-and-chain-clad black bouncer as large as any NFL offensive tackle welcomes us and guides us to an unmarked door. Laura reaches into my coat pocket, takes out the leash, puts the leather handle in my hand and snaps the spring-loaded hook to the link on the front of her collar.

Our eyes adjust to dimmer lighting as we check our coats and I pay our $25 per couple fee to a large dyke, only one notch smaller than the offensive tackle, wearing denim and dozens and dozens of keys and key chains. There is an absurd amount of clattering. She smiles at Laura, keys clinking, jangling and rattling with every move. She gives me a stern glare, the same scary scowl I've seen from boxing opponents just before the bell of the first round rings.

Laura walks in front of me, anxious to see what there is to see. She strains at the leash, and I growl comically at her to "heel" which she immediately obeys. We walk past an empty dance floor surrounded by medieval-looking racks and torture equipment, some of it in use. As we enter the bar area the room freezes, all eyes on Laura. At me they squint quizzically, trying to figure out why or how I'm with this exquisite female.

Most of the people in the bar are half-dressed or completely undressed submissive men wearing chains, ropes, nipple clamps, and jockey shorts. Some are nerdy wimps but many are in great physical shape, with well-groomed hair and polished nails. These must be the doctors, judges, and Captains of Industry who I'd heard are the big spenders, the meat and potatoes of the commercial humiliation biz.

Some are arranged in small herds of five or six male slaves, each little group milling around one or two mostly fattish dominant females who bulge out of ridiculous dancing-hippo-in-a-skimpy-tutu costumes, exposing lumpy parts of themselves.

There are a few moderately unattractive and/or bruised submissive women in a variety of cheap lingerie, each too fat or too thin, paired randomly as to weight and size with men who also are too fat or too thin.

The dominant men wear black leather or denim for their role of master, complete with studded belt and wristband. A few dominant men appear to be slaveless. Freelancers out looking for someone to hurt? There also are some straight looking single guys in civilian clothes and a few tourist couples with the unmistakable air of Queens or New Jersey.

With her very high heels, teased hair and mildly muscular, well-proportioned leanness Laura appears about six feet tall. She is, as usual, the hottest looking, the most valuable woman in the room, she is the rare unicorn sighting. I lead her around. We whisper, trading observations, munching nuances like peanuts.

She wonders why all the submissive women look so flabby, even the thin ones; so pale, depressed, unhealthy, and unathletic. She is not like the other female slaves. Laura's slave side is a deviant addition, a cathartic sideshow to her day-in, day-out happy optimism. Her physical prowess, beauty, brightness, and energy put her in a different class from females I see here. For them, this evening is merely an extension of their negative self-image. They don't have another side; this is their only persona.

Laura is one of life's winners even when she is being tied up and whipped. Her demeanor is similar to the better-groomed slave men, strong and successful in the world, who are exploring their submissive "flip side." Beyond that one thought there is no further analysis. I do not think about what she's working out and neither does she. And I have no idea what I'm working out. I don't even consider that there is anything to work out. During sex she is my slave; in all other facets of our life we are in the ballpark of equality.

But as sure as she is knee deep into this bizarre sex trip, I am in just as deep. We are sharing the essence of existence: no precedence, no plan, no plan "B." We are a second cousin of Heisenberg's Uncertainty Principle: You can do something or analyze it but not both.

People are magnetically drawn toward us. Two submissive men are already on their knees bowing down in front of Laura. One of them touches her foot and, out of character but adaptive to the moment, she spits on him. He thanks her profusely as I gently kick him out of our path.

Harnessing our power, I lead Laura around on a tour of the premises after warning our entourage that they dare not touch her. I walk out onto the empty dance floor and observe the surrounding walls. Bodies, some male, some female, are tied to racks, chained to the wall, or on their knees sucking various cocks, anuses, pussies, and toes. The slight smell of disinfectant is broken occasionally by stale beer, sweat, urine, the musk of sex play, the pheromones of perverts and a variety of perfumes and aftershaves. A corridor leads off to rooms of different sizes—some small as closets, others as large as an average bedroom, some with their doors closed, some empty, some with doors open and filled with twos and threes and fours in the middle of their pain games.

The audio track is a boring mega-mix of unceasingly repetitive 120-beat-a-minute disco with the same too-loud kick drum that seems to follow me nearly everywhere in 1980. This is combined with the deranged libretto of people talking, whispering, begging, crying, ordering and shouting, layered with a special-effects *L'Opera de Pervo*—whip cracks, slaps, yelps, clanking chains, slamming doors.

Our fans follow our every move—mumbling extras in the walking crowd scene. Out to greet us from one of the smallish rooms steps a rather attractive sturdy blonde middle-aged woman with deep set dark blue-grey eyes of great intelligence and determination. She is wearing an amazingly normal print dress and holding a riding crop in her hand. With false regality but excellent posture she inquires, "And what do we have here?"

"We have my slave girl, Countess Zero, Grand Slut Of the Galaxy," I ad lib. I see behind her a slight girl hanging on the wall. "And who are you and what name does the girl go by?"

"She's so insignificant that she has no name," the woman with the riding crop tells me, "I am Mistress Eleanor. And yours?"

"Call me Sir Guy, Mistress Eleanor." The fans "Oooh" and "Ahh" on cue. This existential theater's Act One has finally begun.

"Why don't you get rid of the riff raff," she suggests, "and come inside and maybe we can come to an understanding."

Laura smiles her approval and I tell the crowd to get lost. We walk inside a pantry-size room carpeted with thin wrestling mats. We shut the door behind us and the crowd sighs in disappointment.

Handcuffed to the wall, facing us and completely naked, is a small, skinny, barely legal, badly bleached frizzy blonde with large breasts, which if I am lucky will be as firm as they look. She has dead-looking eyes with bags underneath, mousy brown pubic hair, not a lot, and her thighs are thin and decorated with fresh red crop marks. Even in dim light I can see her body is covered with red welts, teeth impressions, and fading black and blue bruises. The handcuffs are high and her arms stretch above her head. She stands on her tippy toes, like she is having a dance lesson with a Nazi ballet instructor. Her face isn't that pretty but she is fucky looking; hard, used and skanky. Just the kind of slut I fancy as a counterpoint to Laura.

"What games does The Countess play?" asks Eleanor. "Does she crave submitting to a woman?"

"Countess Zero does whatever I desire," I boast, "and, no, I have never loaned her to a woman. What do you wish to do to her?" I certainly don't want her to be abused in the manner of the girl with no name. I check Laura again who continues to beam an A-OK.

Eleanor, about half a foot shorter than Laura looks up into her eyes as she describes her wish list. "I want to make her cry, to hear her beg for me to stop. Then I want her to eat me until I've come in her mouth." Laura flinches demurely and lowers her eyes; on purpose I think.

"The Countess won't cry and only ever begs for more. You must be used to inferior, weaker slaves. Besides, The Countess is my woman and I don't want you to scar or damage her. I'll let you hit her with your riding crop five times and only on the ass, and then she will suck your pussy. And I get to fuck the girl with no name."

"No, please, not with a man!" the girl with no name interrupts.

"Shut up, bitch," bellows the Mistress, "you'll do what I say with whomever I say. Right?" She demands, "Right? Right?"

Now there's rousing verbal foreplay! I actually find a girl who would rather be poked in the eye with a sharp stick than fuck me. I'm thinking this might be a bad scene; the Mistress hits the girl across the face open handed so hard it scares me. Some play this game more earnestly than others. Laura lets out a gasp and looks at me with real fright in her eyes. I note Eleanor's use of "whomever," instead of the more common and incorrect "whoever."

Am I dealing with a perverted lesbian English teacher?

"Yes, Mistress Eleanor, whatever you say." The girl with no name is really crying, which turns me off. As much as I could have enjoyed fucking her I don't fancy having sex with someone who doesn't want me or isn't being paid to want me. It is the same reason I never have a rape fantasy. I might be fucked up, but I want to be loved and adored.

"Hey, I think that we are on a different plane than you two and it's time for us to leave." I tighten Laura's leash and make a move to open the door.

"Wait," Eleanor pleads, "Sylvia," she says giving the girl a name, "tell Sir Guy that you are sorry and that you'll be happy to service him whatever way he wants. Tell him, honey. I want you to do this for me. I want you to let me play with Countess Zero. Tell him the truth. Tell him how you've been fantasizing about getting fucked by a man. C'mon, honey, tell the truth."

"I'll fuck the man for you, Mistress Eleanor; I'll do whatever you want."

This is too fuckin' weird for me in a club full of weird. I'm about to exit when Mistress Eleanor tells me that Sylvia only likes to fuck men when she is forced to do it, and then she really gets into it and that it will be worth my while if I just, "bear with them for a moment."

She offers that I can fuck and beat Sylvia even if I won't let her use Laura, that I am a man of obvious great power and that she would be honored to have me use her slave girl. I don't know if this is patronizing psychotic drivel, but I'm interested in their bizarre story so I ask Mistress Eleanor to tell me about their relationship.

"We are bisexual but mostly lesbian," she tells me, "I guess you could say. We've been lovers for three years since Sylvia's seventeenth birthday party. I used to be her mother's best friend (long pause) but not anymore. We're happy living together. We get a kick out of doing things in public, especially at this club. Sylvia is totally devoted to me and likes to take a lot of pain. We both have desires occasionally to fuck a cock."

Laura whispers in my ear, "I want to watch you fuck the lesbian. And I want this woman to whip me. Permit her ten lashes."

"You can have ten lashes. Is it a deal?"

Mistress Eleanor jumps in, "A deal, Sir Guy, but one thing at a time. First, I want to see you whip Sylvia and fuck her."

I move over to Sylvia and stick out my chest up against hers. My God she has big beautiful tits! Nearly perfect. Textbook tits, like from God's original production manual. I peel off my shirt, and rub my hairy chest against Sylvia's now erect nipples. I kiss her on the mouth and she responds eagerly, no different from a heterosexual. I undress—slowly, deliberately, theatrically—aware that the show is more than half of this game.

Laura is standing behind me being pawed by Mistress Eleanor. I turn to make sure that Laura is happy, also to get the handcuff key from Mistress. Eleanor is rubbing Laura's exposed buns with the riding crop. She stops to hand me the key and the whip and says, "Après tu, mon amis."

I uncuff Sylvia, lay her down face up on the floor, and begin to explore her. She looks up with apprehension and I am not sure whether it's real or an act. She continues to move like a hostage. This doesn't feel like a place for foreplay so I hold her arms against the mat and work my cock into her vagina. She becomes delightfully cooperative and naturally passionate.

Her pussy is even tighter than Laura's. She has no real waist and sweet, smallish hips and a lightly padded ass. She possesses the slim straight body of girls who are flat as a board except she isn't. Altogether she has an oddly built body that is constructed from disparate parts. But it works. It looks and feels sexy. I have no trouble getting or keeping an erection.

I grip her under her ass and while giving her some deep pumps I gently work my finger, then two fingers, up her asshole. I take my time and get quizzical looks from Sylvia that make me believe no one has ever been up that particular route.

I whisper, "Give it to me. Relax." For a moment I ponder promising that I won't hurt her but that might be a turn-off to her. As I feel my climax approaching I pull my hard dick out and hold it and let the climax climb back down. Then I slide into her second opening.

Eleanor, sensing what I am doing grabs my shoulder with a "Hey...!" but is cut off by Sylvia who gasps, "No. Please, let the man do it."

I stroke in and out of her snugness, retarding my climax till I can do so no longer. I come with surprising force. With every squirt shooting inside Silvia's ass, her eyes gain life and she enters into an orgasmic spasm.

She gapes at me in disbelief, continuing to quiver, gurgling like a baby at play. I look her straight in the eyes, now completely alive and nearly beautiful in their sparkle. After a long pause she says, "I never came like that. I never came from there before."

"Great for me, too," I contribute.

Laura is breathing heavily as if some of the orgasm had splashed on her. Eleanor says, "Well, well, Sir Guy. You seem to have made a big impression on Sylvia. Or should I say in Sylvia. But you never whipped her. I want to see you whip her."

I'd forgotten. I really had no desire to whip anyone, except Laura. "I chose instead to fuck her in the ass."

Sylvia looks up to me and pushes her face out at me, "Hit me, please." I minimum bitch-slap her.

"Oh no," she cries, and I figure I've gone over her line till she pleads, "Not so light. Please slap me harder." I hit her just hard enough to scare me and make up for the lack of torque with a vicious scowl and a loud growl.

Sylvia thanks me. I see marks on her face that match my fingers. Laura leans forward and softly says, "I want you to do that to me, please, Master."

I nod.

This is the first time I am an "S" to any "M" other than Laura. While not as complex emotionally as hitting Laura, it's just as hot. I may be a pervert or a bastard, and they may be sickos—but I like submissive women who want me to use them and if they want it, for me to use them hard. And in these surroundings packed with other perverts, bastards and sickos, my behavior is not outside the norm.

"Now it's my turn with The Countess," says Mistress Eleanor, more sibilant than before. I guess it is the sound of her mouth watering.

Eleanor faces Laura to the wall and handcuffs her to a high ring. Laura, taller than Sylvia, isn't forced to stand on her toes. I crouch down, petting Sylvia who enjoys the fondling while Eleanor pulls down Laura's bikini thong and begins exploring her crack with the handle of the crop and then without warning flails the business end against Laura's sweet cheeks. The whoosh of the whip foretells the strength of the impact. Laura lets out a surprised, "Ahhrrh," broadcasting just enough pleasure in her pain to relieve my impulse to kill Eleanor.

"Ask me for another," demands The Mistress and Laura complies. And so it goes. Eleanor savors the nine more slams of the crop against my baby's flesh.

Laura loves it.

More than I do.

I flinch with every thwack. Laura moans with pleasure, sticking out her round and red striped buns after each recoil for the next instance of abuse.

After Eleanor's ten, Laura begs for me to hit her another ten. Mistress Eleanor offers me the crop and not to be outdone, I equal or better the hardest of Eleanor's blows.

Laura thanks me after each stroke and pleads for the next. By number seven I'm hard again. I bend Laura over and massage the inside of her pussy with my stiffened cock. She moans her sex-song, the tune I live for and comes several times. I fuck her but I can't come and that's OK.

Laura and I get dressed. Eleanor and the Girl Who Now Has A Name are staying for more games. We all hug and bid each other a warm farewell like intimate friends. Laura and I collect our coats and leave. At her request I don't look at her going down in the elevator.

30
The pleasure of pain

In addition to our edgy real life in the outlands of perversity, Laura and I share an even more outlandish fantasy life. We both feel some things develop in fantasy and it's our goal to bring them into reality, and some things are better suited to existing only in fantasy. We don't discuss what goes where, it just falls in place and I am the gatekeeper. There is also a list of perversions that neither of us has any desire at all for and just never come up: the bestial, the scatological, the pedophiliac or anything that doesn't involve consent.

I have no idea why but I know that taking our S&M relationship into Laura's whoring world would be wrong. Laura's whore sex is 97 per cent vanilla. A tiny toe sucking kink here, a piss drinker there, and lots of ass licking body worshipers, but most of her whore sex is what healthy horny teenagers do in back seats of cars.

In our own bed, I whip and spank her ass and back and belly and pussy and slap her face, as she looks into my eyes while I fuck her into the next level of beyond. She never says, "That hurts," or, "That's too much," and only ever asks for more or harder. "Use me harder, hurt me" is her mantra.

I am never brutal; never want to take it to a point that will leave a scar or injury. I just want enough to make her rev higher. Sometimes, not taunting me or dissing my masculinity but only as post-game analysis, Laura says, "You could hit me harder. I want it harder." I say, "Next time," but it's up to me to keep some kind of balance, some kind of clarity. Although I am deep into this dance of pain, I do love her and never want to go past the point of amusement. To me there's playing the Sadist and being the Sadist, and I just want to have fun.

More than being a Sadist with a conscience, I am a Sadist with a need for absolution, not because I have guilt but as a way to avoid guilt. Our sex talk almost always ends with me steering the conversation into her telling me whatever she is doing is from her own volition and doing it because it makes her feel good. I need that. I have no idea what kind of synesthesia Laura is blessed or cursed with or what kind of psychic minefield she is crossing but as long as I can somehow justify my actions I don't feel like I am an evil hedonist sucking the devil's asshole.

"Why do you love being whipped and hurt by strange men?" I ask Laura. "And by me? Why do you like pain?"

"Because it feels good to me. It makes me feel good and used and I need it. And when I feel the pain, it's the feeling of it leaving me and I am lighter and that pain is gone forever. I need you to get rid of my pain."

Our fantasy life, however, is more than one step weirder and pretty much without limits. We talk about traveling around and selling her pain to rich perverts who want to hurt her. That excites her, which excites me, and after the first visit to this black and blue fairy tale there is no way to tell who is leading whom. I would say anything to juice her and she was so juiced she would say anything to energize me.

I would fuck her in some slow rhythmic groove looking down deep into her eyes.

"What would you do for me?"

"I'll do anything."

"Anything?"

"Yes. Anything."

"Tell me what you'd do."

"All my holes are yours. You can use them, give them away to men and sell them."

"What else will you do?'

"You can have my pain."

"How much pain will you let me take?"

"As much as you want."

I would probably spank or slap or whip her a bit for emphasis.

"Can I sell your pain?"

"Yes, please. Sell my pain. Watch men hurt me and know I am giving them my pain to please you."

"Will you do it every day?"

"Yes, everyday."

"What if we find some really rich really perverted man who wants to whip you and beat you hard?"

"I would love for a man to beat me hard."

"How hard?"

"Very hard."

"What if he wanted to whip you till you were unconscious?"

"I would let him do it if you were there to watch me. And when you sell my pain I am rid of it."

"Do you trust me to protect you?"

"Yes, I trust you with my life. I know you will always protect me."

"I pledge my life to protect you, you know that?"

"Yes, I love when you tell me that. I know you will beat me and hurt me and I don't have to worry about anything."

"And when other men beat you?"

"If you are there I can have it all without worry. No one will go too far if you are there."

"Do you like it when we go into clubs and I let men whip you?"

"I love it. I need that. I need men to whip me and use me."

"I *did* love it," Laura remembers about one night. "I was all dressed up in my lingerie and my collar and my leash and everything, and my high heels, and lots of make-up. Jeffrey would take me around, and we would walk through the rooms and I would say, 'Let's get that one, and let's take that one, and let's take that one.'

"We walked through this building, and there were four or five floors, and we went through all the different rooms and picked about eight guys, and took them up to this loft on the top floor and there was a big futon.

"And a different man was doing something to every part of my body," Laura continues. "Someone was kissing me, and somebody was sucking my toes, and somebody was sucking my fingers and rubbing my arms and somebody was....

"Was I sitting on someone's cock?" Laura ponders; "I might have been sitting on a cock and getting fucked in the ass at the same time. And someone else was whipping me. Jeffrey was the master of ceremonies, the director. He would stand right there, make sure I had cocaine up my nose; he would give me cocaine as it was lying there on the side—and every single guy there fucked me.

"All eight of them, and the guys were really good looking! I always think of them as my sports team, ha, ha, ha, my little baseball team and I was the catcher ha ha ha... They were really good looking, they were all incredibly strong and muscular and into it—*and into me!*

"It went on for a long time, and they just fucked me in my ass, I sucked them—I had a cock in my mouth and my ass and my pussy all at the same time. Every one of them was touching me and rubbing me and sucking my fingers and rubbing my feet—and it was as exotic as you can possibly imagine—and it went on for hours and hours and hours, ha, ha, ha!

"So I came with every guy," Laura sums up, "I came multiple times with every guy. And then Jeffrey fucked me..."

31

Relationships and drugs

There is a progression in relationships. It's like the high jump. The bar keeps getting raised. Couples keep getting eliminated. As Norman Mailer said: "There was that law of life, so cruel and so just, that one must grow or else pay more for remaining the same."

Here's how it goes: Three hours are all you can endure on a nowhere date. Two dates are all you can manage with someone you don't fancy. Lots of new couplings split up at three weeks—what I call The First Hump—when the new glory can no longer survive on the glow of its own raw energy. This is when the light shines on each other's less obvious flaws.

At about three weeks, if the bond is to last, the "YOU," "YOU," "YOU" that your heart has been singing has to become an "US," and it takes more than hot sex to do that.

The Second Hump at three months is also where lots of couples split up. By this time every little interpersonal annoyance is no longer cute. It is here at The Second Hump where something has to exist between the two of you that is stronger than simply hot sex, superficial connections, and a few mutual interests. The road to The Third Hump, one year in, is littered with the carrion of ex-couples.

Laura and I have been together for about ten months, that point where stuff really starts to get annoying. I am bothered by her drug intake, her not calling on time, her showing up late, her flaky answers to serious questions, and her dirty feet leaving their trail on our sheets.

She is beginning to get annoyed by my strong dominant personality that she loves in bed but that rankles her in other parts of our relationship. She begins calling me "Mr. Push."

In the first six months we had nary a fight except for the few about her giving her money to her husband, Sandy. Now we let off steam daily. We find one reason or another to have a minor spat or a bickering spasm. For about ten minutes. Usually in the afternoon. Then our love impels us to work it out. Then we fuck and have terrific makeup sex, sometimes even if it means pulling the car off the road. We are aware of our ten-minute glitches, and sometimes just pointing them out and laughing defuses them. Sometimes it is more difficult. Sometimes we stumble and just make it over the high bar. But generally we keep the unpleasantness trapped in those ten minutes per day.

More telling than the quantity of time couples spend bickering, arguing or fighting is the quality of the civility exhibited at the lowest point of the clash. During this period and well into our relationship, Laura and I both keep a polite tone when arguing and never require police intervention. Most of the arguments we have are about her coke habit.

Too many people I knew were doing too much coke. One friend burnt out the cartilage in his nose and needed surgery. Another friend suffered a heart attack attributed to his overuse of the drug. I was in the middle of a love affair with pot and I was not a drug prude. I had tried nearly every drug that didn't involve shooting or suppositories. Well, to be honest, I did shoot demerol twice and morphine once with an anaesthesiologist and his nurse girlfriend, but a needle full of anti-anaphylactic shock medication at the ready and their white uniforms made it seem acceptable and safe.

And to be completely honest I did do an opium suppository once and was high for two days. But I was never into drugs so much I needed to say, "Hi, my name is Jeffrey and I'm an addict." I just didn't love coke. It's not a matter of having good ethics or a refined recreational drug palate. It's just biology, like being horny, liking or not liking Brussels spouts (I like), cilantro (I don't), or being tall or short.

Some people I knew were already smoking coke. First there was high-end bourgeois "freebase" and then came its cheaper less pure proletarian cousin "crack." One night, sitting in a car by the Delaware River near New Hope with one of Laura's friends, we smoked freebase. It was apocalyptic. I felt like I was talking one on one with God. Laura was so taken by her first hit tears filled her eyes.

Then, in a few minutes it wore off and the second hit wasn't so elevated. The third and fourth also missed the mark, although they were certainly pleasant and airy. I stopped there while Laura and her friend kept going till it was all gone.

I had, thank God, an immediate revelation. I knew right off the bat what was evil about smoking coke. You can never get back to the feeling of the first hit. Insidious if you think about it. The ultimate intracranial cock tease. Who would have guessed then that freebase/crack would soon change the worst parts of society and make them even worse?

Mothers sold themselves or the use of their kids' orifices for a hit. Mothers sold their children outright for a hit. When I heard these stories I remembered my first hit and how close to God I felt, how nearly equal, and in retrospect how singularly megalomaniacal that feeling was. I know that if the devil has a tool belt, its pockets are filled with crack.

But this was before coke got the bad rep it deserved and when recreational drugs (something most of us, some way too late, came to understand is almost always an oxymoron) were still considered hip. Just as now you would be shocked to see anyone, even at the hippest parties, doing coke openly on a Saturday night, in the early '80s it was not only acceptable it was the fashion.

32
Two tricks

October 1981

Laura asks me if I would like to watch her turn a trick.

"Right in front of me? And the guy won't mind?!"

"Two of them, actually. One after another. One is not just a trick, it's Walter, and he pays me, but he's my friend. I asked them if I could bring you to watch and they both said yes."

"I'd love it." There is nothing not to like about watching Laura have sex.

"I'm seeing Murray after work at his office in the garment district and then Walter this evening. Walter wants to meet you. He wants to know if you're available to come for dinner. Nothing fancy, just bistro or sushi."

"Sure. All of it."

Laura pulls out some coke and offers it to me.

"No. Not for me. Don't you think you're doing too much of that shit?"

"No. I like it. And it's my business."

We are going through that period in a relationship coming up to the first year, when the newness peels off. The question is, what's next? The savory pleasure of deeper emotions and the tummy-filling security of tender routine, or the souring of compatibility, the bad taste of stale sex and the hunger of alienation? Time will tell.

I walk Necort; Laura goes off to meet a friend. After walking Necort I am so excited about our upcoming threesomes that I go to the gym and work out.

I get back to our apartment around four and find Laura getting ready. She is in the bathroom perched on the sink, cave girl style, in front of the mirror, once again in the position of a baseball catcher. If she wants to talk seriously with you, she will either get on the floor in that position and expect you to join her or she'll crouch like that on the seat of a chair.

She is in one of the world's most sophisticated cities playing at the world's oldest profession yet there is something fresh and innocent about her. She's like the country cousin in the big city or the Stone Age child who comes out of the rain forest and learns to adapt to the concrete and steel jungle.

I watch her on her haunches, a feral child playing with civilized make-up toys and ask, "What should I wear? What does one wear to watch his girlfriend turn a trick?"

"Wear your black leather jacket and jeans, that's what I'm going to wear, too."

"Okay." I wonder what these men will think of me. Who is this guy that Laura fell in love with who lets her continue to be a whore and is so bent as to want to watch her work?

We arrive at Murray's office around 6:00 p.m. He greets us politely, eyeing me hard until he sees my sweet Jewish smile. He looks like the faux-hip character in a Woody Allen movie and talks in that "I grew up tough" cadence of male Mafia groupies. He is about 5'7" but I can tell he is wearing Cuban heel boots so he must be about 5'5". His silk shirt is open too wide and he wears too much gold around his neck. He is balding but his comb-over says he hasn't come to terms with it.

He shows us around the factory, takes us to the shipping room and points out that we are looking at $250,000 worth of shirts. He asks me my size and brings out half a dozen lovely all-cotton long-sleeve 15.5/34, fall and winter shirts in wide plaids and small checks that are exactly my taste. So far this is fun.

Murray is one of the quickie blowjob big-tip tricks Laura kept when she left Eureka. Laura breaks the ice by telling Murray to take his pants down right there in the shipping room, that she wants his cock in her mouth. Murray looks at me with a polite "Is this okay?" tilt to his head and I respond with an agreeing nod. We could have been two guys at a Bar Mitzvah, one silently questioning the other whether it was okay to have the last knish off the hors d'oeuvre tray.

Laura unzips Murray's pants, slides out of much of her clothing and takes out his average size-cock, which is nearly hard. I stand there with my shirts in my arms and move in closer for a better look. She bends over to put him in her mouth and then squats down. She tells him, "I want you to talk to me the way you always do. Jeffrey will love it. Don't be shy."

He then performs two opposite functions simultaneously that are so compelling that during the entire blowjob I pay more attention to him than my Laura. He caresses her face and hair in the most profoundly gentle manner, more fatherly than sexually as he whispers the most degrading vile commands.

"Suck my cock, you filthy slut."

"Take it from me, you trollop."

"Eat my come, you unclean bitch."

He utters one phase after another non-stop, each with exactly a second-and-a-half pause, each one different than the last, even if just slightly.

"Suck my jism, you low harlot."

"Take it down your throat, you dirty whorebitch."

Now here is a man the thesaurus was invented for. I can see him sitting in his office, practicing, with his Roget's in one hand while he jerks off with the other.

Murray continues this naughty phrase-mongering until I hear what sounds like a duplication and then he comes with gasping breaths like he's drowning followed by a protracted sigh. Laura moans and makes a big deal out of his orgasm, opens her mouth to show him her mouth full of his come, and then swallows with exaggeration.

After Murray finishes, without changing his gentle whisper, he changes his words to the dearest praise.

"That was wonderful, you sweet, sweet princess."

"Thank you, angel face."

"God bless you, shana madela."

"That was a blessed gift, lovely lady."

I wonder if he is going to go on just as long as he had with the vile stuff as some sort of matter/anti-matter psychic cleansing, but thankfully he stops after about six blessings.

He asks me whether I liked watching and I say it was fascinating. Laura gets dressed and Murray hands Laura two one hundred dollar bills and goes on and on about what a beauty Laura is and how she gives the best head he ever got and how his wife won't put his penis in her mouth and how Laura is the reason he doesn't divorce his wife.

Laura and I say goodbye and leave. Going down in the elevator, she says, "You were so quiet. Was that all right with you?"

"Sure. I like him and I love the shirts. I applaud his vocabulary. Plus you are saving him a fortune in marriage counseling. What's next?"

I'd been hearing about Walter since Laura and I spent our first weekend together. An oilman and banker in his early fifties, he was a self-made man, a big man who fought his way out of the Bronx, went to college on a football scholarship as a linebacker, all the while making a tidy sum playing pool and cards to pay for business school and to seed his stock market investing. He then parlayed his small stake into a small fortune by investing while simultaneously learning French, Arabic, and Japanese. By the time he got his master's degree he was already a millionaire and an intimate of several children of Arab sheiks and princes whose families were neck deep in petrol and petrodollars. He was constantly just off to or just back from Dallas, London, Paris, Tokyo, Kuwait, or Riyadh.

He was married and had grown-up kids; his wife, a cool and

obviously tolerant and/or oblivious Swedish beauty was usually at their farm in Sweden raising Swedish Warmbloods, among the most prized jumping horses in the world. He had several other homes and owned a few apartments in Manhattan, one of which was on the East River near the UN that he used just for guests and sex, and I guess sometimes sex with guests.

He smoked very expensive, very smelly Cuban cigars, which left their stench in Laura's hair whenever she'd been with him. He was fond of over-ordering sushi and always sent home a doggie bag for me that also smelled of Havana. And now I'm on my way to meet this cross between Jesse Ventura and Sam Walton who smells like Fidel Castro.

We get out of the cab in front of a huge building set far back from the street behind some precious Manhattan land used for nothing more than flowers and trees. This gives me an idea of how expensive the apartments here are. We pass through security and the guard smiles, greets Laura by name and tells her that Walter will be a few minutes late. He hands her a key and we take the elevator up to the thirty-first floor, walk down a long hall and open a door that leads into a gigantic foyer, as big as a one-bedroom apartment. Beyond the foyer, and two steps up, is an even bigger living room nearly as large as a basketball court, with a huge glass wall overlooking the river and Queens.

The living room furnishings are white leather and chrome, with big ultra-modern brass, bronze and chrome sculptures. On the non-glass walls are massive abstract paintings in sweeping slashes of bright colors, some fluorescent Day-Glo. One looks like an LSD hallucination of a fatal auto accident minus the bodies but with all the blood. It's stark, powerful, cold, and looks expensive. Off this is a dining area done in smoky glass and black.

I walk around for the grand tour. This is one of the biggest two-bedroom apartments I've ever seen, maybe 3,000 square feet. The oversize kitchen is diamond white and chrome. It has a center island, a breakfast nook and a fridge (I open it immediately) containing five kinds of beer, three bottles of Dom, a jar of olives and a platter of leftover sushi, the last food on earth you want to eat three days old.

The counters hold one each of every kitchen appliance in the world and although Laura says Walter has owned this place for a few years I feel that most have never been touched, except the dishwasher and a new-fangled thing I'd heard of but never seen—a microwave—which is obviously used because the inside is dirty.

Laura shows me how it works and I boil glass after glass of water and cook tiny pieces of aged fish and globs of rice. Several times I quick-open-the-door to feel the heat that isn't there. I feel as if I am in *Star Trek*.

Before I'm done trying to figure out where the heat comes from, Walter comes through the door and we walk over to meet him. He is a round bear of a man, maybe 6'3" weighing 250, with a dozen roses in one hand and a briefcase big enough for an airline navigator in the other. With his hands still full he hugs Laura, lifting her off the ground. They peck kisses like a father and daughter, then he puts her down, puts the flowers and flight case on the floor and kisses her slowly like a lover. Laura turns to me.

"Walter, this is Jeffrey."

"Hello, Walter," I say and extend my hand, which does not quite fill his. His is too wide and I can't quite get the grip I need to give the firm macho handshake a man wants to put out at a moment like this.

"So you're the man who stole Laura's heart!" he says as he pulls me to him and gives me a gentle bear hug and lifts my feet off the ground with the ease of picking up a kitchen waste basket.

Though mildly overcome by his tobacco breath and still airborne I hug back with enough strength to ever so slightly hinder his breathing, a manly signal that half makes up for my ineffective handshake. He smiles and puts me back on the floor. It's a wonderful smile that makes me feel comfortable immediately, even in this lair of opulence. There is something special, an unrehearsed openness about this man that even a cynical Arab billionaire would fall for. He reeks of confidence and success and honesty and compassion as well as cigars. If he hadn't been drawn to money, he would have made a great cop or priest, albeit with cheaper, even smellier stogies.

"First the coke," Walter says. "This is as good as any shit I ever snorted."

He goes to the glass table in the dining room and spreads out way too much white powder for three people for a week. He rolls up a hundred and snorts three lines in each nostril. Laura does the same. I do one each.

"I want to fuck!" the Great Bear bellows.

Laura giggles as he takes her hand and leads her into the master bedroom, the size of a handball court, decorated in black and red Chinese lacquer with an emperor-size bed covered with a huge, fluffy cream comforter stuffed with the feathers of several flocks of geese. Walter pauses at the dimmer control panel long enough to delight me with his sensitivity toward getting just the right lighting. Then he pulls back the comforter and undresses with the concentration and deliberate precision of Houdini taking off shackles under water.

"Get undressed slowly," he instructs Laura. She smiles and looks into his eyes with her big eyes wide open, like a Keane painting. With a teasing half-time tempo she slips out of her jeans, pries herself out of her too-tight T-shirt and in exaggerated slo-mo, removes her black lace bra and panties. Walter stands naked, a big bear wiggling in anticipation. He's got big balls like me and a cock that's larger than mine.

Laura walks to the other side of the bed. Walter falls onto the bed on his hands and knees and lumbers toward her as she squeals and giggles like a child. Naked, Walter looks like a retired professional wrestler, flabby but powerful with a belly large enough to give birth to a forty-five-pound baby and arms that retain most of their shape if not definition, and a massive chest just turning from pecs to breasts.

Laura jumps onto the bed and they tussle and kiss. He lies on his back as she moves her head onto his cock then pivots around till her vagina is on his face.

He moans contentedly. Her Hawaiian princess olive body looks more youthful than usual as they pleasure each other's favorite parts.

"Sit on me." he half demands, half requests.

"Yes, Papa Bear," she replies in what I imagine is some naughty child-like dialog they worked out long ago.

She squats over him, on the heels of her feet, in the same position she puts on her makeup or pisses, and grabs his prong with her right hand and teases herself and him with it before sliding it inside her. As she rides the cock up and down, his hands play with her small lovely tits. She works at this until tiny beads of sweat form all over her body, not droplets, just a zillion minute glistening molecules, each potent with her scent. From about six feet away I can smell her through Walter's lingering tobacco cloud (and I have yet to see him light up!) and she's powerful enough to wake up my guys that run my hormone control room.

Just as I am wondering whether it would be cool to join in Laura says to me, "Put it in my ass, Jeffrey. I want the two of you." I don't need an embossed invitation or a road map. In seconds I am nude, hunched behind her with spit in my hand lathering my dick. I do a gentle push and pull to stretch and enter her without hurting her.

"Shove it in. Hurt me. Hurt my ass," she orders, shoving against my dick until it's deep in her ass. I can feel Walter's cock through the flesh wall and after a few awkward seconds, the three of us tap into a slow groove and boogie in unison.

Walter and I give each other a cool dude smile. After ten minutes Laura comes first. And second. And then Walter comes and I can feel his every pump, and it is sexy and strong and exciting and it transcends fagdom and somewhere in the middle of this euphoric state I am building and hit my point of no return and Laura comes again. I am lost in my orgasmic rush and the polyphonic aural symphony as the room fills with, "Oh my Gods," from me and, "Yes! Yes! Yes," from Laura and loud ursine grunts from Walter. As the fluid dance slows and stalls, Laura leans over to rest on Walter and I lean forward to rest on Laura and we stay motionless like that, me still in her, long enough for it to seem odd.

Finally Walter makes noises. His breathing is labored which isn't surprising so I lift myself up and support my own weight and Laura sits up and my penis squiggles out. We disengage and all lie next to each other, Laura in the middle.

Walter finally lights up a Monte Cristo and offers me one, which I decline, although they actually don't smell so bad live.

Walter explains a little about the oil biz and banking and just how much we are in bed with the Arabs and what a diplomatic and economic juggling act it is to placate American Jews and still keep our cars running with Arab gasoline. He and Laura chat endlessly about shrubs and veggies and sushi and health food diets and people they know.

> "I still get Christmas cards from Walter," says Laura. "He was always surprising to me because he wanted to be taken. We were doing experimental things but he was so shy—eager, but not really experienced. He was ready to experience anything but he didn't really know exactly what to do.
>
> "I used to drip wax on his nipples. He liked that. And he liked me whipping him. He wanted me to be like a dominatrix. But we were like teenagers about it. I didn't act like, 'OK, this is what I'm going to do to you now.' He would say, 'Why don't you try doing this?' and I would just become that. We'd role-play. Sometimes he was more dominant, but he was never aggressively dominant. He was like, 'Is this OK, am I being too dominant?' But his favorite thing was for me to take him, ravage him.
>
> "I remember one thing that I loved that he used to do. When we would get really really hot and sweaty, he would blow on my face to cool me off."

Walter suggests he pick up a lady friend of his and we'll all go to dinner at one of his favorite French restaurants on First Avenue. He'll introduce us as a couple he met on an airplane. We wonder if we are suitably dressed and Walter says not to worry, "I own a piece of the joint."

Walter and Laura inhale more coke. I pass. After their snorts, Walter sweeps what's left—several hundred dollars worth—into an envelope and gives it to Laura.

We shower, dress, and continue our chitchat as we go down to the garage and get into a brand-new factory stretched Cadillac Fleetwood Brougham. This is his personal car, the largest production car made in America. (Other than this factory stretch all other stretches are made aftermarket.) Laura and I sit in the back and we head uptown to pick up Jennifer.

We arrive at a newish building with a posh-sounding English aristocratic name in the East 60s. Walter gets out and asks the doorman to ring Jennifer. She's a tallish girl with fine light brown hair and a long forehead that took a minimum of six generations to evolve. She has that frail yet healthy look that only inbreeding Protestants can create. It's only late October and she's already wearing a full-length fur that I assume isn't faux. I beg Laura not to go on an anti-fur tirade and she agrees.

Jennifer is pissed that Walter is fifteen minutes late, which is unfair because it's well within the rules of being on time in Manhattan. She sounds like one of those well-bred WASP girls like Becky whom I dated just before Laura, an apple-pie, ethnic-less All-American with a prudish exterior and, I suspect, because she's sleeping with The Bear, a secret Hester Prynne fantasy under her pillow.

Dinner goes well with lots of snails and laughter and *blanquette de veau* and *canard a l'orange*. Walter tells us how he bought a zillion gallons of aviation fuel and crude oil that day and how he will create trades through straw parties and conduits so that warring or at least spitting-mad factions can trade with each other with a wink and a nod. Then we have some fabulously gooey desserts.

Walter says he'll drop us off downtown before he heads back to his place with Jennifer. We pile into Walter's Caddy and are driving down Second Avenue when all of a sudden the car spurts, burbles, then dies.

"I'm sorry. I think we've run out of gas," says Walter with an interesting use of the first-person plural.

"I think there's a gas station a few blocks down," I remember.

"Let's let Jennifer steer and we three push," says Laura.

And there we are on Second Avenue, pushing the car of the man who just that day bought half a gazillion gallons of aviation fuel and West Texas Crude. (Now there's a name for a rock band!)

Without saying anything, the three of us look at each other with tacit understanding of the absurdity and laugh all the way to the gas station.

33

Living weird is the new normal

1981–82

In 1981, the world takes yet another leap into insecurity. Reagan gets shot and survives. The Pope survives an assassination attempt and Sadat, a man I admire and who had intelligence, a large sense of destiny and the biggest set of balls in recent history does not survive.

The Professional Air Traffic Controllers Organization strikes, which to my surprise and I'm sure all the striking air traffic controllers, leads to the permanent firing of nearly an entire work force. Marshall McLuhan and Moshe Dayan, two of my heroes, pass away. Lech Walesa makes Polish jokes obsolete.

One non-sex oddity happens in the Los Angeles airport while Laura and I are waiting for a flight back to New York. There is a small herd of American Olympians, male and female. All are in red, white, and blue official clothing; all are in great shape and most are smoking cigarettes.

Athletes smoking? Laura and I ask them why. One of the men, a tall blond and handsome All-American Olympian poster-boy says that they smoke because it doesn't have any effect on their sport. Laura figures it out in about three seconds. It's high diving.

Laura turns tricks, buys and sells coke, does too much coke and begs me to whip her just about every time we fuck. As for me, I am doing too much coke and too much whipping her.

I'm really getting into it. She takes the guilt away by telling me over and over and over that it doesn't hurt, that it feels good to her, that it makes the sex hotter. I don't exactly understand her words but I get the meaning when she says, "I beg you to love me, to do me, to manipulate me into you. I need you to own me."

Whatever her kink is, it suits me.

In New York we go to Club O, the Hellfire Club, and Trapeze. I especially like Trapeze, a disco club that had coasted into the sex club scene. It was the only on-premises club I knew with a great sound system and a large, hardwood dance floor. Dancing at an on-premises sex club has no limits. You can dance naked or start out clothed and end up naked having sex right there on the dance floor. Laura sucking my cock while I dance with her head in my hands is a legitimate dance step.

We also visit half a dozen other sex clubs in L.A. and Miami. Playhouse South in Miami is a favorite, full of good-looking Floridians and winter snow bunnies. One night, Richard, a cokehead lawyer friend in Miami comes over at 8:00 a.m. to our hotel room at the Fontainebleau to consummate a trade I arrange for him. He gives Laura $100 and a gram of pure uncut Miami drug-dealer coke in exchange for the first hooker sex of his life. I get to watch Laura in her favorite hunch-down primitive squat, ride up and down on his cock, slowly at first then very quickly, touching him only with her pussy until he comes. He softly says, "Oh my God," about sixty-five times until I ask him to stop.

Laura and I fuck secretly or not so secretly in semi-public places: in a doorway, a quickie in an express elevator, on a rooftop, against a car hood in an empty parking garage, blowjobs in cabs and highway blowjobs with truckers as the audience.

We go to adult bookstores in a variety of cities. One night we chat up a black uncle and his nephew. Uncle says they like to go out and drink together, then come here and jerk off separately in different booths. We invite them into a large booth with a couch. Laura does each of them twice simultaneously—one in the mouth, one in the pussy, and then they switch positions. She says she will never forget "the ravenous intensity," of the younger man who says, "You the most beautiful woman I ever seen."

I take lots of walks with Necort for an hour or two when Laura turns tricks in our New York apartment. When I come back Laura and I are both so horny we fuck immediately, sometimes before we reach the bed.

One day I run into Al Goldstein, the intermittently fat, always sassy and fabulously hedonistic publisher of the porn newspaper *Screw*, whom I have known for years. Al had just lost a lot of weight, maybe a hundred pounds, and wants to join me for Saturday Morning Boxing. He is the only dude who ever arrives at the gym in a chauffeured car.

Laura comes down to meet me after boxing and meets Al, who is quite taken with her. The next time I run into Al, he tells me that he thinks Laura is gorgeous, sexy beyond mere mortals and that he wants to fuck her more than any other woman in the world.

He doesn't know she is for sale; it is just his way of giving a compliment. I ask him how much was the most he ever paid for sex, and he says $500 for Seka, that year's current blonde goddess of porn. I tell Al that Laura occasionally turns tricks and would be available for $600, just to make sure she is the most expensive pussy of his life. I also get him to agree that I can be there and watch.

"Jeffrey hooked me up with Al Goldstein; I got $600," Laura laughs. "I was the highest-paid girl Goldstein had up to that point, which Jeffrey took a lot of pride in, ha, ha, ha. That really turned me on—that Jeffrey controlled me and once in a while would sell me to men who would use me for their pleasure.

"They would pull down their pants and make me suck their cocks or eat me or both and then spread my legs and shove their cocks in me and use me and shoot in me, come in me, and be as happy as they could possibly be. I liked that men used me for their pleasure. I liked being able to do

that for them. I could make a difference. For a moment or
two they would love me more than anything in the world.

"Jeffrey would sometimes get the money and then he
always gave me the money in front of the guy. That was
so much fun! And I loved the money! What an insane way
to make money. Have the best time of your life and make
hundreds or thousands of dollars in just an hour doing
what I would most want to do even if it was for free! I
mean I would have paid for it if it was offered to me. I
mean there was nothing I'd rather do than do drugs and
fuck. I loved it all!"

One afternoon, in some little apartment that Goldstein keeps near
his office, I watch Laura fuck Al, and I enjoy every moment of his
pleasure. Al says she is worth every penny.

He becomes a semi-regular of hers and, I think, quickly
negotiates a volume discount. I go the second time but not after
that. Laura says he always treats her well and can eat pussy better
than not only me, but also any man she'd ever met, even better than
her film director ex-lover, so she especially likes him as a client.

By late 1981, Laura starts divorce proceedings against Sandy and
with Walter's help, buys out Sandy's half of their house.

We commute regularly between my cabin, her house in New
Hope and our apartment in NYC. Sometimes we are separate
and sometimes we are together. We are a movable feast. And
an expensive one. That's three sets of everything like toothpaste,
shampoo, toasters, frying pans, stereos, bagel slicers, sheets, TVs,
beds, sofas, refrigerators. All of it. Thank God Laura's cash-cow
pussy holds up her half. With our three domiciles we have the
lifestyle of the rich and famous but without servants, fame, or a lot
of money.

Gastronomically, Laura and I have become full-fledged Sushi
Junkies. We have a $400 a week habit. I go from never wanting to
try the stuff to loving it on a near daily basis. Repetition makes our
peculiar lifestyle normal.

34

Lynne Something or Something Lynne

Late spring 1982

Laura and I are in San Diego at an adult magazine convention promoting *Puritan*. We talk to our distributors and look for new ones. At the *High Society* magazine exhibit we meet a hot, corn-fed Miss America-looking spokes-porn-star. The three of us chum around and soon become fast friends. (I should remember her name but I don't. I think it was Lynne Something or Something Lynne.)

She is spectacular—movie star gorgeous, and, to be honest, a notch above Laura. She's a tall blonde with blue eyes, big tits and a cheerleader smile. In her films I've seen, she fucks at the edge of sanity. Maybe beyond. Although new to the business she is making a name for herself.

On the second night Laura and I are asleep when a knock on the door around 3:00 a.m. wakes us up. It's Lynne Something or Something Lynne in tears and pulling a pink suitcase with wheels. After trying unsuccessfully a dozen times to fuck her, a slimy, rude male representative of *High Society* asked her if she didn't want to fuck him who the hell did she want to fuck? She says, "Jeffrey and Laura," so he throws her out with the $500 he owes her and tells her to go fuck us.

She apologizes for the disruption, tells us the hotel is sold out and asks if she can stay the night even if she has to sleep on the floor. I look at Laura and ask with my puppy-dog face if I really can take advantage of this once in a lifetime offer. Laura smiles her consent.

I ask out loud if Laura is sure this is okay and she reconfirms it. I kiss the distressed damsel and Laura welcomes her by putting her hands down her pants. Soon she and Laura are each straddling one of my legs, looking up at me with smiles, sharing my penis, rubbing their tits on my thighs. The two of them kiss each other with winding exploring tongues. I am aware that these are the two most beautiful girls I have ever been in bed with at the same time. This is it, the magnum opus of my life's work in sex. I hope it's not all downhill from here. They sixty-nine. I watch. Laura is on the bottom and the porn star tosses her long blonde hair back and forth in a move right out of one of her porn flicks.

I fuck Laura for a while and then I fuck Miss America. I hold all my come. I want this to last. Miss America is going wild and suddenly Laura runs to the bathroom crying. This is totally unexpected, the first evidence of jealousy I have ever seen from Laura. I don't know what to do. A porn star who looks like Miss America is under me and I don't want to miss a frame. My Ethics Committee convenes and votes five to four to go talk with Laura.

It's clear what's wrong: We've never had a threesome with another girl and Laura has never seen me fuck another woman as beautiful and stunning as Miss America. Me either. Most of the sex Laura and I have with other people is with men fucking Laura and me watching and/or joining in. When I'm fucking another girl, she is never as good looking as Laura and while this is going on Laura is probably fucking three guys.

Laura says she wants to go back out and say what she feels in front of all us. "I'm going through some emotional turmoil but I don't want to be controlled by its spell," she says. She wants to work through it in Enlightened Be-Here-Now Hippie Fashion.

We go back out to the bedroom and Lynne Something or Something Lynne is sitting up in bed and she's crying too. Laura admits to being jealous. She says she knows she shouldn't feel this way but she does and she can't help it. She says she's never seen me fuck a woman as beautiful. Miss America showers us both with hugs and gushes, "You are the best couple I ever met, and I would never do anything to break you up and if you don't want it, I won't fuck Jeffrey."

I pray to God: "Please give Laura the strength to sanctify the continuation of this blessed celebration."

Laura tells Miss America that she is the single most delicious and beautiful girl she ever kissed and she wants to kiss her more. After a red flag and a yellow flag, the green flag waves and we are off and running. I am a religious believer at that moment more than anytime since my Bar Mitzvah.

Lynne Something or Something Lynne does some of her best work with us. I wake the next morning between them; surprised it wasn't just a dream.

(When I die and my life flashes in front of me I hope it slows down for that San Diego night. And I might not even edit out the Laura Bathroom Freak-Out Scene because it added drama in our Second Act.)

35

Puritan interview with Timothy Leary

Summer 1982

The owners of *Puritan* magazine like our interview with Norman Mailer so much they commission Laura and me to interview Timothy Leary.

My fascination with Timothy Leary, both as New Age Avatar and Drug Guru, dated back to the '60s—when I was in high school in Newton, Massachusetts, and he was at Harvard experimenting with the newly popularized psychedelic, LSD-25.

In many ways Laura and I are at the confluence of the Mind-Expansion Movement of the '60s, over which Leary presided, and the Sexual Revolution of the '70s that gave birth to *Puritan*. We see *Puritan* representing the erotic part of that movement. Again, Laura and I spend a lot of time preparing with *Puritan* editor Stanley Bernstein. We see fertile ground for an interview. We read several dozen of Leary's old and new interviews. We want to know what the Leary of the '80s has to say about the '60s and '70s, and what's coming next.

Dr. Leary suggests we spend some time with him before the interview to get to know one another. Laura and I fly to L.A. and drive to meet him and his fifth wife, Barbara Chase Leary at their house in the hills above West Hollywood. The four of us get on great from moment one. Tim is sixty-three, looks younger and moves with grace and energy. He is humble and unpretentious, maybe on purpose, but very sweet and generous with his private stash.

> "I wouldn't say Timothy Leary was sexy," Laura recalls. "No, he was way too into himself, he definitely was very much all about himself; 'The Great Tim Leary.' You know, 'I AM THE SHOW!' "

Hanging out with them for a few days by his pool, enjoying Barbara's California fresh cooking, going out to his favorite Thai restaurant on Sunset Boulevard and consuming vast quantities of coke, grass and hash puts us all in a relaxed comfortable mood.

I don't know whether it is a good thing or a bad thing, but when we finally get down to the work, we all sit on the floor around a low table and smoke and drink and puff and snort our way through three hours of questions and answers.

> "We did the Tim Leary interview at his house in California," Laura remembers. "Leary said that he would do the interview if we brought the three Cs: cocaine, champagne and caviar. So we did. That was fun."

Here are excerpts from our 1982 *Puritan* interview:

LAURA BRADLEY: Is the country ready for a "free sex and drugs" government?

TIMOTHY LEARY: I think it's a primitive barbarism that in our country our health departments haven't had a crash program to develop a drug that is a safe euphoric aphrodisiac that you could come home at night and sip in a glass with or without ice to make you feel wonderful and a thousand times hornier than you ever felt in your life.

LB: What exactly is sexual about acid, or in what way does acid release this orgasmic energy?

TL: The first time you take acid, if you're alone in the desert it's not going to be an aphrodisiac. It's when your wonderful lover takes you into his or her perfumed silken boudoir and turns you on to acid that erotic awareness deepens. Intelligence is the ultimate aphrodisiac. If you want to be a better lover or enrich your sex life, you've got to increase your intelligence. Acid is basically a philosophic experience. It opens up your brain, makes it think long and deep. You get greater sexual awareness when you turn on and access those circuits in your brain that are performing those wonderful functions. You get tremendous pleasure and bliss and aesthetic kick.

LB: And more powerful orgasms?

TL: Of course... You see, we're just learning now the way that specific drugs become associated with sexuality. It's as though you were first laid in the back of a Chevrolet, so therefore you always need a Chevrolet. There's always the trap of tying yourself to one chemical stimulus. There are people who can only fuck well if they think they are on one particular drug.

LB: How do you react to the numbers of people who have abused or ruined themselves with drugs?

TL: Do you realize that drugs are safer than any other form of recreation? They're safer than jogging, safer than skiing, safer than high school football, which ruin, what, 100,000 knees a year permanently? Mountain climbing, swimming, not to mention driving... drugs are the safest recreational opportunity around on a statistical basis.

JEFFREY MICHELSON: What are your thoughts on the tremendous upswing in popularity of sadomasochism?

TL: These are phases that people are going through. There's a phase now of getting off on discipline and bondage, which is obviously childish.

JM: Do you mean literally childish?

TL: It goes back to spankings and really infantile sexuality.

LB: Is that it, are people now getting into that part of their childhood?

TL: There are circuits in the brain that are physically animalistic, for grabbing and forcing... We all have these circuits. And as kids we are much more into immediate violence, wrestling, being punished. Our species has gone through a reversion to the same stage in the past—take warfare, swords, battlefields, hand-to-hand combat, inflicting of pain. These are phases that people go through. But I think it's sad for someone to spend their whole life going through the same ritual of being tied up and punished. That has to do with guilt and shame that's imposed upon us by Judeo-Christian religion. Anything you do to enjoy yourself sexually, you have to be punished for. The first time you were found masturbating, you got spanked. Of course, every time you got spanked you came in your pants.

LB: I was wondering, have you ever paid for sex, and if so, what have these experiences been like?

TL: Everyone pays for sex, one way or the other... Yes, before I was married I had experiences with prostitutes.

LB: Did you enjoy them?

TL: Oh, of course. I enjoyed and learned from them and every sexual experience. Most prostitution is sordid and power-oriented. But it is possible for any intelligent person to meet any other intelligent person and exchange life experiences at the body level. Money is not an issue—intelligence, goodwill and elegance are the real issues there.

LB: Have you ever had experiences with group sex? What are your feelings about swinging?

TL: I've been in rooms where I have made love to people when other people were present. But no, I am not a swinger; I am not an orgy person.

"I don't know if Leary even looked at me sexually," Laura muses. "Maybe he did but like I said, he wasn't particularly sexy. I had a good time because he had a beautiful wife, Barbara. I was turned on by her. Absolutely. And she was much more real and nicer than he was. He was nice enough, but not like her..."

After the interview Tim gives Laura and me two tabs of Tim Leary-Approved™ Acid. Tim tells us the last time he did acid, a few weeks before, he went out and bought a Mercedes.

A few weeks after the interview Laura and I drop the acid at my cabin. We have loving hippie psychedelic sex: ultrasensitive, shape-shifting, time-traveling, out of body, Garden of Eden with an exploding synesthesiac rainbow/maple fudge/trumpets orgasm. No whips, no pain, no roles. We just do all the things early Homo sapiens did before other people told them they shouldn't.

Then I mow the lawn while Laura plays with the cats and then we do the laundry together. We are the ultimate suburbanization and bourgeoisification of the hallucinogenic experience. Turn On, Tune In, Do The Laundry.

36
Alea Iacta Est

Two days later

Two days after we interview Timothy Leary we read about a swingers club in the *Los Angeles Free Press* and decide to go. Laura does about three lines in each nostril before we leave the Hyatt House on Sunset, nicknamed the "Riot House," because of the rock bands that stay there and their famous commotions including several Keith Moon incidents that were early warning signs of his demise, and where Moon, Keith Richards and John Bonham each allegedly dropped a TV out of a window at different times for different reasons.

I say to Laura, "I love you, but you need to stop doing so much coke."

"Don't tell me what I need," she says with a hard edge.

The club is on La Brea just south of Hollywood Boulevard in West Hollywood.

We pay our $50, go to the locker room and come out in standard swing club uniform: Laura in black lace bra and panties and me in bikini briefs and an open shirt. The crowd is *sooo* very L.A. and definitely the most attractive I've ever seen at an on-premise swingers club anywhere. I can see that every guy in the place spends more time in a gym than me.

We stop at the bar for a vodka and tonic, and then head off to one of the swing rooms. I'm not sure how well I would do in this L.A. babe pool with a lesser being by my side, but with Laura I'm getting some nice eye contact from what I assume are would-be starlets.

Laura and I lie down next to each other in the far corner of a large, dimly lit room carpeted wall to wall with mattresses. It looks like there are about eight or nine couples and half a dozen extra guys, two in threesomes with couples and the other four playing with themselves while standing in line to fuck one babe who is somewhere in the middle of a gangbang.

Like many on-premise swingers clubs that are supposed to be couples-only, this one has a small herd of single men who are either friends of the owner or bribers of the bouncer. Guys who want Laura bring over their Vaginal Offerings for me to inspect. Uncharacteristically, in a perversion of my normal depraved preference for steamy sluts, I choose a wholesome surfer babe. Laura selects a guy who could be the fourth runner up in a Teenage Troy Donahue Look-Alike Contest. The couple next to us is another hot guy on his back being ridden by another surfer babe who looks remarkably similar to mine. Both have the same build, medium long bleached blonde hair, natural breasts on the small side of a B-cup and suntans everywhere except where bikini bottoms once resided. They look like they could be cousins. But I'm wrong.

During a rest stop I ask my Surfer Girl if she knows the other Surfer Girl. She laughs and says of course she does, they're sisters. Then she leans over to give her sister a slow theatrical two-girl porn kiss and all I can think about is that I'm sorry I didn't grow up next door to them.

Sister Two finishes with Hot Guy, joins us and starts playing with my balls as I fuck Sister One. I'm having another of those moments I feared would never happen to me when I lay in bed jerking off as a teenager.

There are few things more pleasurable than having your balls played with, licked, caressed, kissed or gently sucked at the beginning of an erotic event. The yin/yang of balls, and I don't know which one is yin and which is yang, is that they provide a man with just about the most pleasure that can be had, or, in different circumstances, just about the most pain.

Some guys have big balls and some small. Mine are on the large size, the size of jumbo eggs but smaller than goose eggs. It's great having your balls touched even if you have to do it yourself. Many men, including me, play with their balls with one hand while jerking off with the other. Certainly it's best when a girl (or preferably two) touches them for you. Balls make great foreplay on the way to an orgasm and long after, having a girl caress or scratch you there can fill hours with joy.

I was taught that if you are knocked down in a street fight and you're being kicked by one or more guys, use your arms and hands to protect your eyes and your balls. Everything else will heal faster than those two regions and permanent damage to either place will bring daily lifelong misery.

The fact that humans have external testicles is just plain wonderful. It's got something to do with their functioning better as a sperm factory in temperatures lower than the body. It could have gone the other way and instead of being like horses, dogs and cats with the gift of external balls, we could have ended up like other mammals such as elephants, rhinos, sloths, whales and dolphins with internal balls which, now I'm just guessing here, I don't see being as much fun.

Balls as a metaphor stand for courage. We say, "He's got balls," "You've got some stones," and, "You got to give it to him but that bastard has major cahones" as a tribute, while penis metaphors like: "He's a prick," "Don't be a dick," and as Elliot called his brother in E.T., "penis breath," are not compliments.

Laura as usual now has a group of guys around her, with the bravest ones already in the dance. She is on her hands and knees with one guy behind and one in front. She is right next to me getting a triple dip of Vanilla Nookie to which she adds some Chunky Monkey, Moose Tracks and Rocky Road by pleading, "Spank me," "Use me hard," and "Hurt me with it."

After I finish with the Surfer Sisters, fucking but not coming in Sister Two, Laura takes a break and we head off to the bar. It's about ten stools long, kind of like a bar in a social club for Veterans in a small country town. About fifteen people are in the room, some dressed, some completely naked and some in-between. Laura and I are among the naked. She orders two vodka and tonics, which are made with something that tastes a little bit like vodka and something that tastes a little bit like tonic.

Standing, Laura rests her arms on the bar. A guy next to us, Soap Opera handsome with good manners asks if he can touch her. He starts stroking and rubbing her ass. She loves it and pushes back and jiggles around. Soap Star, also naked, compliments Laura on her lovely bum and then looks at me and asks if he can put his cock in her. I nod yes.

He does. She never turns around. He finishes and another guy asks me for permission. This goes on for seven more guys who each fill her with his jism. I am so turned on I become her eighth. Once again I'm not crazy about the cold fluid dripping down her thighs but the erotic outweighs the cold viscosity and I get past it.

She turns around. The guys shower her with "Thank yous," while she kisses me for a very long time. Then she says she must retrieve her purse from the coat check and "clean up" in the ladies room, which I know means do more coke.

As she walks away a small flood spills out of her and onto the floor. I watch her and wonder how often they have to shampoo the carpets.

She comes back annoyed, complaining that she spilled her coke in the bathroom. She licked up what she could but needs more. She walks around the bar trying to hustle some from each guy. I am embarrassed. I call her over, talk to her gently.

"Let's go home. We had a great evening. We'll go home and have some more fun."

"Soon. I just need to get a little more coke."

This is the first time I hear her say, "Need to get." It's Epiphany Time, the first of three I get in the next ten minutes. She's crossed the Rubicon. As Caesar said. "Alea iacta est," "the die is cast."

"We'll get some tomorrow. Let's go home and fuck."

"Don't tell me what to do. Get me some coke."

"Tomorrow, baby. Let's get dressed and go."

"No," she says with stern resolve. "If you want me to be your slave, you have to do what I want." Epiphany Number Two. I know she's right. I am her slave.

"Do what I want. Get me coke," she commands. Epiphany Number Three. This is the first time I see that she can be a total perineum, a complete taint, somewhere between a cunt and an asshole.

I always said I would do anything for her. I guess helping her feed her drug habit qualifies as "anything."

One guy at the bar says he knows a dealer who will trade coke for sex. Laura jumps on it and agrees. I tell the guy to have his dealer buddy come and meet us in the parking lot.

The guy uses the pay phone (remember them?) then comes back and says his buddy will be outside in ten minutes. We get dressed and exit. Laura is the most jittery I have ever seen her. The Dealer drives up with two other guys in a huge Lincoln. The Dealer offers Laura a couple of spoonfuls immediately and as she's powdering her nose through the car window he pulls out one of those ubiquitous tiny brown bottles. He playfully teases her with it, moving it slowly in front of her face, and says she can have it if she'll blow all three of them. She accepts in the middle of the offer. Laura gets into the back seat and one after another gives each guy a blowjob for the gram. She doesn't skimp. Each cock is adored, licked up and down. She sucks each one to completion and makes a show of swallowing each load. I stand outside the car. I am excited by her raw sexuality, exceeded only by my distress about her coke habit.

37

The cocaine Ponzi scheme

Coke was everywhere and everybody was doing more and more of it and acting crazier and more paranoid, and no one spoke out against it, other than the anti-drug forces that seasoned dopers were programmed not to believe. Very few members of the hip community saw that the Emperor was naked. Few things are more dangerous than a hard drug with a good reputation.

It was in more and more places and more overtly displayed. It was one of the biggest fads to hit the baby boomers since the Hula Hoop, the Twist and bell bottoms. It even gave pot a run for the money. And speaking of money, dope dealers loved coke. A shoebox full of grass, which can't be cut, might be worth in 1981/82 a thousand dollars; a shoe box full of uncut coke, which will definitely get cut, is worth tens and tens of thousands.

It's hard to conceive of it now but in the early '80s, business meetings would often start with lines on the table. And I don't mean just record and movie business meetings. Lawyers and Wall Street traders were fuelling their overtime-driven careers on it. Most of the players were self-deluding themselves that it was not only safe, it was good for you. Cocaine led to mass hypnosis.

Middle-class and upper-class parties would often have a bowl of it for guests. The only difference was the size of the bowl. I saw it handed out to adults at bar mitzvahs and at Irish wakes.

Coke was so expensive that half of us were dealing to the other half just to make our stash, like some Colombian-backed psychotropic Amway multi-level marketing scheme gone mad. If I could have invested in Bolivian Agriculture Futures or Colombian Processing I would have.

Coke was so much more expensive than the previous highs of pot, alcohol and speed that cocaine altered the very fabric of hipster finances. Great pot in 1981 was maybe $50 an ounce, which would take two normal potheads at least a few days to consume. Alcohol as always, except during Prohibition, was legal and cheap. And speed, at maybe $2, $3, $5 or even $10 a hit or a snort would last for more hours than nighttime, even on the winter solstice.

But coke had the shortest half-life of them all. A $100 gram could be used up by a couple just getting dressed on the way to a disco. One-hundred-dollar-a-week pot or speed habits became $200-a-day coke habits. And freebase was the Hoover cash vacuum of all drugs—$1,000 up in smoke in just a few hours. People developed five-figure-a-week drug habits. Heroin dealers were eating their heartless hearts out.

I knew several people who went through $10,000 to $20,000 worth of freebase in a week. Inheritances went up in smoke—as did paychecks, savings accounts, children's college funds, businesses' cash flows and lawyers' clients' escrow accounts. Then they started stealing from strangers.

I knew enough from indulging in speed a bit too frequently earlier in my life that you can't keep borrowing from the future. You can't cheat life, but in the early '80s a whole segment of the hip middle-class thought they could. Coke pulled the wool over our eyes for half a decade. The courts were being lenient on middle-class coke busts that didn't involve big weight, so there was no bogeyman under the bed, only the one coke paranoia made you think was there. Hipsters, not being so hip, were in mass delusion.

With our conspicuous consumption and Laura's drug habit expanding, she started dealing more than hooking. First for her habit, which I protested against funding, and then for the money itself, which was easier and faster to make than by turning tricks.

Most often she sold both to the same people—a horizontal marketing expansion, a hooker with an upsell.

Lots of rich clients would buy a gram of coke from her for $100 and then give most or all of it back while fucking her. Others would order larger amounts and share some. She had a few clients, nice middle-class guys who had become biggish dealers, who would trade coke for sex or sell it to Laura at wholesale, or both.

Soon we had a scale and a grinder and little gram bottles with coke spoons and a thriving cottage industry just like many of our friends. Just like tens of thousands of other user-dealers obliviously on the payroll of Pablo Escobar. The one part I liked was the grinding, weighing, and cutting because it was like being a kid with a chemistry set. It was all a bit like alchemy—with coke instead of lead. You mixed coke with mannitol and turned it into gold.

The returns were phenomenal. You would buy an eight-ball— an eighth of an ounce or three and a half grams—of really high quality coke (coke's one saving grace was that it taught a lot of us the metric system) for say $200 to $300 and cut it in half or more with mannitol and sell seven or eight grams for a hundred apiece and make $400 to $500 profit and do it twice a week or twice a day depending on the width of your customer base and the depth of their habits.

It was, looking back, a mass insanity that ultimately did none of us any good. Even before AIDS, it spelled the end of an era.

38

Mr. Tall and the world's ugliest swing club

October 1982

From 1981 into 1982, Laura slides from fucking with some S&M into S&M with some fucking. Laura is black and blue by choice much of the time. She likes it. She wears bruises like jewelry.

Less and less she talks about sex or orgasm or pleasure. It's now about taking pain, being used and completely being owned by me and being used and whipped by men she doesn't know and will never see again.

The politics are weird. The power in an S&M relationship is more fluid than static. It's hard to tell where it is at any given moment. Does the slave need the master more than the master needs the slave? The reason why these bizarre relationships work, sometimes for a while, sometimes for a lifetime, is because that question's answer is situational and not etched in granite. The sliding power differential is the attraction. She is my preternatural sex Goddess. She is my slave, but I worship her and need her.

Watching her in sexual ecstasy is freebase for my penis, except unlike the drug the emotional payoff keeps getting better instead of progressively falling short. We come home from some sordid public display and I am steel rod insatiable for the rest of the night, shooting come every hour or three in one hole after another. It is, at the time, my idea of heaven.

One of the reasons I tolerate her coke habit is that coke makes her horny and slutty, and I enjoy fucking her into a more mellow state. Usually.

The first time I notice a quantum change in Laura's attitude, the beginning of the S&M slide, is one blustery Sunday in late October 1982. During the day Laura has two tricks that are well paying but are sexually boring. By sundown she has fucked me out. By Sunday night, she's coked up and jittery and even a decent whipping doesn't settle her down.

I slap her face, which is one of her new favorite perversions. Slapping someone you love across the face is even more counterintuitive than spanking. I slap her face gently and she complains. I hit her harder and she says it's not hard enough. I slap her with force and she thanks me and my dick gets harder. I am Pavlov's Dog. That's how easy it is for a sex maniac to fall into something. She tells me that when I hit her, spank her, slap her, it doesn't hurt as much as it feels good to her. She gets pleasure out of acts that would give me pain. I have no idea why she has this perverted sensual interpretation or what it means but I know it turns me on. And it comes with free absolution, an ecclesiastical declaration of forgiveness of sins complete with free indulgences.

Laura wants it hotter, but it's Sunday night. Almost every place we know is closed. We find an ad in *Screw* for a 24/7 on-premise swing club so we get dressed and head there. On the cab ride over she whispers to me her anticipation of being used by strangers.

"I want you to look into my eyes. I want to be hurt in front of you. I want you to slap my face hard while another man whips me."

The club is just off Broadway around 49th Street. We are let in for free by the man at the door who looks at Laura and lights up with a smile. Lots of swingers clubs during this period are fronts for whorehouses. Single men are the rule rather than the forbidden or the exception. Couples or women get in for free or next to nothing and single guys pay $75. The owner hires shills, sometimes classy hookers, most often street hookers so single guys can get sex. The whorehouses use the semi-legal permissiveness allowed at swingers clubs to their advantage.

Nearly all true swingers clubs are couples-only except on rare nights when single men are allowed. A normal Joe needs to find a girl or at least hire a decent-smelling hooker. Real clubs are open only at night, with one or two dark nights. The fake clubs, set up for single men, are open twenty-four hours a day, seven days a week, like whorehouses, which is what they are.

We go up the stairs and enter a large loft. It's mostly empty. The floor is dirty. There is an area with gym mats covering the floor surrounded by folding metal chairs; the kind you would rent for a funeral except they wouldn't be this rusty. It's set up like a boxing ring without the ropes. The lighting is gloomy and dim, not moody and sexy. The place reeks of stale sperm, body odors, old piss, two or more warring camps of cheap institutional air freshener plus an undercurrent of ammonia. The ammonia is the friendliest aroma.

Half a dozen badly-shaped, mostly middle-aged men, naked or in their Jockeys, are seated around the ring, all playing with themselves, watching a lone plump black whore with bad teeth and a few massive body scars sucking off the semi-hard penis of a fat guy with a stomach so big that he probably hasn't seen his own dick without a mirror in a decade. Not one man ringside has a decent hard-on.

Laura never opens her lavender down coat and is already asking to leave. I am fascinated by the unrelenting ugliness. This is sex hell. Forget the sex, I tell her. Let's just stay a minute or two longer. I am in the middle of a once in a lifetime experience. It would be hard for a set designer to duplicate such a rancid mood. It is not simply unpleasant; it is spectacularly disgusting. I'm captivated, like a rubbernecker passing an automobile accident. (If someone showed you his infected pus boil, wouldn't it be hard not to look?)

I slowly pan around the room; not one spot isn't frayed or putrid. Of the five large, decade-old, huge, semi-nude girly posters on the wall, all are torn and surrounded by peeling paint. Two are falling down as if they were caught in an attempt to escape and were left hanging, wounded, as a warning to the other posters. If the devil were feeling generous, this is where he would send you for Christmas.

Finally, I've had enough and as we turn to leave we come face to face with a well-dressed, nicely handsome tall man who says, "If you're leaving, I'm leaving. If you're staying, I'll stay."

Laura smiles at me, then at Mr. Tall. He is not yet forty, obviously an executive with his wingtips and Brooks Brothers suit. "I'll stay," she says without looking for my approval, pulling off her beret and coat. The three of us head to a corner with lousy lighting and a sea of dead sofa cushions and padded chair seats, maybe twenty of them. The three of us take off our clothes and, showing good breeding, neatly fold them in little piles. A few of the crowd come over to watch as Laura drops to her knees and starts sucking the tall man's biggish cock.

It hardens fast and points straight up. Laura turns around, grabs his cock from between her legs and, leans forward balancing on two big cushions, while Mr. Tall guides his cock inside her as she, all slinky and thin and angular and young, rides it. Soon she is the only one moving, sliding in and out, and making guttural raspy noises like the sound of someone practicing German phonetics. In this sea of ugly she is an island of vivacious sex and beauty. The dichotomy makes her more impressive, magical.

The voyeur peanut gallery, everyone in the room including the fat man and the black whore, surrounds us. Every person, including the black whore, is doing some serious masturbating. Even the fat man now has a noteworthy erection. While fucking Mr. Tall, Laura begs me loudly to slap her face, and I do. The gallery responds with a gasp, masturbating faster and taking a step closer. I put out my hand to signal the herd to stay back. I hold Laura by her shoulders and like power-assisted steering, I help energize her moves.

Mr. Tall stands like a mannequin while Laura milks his cock. Then he reaches out with strong arms to help her ass move back and forth. The three of us look like a rudimentary machine.

He comes in Laura with great bull-fuck snorts. She starts singing her special moan, signaling the beginning of her climax.

"Slap me hard. Lots," she begs. I oblige.

His snorts, her moans and my slaps ring out in the hollowness of the room's hard walls.

She continues her motion another half minute till he pulls out of her and she drops onto a large pillow. He leans down to caress her and whispers to us that if we would be more comfortable in his hotel, he'd love to take us there. Laura looks at me pleading yes, so we dress and leave. The pack follows our every move all the way to the door as we split the toxic pit and catch a cab.

Mr. Tall tells us he is in town for a business meeting. He's the speechwriter for the CEO of one of the big media conglomerates, and he's staying at the Waldorf-Astoria. He boasts that he's also written speeches for the White House and that President Reagan likes his work. He says it's a thrill watching the president read his words at a meeting and especially on TV. He says hearing his words on TV actually makes him hard. He doesn't look familiar but he definitely has a tall patrician private school Ivy League thing going on.

He pays the cabbie and we head up to his suite. He immediately orders half a dozen drinks from room service. Laura excavates the little bottle from her bag and does a few lines. Mr. Tall and I pass. We all start undressing again. Mr. Tall and I simultaneously ask Laura to get undressed slowly. She peels off her street clothes and takes a very long time with her black bra and knickers. Naked, she comes over and rubs up against our arms.

Then she climbs onto the bed on her hands and knees, her pussy wiggling as she begs the stranger for a spank. I sit down in a comfortable chair, which I move closer, just watching.

Whatever hormones she secretes in anticipation fill the room and overpower the cut flowers on the dresser. As soon as her sweet musk hits my nose, my penis, like so many times before and after, hardens and throbs.

"Yes. I'd like to spank you," he replies and lays a tender slap, way too lightly for Laura's liking. She keeps begging him to hit harder but his escalating increments are too inconsequential. She orders, "Jeffrey, spank me. Show him how hard."

I spank her with the force of an angry but civilized father. Mr.

Tall gasps, like the herd did an hour earlier.

"Like that," she instructs Mr. Tall. "Spank me hard like that."

He lets go with one that is hard enough to send her back a few inches and she says, "One. Yes. Like that. But harder, please."

He pulls his hand back farther and cracks her ass again.

"Two. Yes, but harder, please."

"Three.

"Four."

At "Nine," she turns to me and begs, "Please slap my face when he hits me. I need to be beaten by both of you." I slap her face hard enough to freeze Mr. Tall with either excitement or disgust. A knock on the door signals the arrival of the drinks and releases him. He grabs a bathrobe and goes into the sitting room, closing the bedroom door behind him. Laura remains on the bed on hands and knees, smiling, repeating yet again another variation of her mantra. "I like the pain. I like doing it in front of you. I like taking the pain from both of you," she whispers.

Mr. Tall re-enters the bedroom with a tray. Laura stands up and we all slug down doubles of twelve-year-old single-malt Scotch. Laura finds her bag and fixes up her nose again.

"Do the ten over again, please," begs Laura as she gets back into position on the bed.

I stand in front of her and slap her face firmly, open-handed, carefully, but hard. Mr. Tall slaps her buttocks. The front and rear cracks are just a little out of sync and Laura is jolted in two directions and her face is red and her ass is very red and Mr. Tall's hand is sore.

And he is freaked out. We have crossed his line.

"I'm not comfortable with this," he says. "I want to be with Laura alone."

"No dice, not alone," I say. "Get dressed, honey."

Laura jumps up and we begin to collect our gear. Mr. Tall quickly folds.

"Okay, okay. Both of you please stay. Can I please be with Laura, and you can watch?"

"Sure."

Mr. Tall sits on the bed and has Laura lie across his muscular thighs. He begins to spank her.

"Have you been naughty, little girl?

"Yes, I've been bad," Laura says shyly. She looks directly into my eyes with anticipation and a pinch of fear. Mr. Tall spanks her harder and harder and she replies with a "Thank-you," after each stroke.

"Slap me once Jeffrey. Please," she implores. I get up, slap her face and return to my comfortable chair.

I watch this pain show take place in front of me and I cannot understand the reason I like it. But I do. Or why she likes it. And she does. There is something about her desire for pain and her reveling in it that is beyond erotic, way beyond a mere act of sex. There has been no sex, nothing about genitals, kissing, sensuality or warm squishy orifices since we arrived in this room. Only sadism and masochism.

"Let me suck your nice cock please," she asks Mr. Tall. I am oddly relieved that she wants a penis included. He comes around in front of her and my Laura sucks him for a very long time until he comes, stifled, softer compared to his guttural grunting in the sex club—as if his parents were in the next room and he didn't want them to hear us.

She lets the come drip theatrically over her lips and recaptures it with her tongue, swallows, and smiles.

I get up and heave her on her back, mount her, and fuck her hard. Mr. Tall covers her mouth with a kiss until I nudge him aside and slap her face. She thanks me, moves her face toward me and asks for an encore. I rest on one hand and slap her again with the other. Mr. Tall joins in, holds her head up and braces it for my next slap. She cries from pain or delight or both and shouts, "Oh God! Yes! I need it!"

I'm bursting and can't hold. I arch and my ass cheeks tighten. Laura comes with me and Mr. Tall, still with her head in his hands, bends down to kiss her. Her face is blissful, her mouth open, her tongue hanging out slightly.

After a moment's rest I get up to get dressed and Laura follows my lead. She does a few more lines of coke, and stilted talk about the weather ends our visit.

Laura and I catch a cab back to our apartment. As we cruise down Park Avenue, she discovers she's left her purple scarf in Mr. Tall's suite. She decides not to retrieve it. "Casualty of war," she says.

"What did you think of the evening?" I ask.

"It kept getting better. He tasted sweet. He must eat lots of cucumbers."

We get back to our apartment. It is just after 3:30 a.m. I am tired. Laura is still wired. She does some more coke. I think more coke is ridiculous, but I don't want to fight about it. There is no longer getting through to her about drugs.

I'm lying down and she is next to me.

"It excites me to take pain from a stranger while you watch. Being used like that satisfies my soul," she says and then asks, "You love it too, don't you?"

"I do," I say truthfully. "We are erotic bookends."

"What do we hold together?"

"Maybe neurosis? Maybe psychosis?"

"I don't want to know," she says. "I'm not finished with it. I want more."

"I want more, too."

But I'm exhausted now. Laura, still buzzing, sits next to me and rubs me to sleep. I awake the next morning and she is curled in my arms. Her body is warmer some places than others. I pull back the blankets and look at her welts, the embossed ridges from lashes. There are a lot of them, some on her back and sides, but mostly on her ass. She looks as though she was beat up or fell from a moving car. I touch them. She moans. I can't tell exactly what the moan is expressing so I press firmer and she moans louder. There is no ouch, only a pleasant sigh. It is pleasure, not pain she is feeling.

Laura is a masochist even in her sleep.

39
The art of war

The two main factors to getting along in a relationship are annoyance and tolerance.

If one person is not so annoying, it doesn't matter whether the other person is very or not so very tolerant. If one person is very tolerant, it doesn't matter if the other person is slightly or very annoying. However, if one person is very annoying and the other isn't very tolerant, life can suck.

The level of one's annoying behavior doesn't appear to be easily lowered except by long-term psychotherapy, a near-death experience, or actual death, or occasionally, by mellowing with age. The general tendency is to retain your annoyance level or to become even more annoying over time. My mother says she never met a person who got less annoying as they got older.

Tolerance is variable under only two conditions. Men can be more tolerant of women who take good care their penises, and rumor has it that women will be more forgiving of men who are great lovers. Also, it appears that either party can be more tolerant if the other person has lots of money.

With Laura and I taking superb care of each other's genitals, and both of us having enough money, our initial tolerance levels are elevated. This paradigm works for only so long, however, because of our natural tendency to become ever more annoying.

Sometime after our first year together our annoyance/tolerance ratio begins to suck. What had been ten-minute-a-day civilized intrapersonal annoyance reports progressively metastasize into full chapters, loud screaming rows worthy of hot Latin lovers. Laura and I never fight about the things that most couples do, like money, family and sex. Our fights are more mundane. I'd tell Laura, "You're driving too fast/that looks too slutty to wear in public/you didn't put the scissors back where they belong/and you do too much coke."

Laura would answer, "That's the wrong direction/you eat like a pig/how come you get to pick all the movies/stop telling me what to do/fuck you my coke doesn't cost you money and I'll do as much as I want!"

Sometimes our fights are short stories and last a few hours, punctuated by Laura breaking things and me waving my fists. Lots of plates go into the trash in pieces. She throws punches sometimes and I am rough in defending myself more than once but never flat out hit her. I never strike her with my sword but I bang her more than once with my shield.

Then one time, during the swelling crescendo of a loud screaming match, she calls me "Jew bastard," and I slap her face, not so hard but hard enough. It is the first time I hit her that isn't sexual.

Being called a "Jew bastard" is the reason I slap her, but it isn't an excuse. I am wrong. At this point in my life I don't have the ability to walk away when another person is intentionally pushing my buttons.

Laura's sweet and demure personality is shifting toward confrontation and hostility. Long-term coke abuse makes users more irritable, not just when they are doing coke but during all the spaces in between. My low-level selfish acts—the new Newsweek comes and I glom it, I finish the ice cream without offering her any, I am thirty minutes late—small infractions that deserve warnings or citations or at most light misdemeanor sentences—get magnified by coke paranoia and are treated as felonies.

If relationships can be judged by how fair the fighting is, we are becoming unsportsmanlike. As our sex grows more violent so does our fighting. I am aware of it—I suspect a direct correlation—but I don't know what to do about it. I don't discuss it because tacit agreements are binary. They are on or off. You cannot un-speak words or un-ring a bell. It's a no-way-back concept like virgin, monogamous or dead. I don't want to spook the magic.

40

The beast comes out of the bedroom

Early November 1982

While driving on a winding country road in Bucks County one early November night in 1982 on our way to our favorite restaurant, we have an argument.

After being high for days, Laura is now straight but crashing and irritable. Sometimes worse than cokeheads high on coke are cokeheads between binges. Either way it's lose-lose. The more drugs she abuses the unhappier I am and the more we fight. She is screaming at me that I am driving too fast and I do not respond. This infuriates her and she grabs the wheel. This scares the shit out of me and I push her away and slow down. She grabs the wheel again. With a strong right backhand I more than firmly slam her back into her seat and hold her there like the safety bar on a roller coaster.

Something is wrong. She's trying to catch her breath and wheezing. She's crying. My first instinct is that she's faking it but I know I slammed her too hard. She's not acting. I pull over. Several minutes pass as her breath slows and regulates. She's feeling her chest and wincing. We turn around, drive back to her house then knock on her neighbor's door, a doctor. Laura tells him, without my urging, that she tripped and fell onto her bed's footboard. His quick diagnosis is that her ribs, two of them, are slightly cracked and that there is nothing to do about them but wait for them to heal.

That night we comfort each other. She isn't mad and says it's her fault as much as mine. But I'm wrong and I know it. I can't take it back. I swear to her never to lift a hand to her in anger, and I swear to myself the same thing. But another Rubicon has been crossed.

It wasn't the first time I'd gone over the line. I'd pushed or slapped previous girlfriends, but never more than once, and I never punched them, so I never felt I was a physical abuser. Then there was Dian, my girlfriend, and then fiancé, before Sherry. During one argument, I pushed her. Dian was taller than me and quite tough, and immediately kneed me in the balls and dropped me right where I stood. I didn't get mad. I knew I'd bought it. I felt more humiliated than angry.

It was easy enough to blame my lack of control on my parents, who were old school and quick with corporal punishment, or the rough-and-tumble street society I grew up with in Dorchester, Massachusetts, where fighting was a way of life. But none of that mattered. I wanted to be above that. Why I hurt Laura was less important than learning not to ever do it again.

I didn't want to spend years with a psychoanalyst figuring out why. I found a behaviorist to teach me how to not behave like that. The first thing he did was to make me see the entire spectrum of violence, from a light push to a beating, as all the same thing. I had to start by admitting to myself that whether I beat a woman with fists or push her, even just once, I have crossed the line. Unacceptable behavior is not only violence but also the threat of violence. Any use of the size differential is abuse. Shaking a fist is out, so is screaming in her face.

I had never thought of myself as a woman batterer, but I was one. I had an impulse disorder and I needed to identify the impulse and the triggers, and substitute other actions. I started counting to ten, walking away, and screaming (after I walked away, not in her face).

That was the last time I ever hit a woman in anger.

41
Getting stale

In late 1982, Laura and I moved out of our Manhattan apartment because we were spending more time in the country, less in the city. The impetus came when the monthly rent on our car garage was raised to more than the monthly mortgage payment on my cabin.

Serendipitously, a rich, gentle, male cokehead friend of Laura's who kept a *pied-a-terre* in the West Village gave us keys. He was seldom there; we paid the modest stabilized rent, so it was a good deal all around. It was a lovely, first-floor garden apartment on quaint and beautiful West 11th Street. It was also a perfect place for Necort to live in New York.

The first night we were there my car was stolen. It was a brand-new Datsun Maxima diesel that was probably worth three times as much chopped into parts. I'm sure that two hours after it was stolen it was hanging on walls in pieces. We had unloaded all the valuables, clothes and electronics. But my Alvin Dark model baseball glove that I had since I was a kid was in the trunk. That hurt. It was a bad omen.

Laura was still turning tricks and doing even more cocaine. Now she was smoking it, not with me, but she did it any chance she got with tricks or friends who were freebasing.

There was a dichotomy to Laura. She was a cigarette-smoking cokehead city hooker who transmogrified into a whole earth hippie holistic vegetarian health nut organic gardener. That summer she dug up part of my cabin's large front yard and made a vegetable garden. She knew exactly what to do and organized the rototilling and the truckload of cow manure and the exact amount of materials for fencing and a gate.

She planted onions and peas early and everything else in its time and kept the twenty-by-thirty-foot patch flowing with tomatoes, peppers, beans, zucchini, red beets, carrots, basil, broccoli and so on, that not only fed us that summer but also filled our freezer for the winter. Sometimes I'd drive home to my secluded cabin and find her working naked in the garden. She looked like the Earth Princess, even though sometimes she'd be stoned on coke.

I loved her passion and loved her perversion but the more coke she did, and the longer she kept at whoring, the less she was a hippie-hooker and the more she was just a cokehead whore. In the first few years of being together we fucked virtually every time we saw each other, then on the way to sleep and also first thing every morning. Each time it was a fresh discovery and the most wonderful experience of my lifetime. The audio track was filled with pronouncements of love for each other, of love for the acts performed, and declarations of how this thing between us was not only the best thing going on in our lives, but also the best thing that ever happened in our lives.

Our sex became more ritualistic and less frequent. Some of the drop in frequency was just because the newness had worn off; it happens to most every couple. Now when we did have sex, it was as much about tying up and whipping as it was about fucking and sucking. She bought several whips, riding crops, short multi-stranded lashes that had no reason to exist except for S&M, and a cane with a knotted strand swinging from the end. She would get one out every time we had sex. She, me, and the whip became a ménage a trois.

Our sex rap had been about Laura pleasuring another man or groups of men; now it was about Laura being whipped by other men. Her fantasy of being tied up on the wall and being a "whipping ornament at an orgy" was the central theme. I loved it the first 300 times. As Norman Mailer said, "Repetition kills the soul." I understood and accepted as weird but not diseased the fact that I got off on giving Laura to strange guys who knew full well that this was the most striking sexual creature they would ever penetrate. I loved being the Angel of the Sacred Mercy Fuck.

I was Pro Bono Pimp Saint Jeffrey. The more ordinary the man, the more I liked giving her to him. The more that his experience was a once-in-a-lifetime dream-come-true, the better. The hornier and more sexually unfulfilled he appeared, the more the kick in fulfilling his hottest masturbation dream. I loved watching his face as much as I loved watching hers. I was the all-powerful Zeus. I was the genie in the bottle. I knew how he felt because I knew how I would have felt.

I loved owning this woman, being brave enough to have her fuck other guys, knowing she would come back to me. Laura was the proverbial bird you let go and watch fly back. Laura was every dirty, slut-whore, porn film fantasy, the hot babe who takes on two or three or twenty guys. But Laura was real.

Incrementally, I found myself drawing away from Laura emotionally. I saw her crossing Seventh Avenue in the Village one day and she looked too skinny and too coked up. I didn't like looking at her. She didn't see me and I walked away from her instead of greeting her. It was the first time I ever did that. I loved her, but I was losing her to drugs.

When we first started dating and living with each other, there had been times when I really thought we might make it long term. Her sweet hippie side, the way my friends and family accepted and loved her, plus her beauty, wit, grace and my total sexual satisfaction with her added up to the possibility of us doing rocking chairs together. I didn't see that anymore.

In the way that recreational drug use crosses some very hard-to-see line and becomes a habit, playing at S&M becomes not a game or a preference but an addiction.

The sweet lovable hippie who liked drugs and rough sex—and, I thought, herself—had turned into a progressively negative person who hid behind more and more drugs and elective pain.

Our game of light S&M had grown organically out of our natural love of dominance and submission. At first an ancillary sexual titillation, it had become the basis of our sex. Naturally, it was easier to see her faults than mine. And her coke habit made her an easy target to get a bead on. But if S&M was her psyche-administered self-punishment, what was I doing to myself? For the first time I doubted my sanity.

In the middle of this bout of befuddlement and self-evaluation I saw a copy of *Time* magazine with a huge "Herpes" headline on its front cover. I felt the jig was up. I read the article and it shook me to my bones. Here was something you couldn't get rid of. I felt like the Christopher Walken character in "The Deer Hunter" who was invincible at Russian roulette till that moment when through his heroin fog, he recognizes Robert DeNiro and says, "One more," and, "BAM! SPLAT!" He's dead! All day I carried that image with me. The next strange vagina had my bullet.

I went from a less than statistically significant amount of worry to obsessed. The idea of getting something you couldn't get rid of crumpled my immortality shield and scared the shit out of me.

I was talking to Jerzy Kosinski, the writer and actor at a sex club one night. "Did you see the *Time* cover, Jerzy?"

"Yes. It gave me pause," he replied in his cultured mildly Polish accent.

"I think my number is up," I said. "I have never been touched by anything, so far. But I no longer think I'm immune."

"Then you are probably not immune anymore."

"And you?"

"I had a similar thought today also after reading that story," Jerzy said. "You may be right. It might be too dangerous to play some of these games."

I liked Jerzy. He, along with Vonnegut, Hemingway and Mailer, were among the few writers whose books I'd read one after another when I discovered them. In addition to being a great writer, Jerzy was a brilliant raconteur, maybe the best I ever met. He told stories about hanging out with the rich folk, one-on-one polo, life in Poland, and his friendship with Roman Polanski. Jerzy told about how TWA losing his luggage on a trip from Europe to New York to L.A. kept him in New York one extra day and saved his life by keeping him from being with Polanski's wife Sharon Tate and their friend Jay Sebring at the house on Cielo Drive in Benedict Canyon the night the Manson Family killed everyone. My favorite story, and the one I think about often although I have never acted upon it was his claim of sleeping eight hours a day, from 4:00 a.m. to 8:00 a.m. and 4:00 p.m. to 8:00 p.m., the two four-hour periods he found the most boring.

Other than running into him a few times at Café Un Deux Troi in midtown, the half dozen times I met Jerzy was at sex clubs or sex parties. He was a more bizarre partaker than me in these kinds of amusements. I was warned by porn star Jamie Gillis that Jerzy could be so sadistic he was scary.

Jerzy loved Laura's looks and often praised them when we would meet. One night, at a party at Plato's Retreat for *Screw* magazine, just after she read *The Painted Bird*, I left them alone purposely so he would get a chance to feel her personality and intelligence and see beyond her physical allure. When I came back Jerzy tried to take control by telling Laura that he wanted to whip her without me being there and without a safety word for her to utter when she was past enjoyment, and I said no.

"Jerzy was very intense but he wasn't sexy," Laura says. "He was sadistic, but without the sex part. Something else was going on in his head. I don't think it was sexual. He was probably trying to get back at the Nazis for killing everybody. He must have been very angry. I could tell he was an angry guy. Jeffrey wasn't an angry guy. He was just extremely sexual, like me. But Jerzy was out for blood. He definitely wanted blood. And when Jeffrey said no to Jerzy

I knew he was doing the right thing. Jeffrey's number-one job was my safety and his number-two job was my pleasure and sometimes in some situations number one ruled out number two. I trusted Jeffrey to make the right sexual decisions for me."

From that moment, after talking to Jerzy when herpes made the *Time* cover, I began carrying rubbers. And I told Laura that from that moment on she must double check each cock she encounters and search them for any kind of thing that shouldn't be there and reject them as necessary. Also that she had to start using rubbers with tricks too, which I don't think she did religiously. While I was telling her the new rules she added, "At least you can't get herpes from being whipped."

42

The S&M pimple comes to a head

December 1982

One Thursday night in December 1982 we go to Club O for some genial depravity. On Thursdays they let in single guys, and it is a good night for Laura to pick up a really horny man or two. By this time, we are club regulars and are greeted warmly by the door dyke. After Laura checks her coat, we go to the locker room where Laura does a few lines of coke. In the signature color of our affinity group, she's wearing all black: teddy, thong, stockings, garters, high heels, and a studded slave collar. I'm wearing a black shirt, black jeans, no underwear, and carry a small whip—black, naturally—in my back pocket. It's so easy to dress S&M.

After a drink at the bar, we shoo away the unattractive single men we always draw, and take a quick tour of the action. On a wooden torture table in front of the bar, a young, naked woman with the white porcelain skin of an English schoolgirl in February is restrained with leather. The table looks like one you might see in a New Yorker cartoon. Her feet are on the floor and she is bent over one end of the table with her hands outstretched and shackled. She is being gently flogged by a short, bald, soft, blubbery older man in glasses, white jockey shorts, black socks, and shoes.

He wields a multi-strand whip that dwarfs him. It is shiny polished leather with two dozen long strands, and a big leather-wrapped bejeweled handle full of blue and red stones. It is either a movie prop or an antique from the Spanish Inquisition. It's strange to see such a whip used so politely. He has the look of a lawyer or accountant. She has on too much makeup, which is running from either sweat or tears. She isn't enjoying it as much as enduring it. You can tell the difference. My take is that she is a hooker and he is a trick. Or maybe he is her lawyer and she is paying off her bill from her last prostitution bust. Or perhaps she is pre-paying her accountant for next year's taxes.

We move on. In Club O's large, sparsely furnished living room we walk in on an odd yet stylish cluster fuck. In the middle of the room, four girls are on their knees facing the center of a circle, their heads nearly butting. They are being fucked from behind by four guys on their knees. I have never seen anything so choreographed. It looks like performance art.

Each of the eight fucksters is at least moderately attractive, a rarity at a public on-premises swing club. All are in decent youthful shape. Maybe an extra pound or two here or there except for one girl who is just plain plump, but on her it looks sexy. The guys have shortish, definitely non-hippie hair. All are several years younger than not only me, but also Laura. They probably get carded outside New York City. All the girls use more hair spray than I normally see at sex clubs.

One girl with Big Hair, jet-black and teased high says in unmistakable New Jersey Italian English, "Oh, that's nice. I like it like that, Joey. I never knew you could fuck like that." It displays familiarity rather than romantic partnership. A few, "Hey Joey!" and "Go Joey!" from both guys and girls, then small laughs, then all go silently back to the work. They are either a group of swinging friends or maybe just friends. It is more exciting to think of them as orgy virgins than sex hacks.

Light touching, not really sexual, is happening between the females while the guys smile at each other, trying to get their rhythm section in synch. Dance music plays in the background with its incessant 120-beat-a-minute 4/4 time so even white boys can catch the groove. The girls giggle too much for my taste.

Around this center circle, half a dozen single men of varying ages and shapes in varying degrees of undress are standing and sitting, watching and pulling their puds. One young buff fellow is sitting in a huge Victorian armchair with an older, slightly dumpy woman with huge boobs on his lap. She is riding up and down on his big cock. A smaller man, obviously a body builder with big biceps and traps, major magnificent abs, and an equally impressive cock moves toward them. The woman reaches out with her face to give him head. Back in the cluster I'm surprised to see each of the four kneeling males pull out and move to fuck the girl on his right! Synchronized debauchery!

I pull Laura to the circle and ask if there is room for us. All the males welcome us and look at Laura with delight. Two girls look at me; one nods with mere acceptance and one flashes a smile. Thankfully, Smiley is the skinny bleached blonde with dark roots, big tits and small butt whom I fancy the most. Although intriguing to me, this assemblage is far too tame for Laura. "I'll do this for you," she says, "but then you'll do something for me. Right?" I nod my agreement.

I take off my clothes; Laura removes her thong. I place Laura on her hands and knees like the other girls to the left of Smiley, so Smiley will be my first switcheroo. Everybody scrunches over to make the now five-pointed star even. I only need to finger Laura's partially lubricated pussy for a moment to bring it to its full-juice welcoming. Feeling her get wetter makes me hard. I enter her and join the easy to follow rhythm section.

A single dude comes over to the cluster. He slides between the two couples opposite me, lies on his back and starts touching the two girls' breasts. Then a guy, just a regular kind of average Joe, comes over next to us and starts playing with Laura's back and bottom. Something about his touch bothers her, and she turns around and gently utters, "No. Please, no," very quietly to not embarrass him. He moves away and starts massaging the ass of another girl who doesn't mind. Laura doesn't often turn guys away, but once in a while some guy sends her the wrong vibe. Usually it's how they smell or the way their dick tastes. Rarely is it just a touch.

The deal between Laura and me is simple: What she doesn't want to do, she doesn't have to do—unless I demand it. She either accommodates my second request or refuses a second time, and then I know she really doesn't want to do whatever it is and I make sure she gets her way. She has the final veto. We never have a problem. Her safety is my responsibility and I pledge my life to make sure she is never harmed in any way she doesn't want. This might sound melodramatic, but I take it seriously. We are doing some pretty edgy things with strangers in strange places and since I only have my fists and a buck knife, instinctual prequalifying is our chief security. There is rarely a problem that can't be solved by a deep-breath, chest-expanding stern grimace on my part.

> "I trusted Jeffrey," Laura explains; "I felt I could be as wild as possible because I knew Jeffrey was there to protect me. He gave me freedom. I wouldn't trust myself the way I was, the way I used to get *so high,* I wouldn't trust myself to go out by myself into the world, and just fuck around. Jeffrey always took complete charge of it.
>
> "Jeffrey allowed me to be completely incapacitated with pleasure," Laura continues. "All I had to do was have a wet vagina and everything else was taken care of by Jeffrey. Whether we were alone, or in a sex situation with other men, my mind could be empty of everything but having pleasure."

The muscular guy with a Marine Corps tattoo fucking Smiley on my right comes loudly shouting, "Jesus, Mary, and Joseph!" in the manner of Catholic orgyists testing the edge of excommunication. Smiley comes too with a head-waving, hair-twirling shriek—a good sign, I want her more—that would be part of a cheerleading routine if orgy teams had cheerleaders.

Everyone yells, "Yeah, Tony! Yeah, Tony!"

"I'm going to relax for a bit, Terry," he says to the girl to the right of him, not the one he's fucking.

"Thanks, Angie," he says, giving the skinny girl who smiled at me a pat on the ass and a name. I don't know anything about these kids, but they are a fun group.

Tony pulls out, wipes his dick on Angie's ass, gets up and moves into an empty chair. One of the single guys around the circle takes Tony's place and starts fucking Angie. In twelve bars of the music we are all in meter.

I have no idea who's with whom—if it is the case that these are couples. In a few minutes, without any visible signal, all the guys pull out and move to their right. I start fucking Angie. Her pussy is wet and full of come and I like it. It's not so tight, but I'm in no mood to come yet and that makes holding off easier. Angie's pussy is so juicy I can feel that this is more than one comeload I'm fucking into. This must have been going on a while.

Laura is having a fine time getting it from an eager, cocksure, youngish male with a moustache and short hair who—since I need to fill in the personalities of strangers who fuck Laura—I imagine owns a pizza parlor. Another single guy is now lying under Laura sucking her tits and she likes it. Four single males affix themselves to us five couples and are grabbing and sucking whatever female parts are loose. It gets erotic enough that, thankfully, all the giggling stops.

The slightly plump, short girl on Laura's left starts raising her voice in climax. Soon, the guy fucking her comes and the guy Laura doesn't like takes his place. Not good.

I don't know whether he is one of the friends or not. He looks a little older. He's having a bit of a hard time squiggling his not entirely hard cock into the plump girl whom I would have had no trouble tooling. She coos, "C'mon. Get it in me, I want more cock!" and wiggles around so sexy that he gets it up.

He starts to fuck and everything seems to even out. The mood grooves. Except I'm totally aware that the next switch will be unpleasant. Mid-fuck with the plumpster he puts a hand on Laura and she tells him, "Please no. I don't want you to touch me."

"Why not?" he whines, revealing that he isn't Italian but is pretty stoned.

"She doesn't need a reason," I interrupt. He backs off, but thirty seconds later he's touching Laura again. I lean over Laura with my rod still in Angie to move his arm away and say firmly, "That's it. Don't touch her again."

He leaves her alone. When it's time for the next switcheroo Laura looks at me—signaling that she wants to handle this—then looks at him and says flatly, "I don't want you to touch me and I definitely don't want you to fuck me."

He slurs in a stoned drawl with a dash of malice, "That's too bad because I really want to fuck you." He sounds very drunk or maybe luded out more than pothead stoned.

Just what I need on a night of sleazy fun.

In hundreds of orgies and sex club outings, I never saw the mood get so sour so fast. I'd seen fifty girls say "No" to fifty guys. Never once was there more than a casual second lobbying attempt, or at worst, half a sarcastic retort. I'd much rather be an observer to this freak of protocol than a participant. Something inside me grates at having to disrupt my evening but I decide to confront.

"Don't fuckin' move," I say in my most martial voice. I pull out of Angie and still on my knees, face the fuckhead. As I slide out, her vagina and my penis utter disappointed sighs. The cluster fuck sputters, then, stalls. I look at one of the Italian guys and ask, "Is he one of your friends?"

"Nope, he's all yours," says Tony, still on break, sitting on a couch playing with his cock. "Whistle if you need help," he adds. Some of the guys are probably sorry they left their baseball bats in the car.

Everybody is looking at the Unchosen One and me. The room stops moving. The droopy fat woman takes the ab roller dude's cock out of her mouth and looks at us. I'd been a violent kid—but since I learned to box at nineteen, I had never been in a fight outside the gym. Now, here I am, almost twenty years later, full of "Make My Day." I only half want the Unchosen One to back down.

The Unchosen One makes my choice for me. He makes the slightest move toward Laura. I grab at him and end up with two of his fingers in my left hand and his throat in my right. Grappling on our knees we must look like clowning circus midgets. He's throwing lame head and body punches at me with his free fist so I increase my throttle.

Who the fuck does this motherfucker think he is! Ruin my evening? Fuck you, you son-of-a-bitch! His punches get puny as his oxygen decreases, but I feel his rage as he tries to strike me. I take a deep breath, tighten my grips, and stare at his eyes as he cocks his arm. All bets are off, I'm ready to release my right hand and nail him fast with a right cross, my strongest punch from that position if his fist lands on me.

He responds to my new escalation with fear, not rage. He's scared and he's not breathing well at all. I lighten my grip a degree, still vigilant for a sneak attack. I hold then I relax a bit. He lowers his eyes like a dog when it gives up and backs off. I let go of his fingers but keep hold of his throat.

"You're going to get up and leave or you're going to die." I don't write the line and say it. It just pops out of me. I cringe at my own melodrama.

Overlapping deep breaths from everyone in the room. Something tells me I have just become fifty percent more sexually desirable to all the women: Laura, Angie, the older woman riding the buff dude's cock, even the girls who didn't give me a second glance.

> "I knew that Jeffrey wouldn't get sidetracked and forget about me," Laura laughs. "He was very intense and intent on keeping me safe. I knew he loved me and that he would fight anyone who bothered me. Jeffrey was my bodyguard. He always made sure I was having a good time. I could be wild and get whipped and fucked for hours—and he'd make sure every man was respectful—even if they were whipping me. He knew how far to let them go. I never got scared.

Jeffrey was very tough and guys knew it—and he was giving them me to use for a while and they were respectful of that. And if they weren't, God help them!"

The guy I've got by the throat tries to speak but can't, so I release my grip.

He croaks, "Sorry. I'm leaving."

He gets up, grabs his clothes and exits.

"Smooth move," says Tony.

"I didn't mean to ruin your good time," I apologize.

The guys all say stuff like, "Don't worry, he was a jerk," and, "Don't let it bother you." Actually, "Doen let it bodda ya." And three say, "Fugetaboutit."

They are Italian. They understand these things.

"Back to the party!" says another guy.

I move to the girl to the right of Angie who is more excited about fucking me now, but I notice Laura beckoning me so I crawl over and fuck my damsel in distress like a warrior till I come loud and proud. I get a much bigger round of "Yeahs" than even Tony did.

I've had enough of this room. We collect our clothes and go to the bar to see what we can find. It's time to get Laura hers.

We order two vodkas with cranberry juice. I feel more tired than excited by what has gone down. I feel like I feel after boxing well. Good tough manstuff. I think the evening will be easier. I am wrong.

There are attractive people here, but no females in Laura's league. I look among the men for the one or two I would let fuck and whip Laura. Then he appears.

He is cowboy-chiseled handsome, 6'1" and 175 pounds, my dream height and weight. He is dressed in regular civilian clothes, white shirt and dark slacks, as if he'd come from the office and left his tie and jacket in his locker. He looks at Laura and then notices the whip in my pocket. "Does she like to be whipped?" His question is directed to me but he is looking at Laura. He sounds cultured, refined.

"Yes. I like to take pain," Laura cuts me off, looking up into his eyes with a little too much eagerness.

"Why don't we go to a private room," he suggests, still fixed on her eyes and still ignoring me.

"Definitely," she replies. I haven't said a word. This doesn't feel good.

He puts his hand lightly on Laura's shoulder to guide her in front of him. I follow. The giant black security guard in traditional black leather "master" garb who keeps uninvited single men out of the private rooms smiles with approval as we pass. I begin to hear the sounds of whipping, slapping, commands and slut talk emanating from the private spaces; some doors are open, depending on their occupants' desire for exhibition.

In one a man on his knees faces the wall. Three women, each uglier and fatter than the next and each in skimpy leather lingerie, are whipping him hard while calling him "girl," "slut," "toilet slave," "useless," "whore," and "lower than whale shit." His back is raw but he is begging for more. Since most of the slave guys are tricks who pay for their pain, I figure he must be a big spender.

Across the hall is another open door with one guy and one girl. They are both short. The guy is more than slightly fat with a pronounced lack of muscularity. He wears an ill-fitting too-tight denim shirt and leather vest with their buttons popping, and leather pants with lots of rattling chains all over the place. Either he bought these clothes when he was thinner and outgrew them or he doesn't like buying clothes in his size.

Sticking out from his open fly is what would have been a miniature penis even if it had been hard. He has the obligatory huge key ring with the necessary three dozen keys that so many of these cardboard-cutout "masters" carry. He has short hair and out-of-fashion glasses and looks like an S&M nerd. His slave is smaller than he, rail skinny and naked except for a cheap, torn beige bra and ripped panties. She has a too-long face and sunken eyes. Even coke-thin Laura looks healthier than she does. The girl's panties are dripping with what appears to be piss. I don't know whether it is her piss or his.

"Would any of you like to use this bitch?" S&M Nerd pleads in a squeaky voice that matches his looks.

"Thanks anyway but we're busy," I say. "Maybe later," I add generously with a wink to the appreciative girl. Although this wasn't an etiquette situation she had ever envisioned, my mother taught me to be polite and try to say something flattering when someone needs it. The cool dude guides Laura into a larger than normal room with two huge sofas in the middle.

"What's your name?" I ask.

"That's unimportant," he says too coolly.

I don't like him. For the first time ever with Laura I feel something akin to anxiety. I'm not in control and I'm jealous. Laura gets out her little brown coke bottle and spoon that is tucked into her garters and does three heaping lines in each nose. She offers. Mr. That's Unimportant and I decline.

He positions Laura so she is standing, bent over the back of a sofa with her ass jutting out. He pulls handcuffs out of his pocket, shows them to me and gives me the key (smooth bastard!) then puts the handcuffs on her. Mr. That's Unimportant pulls down her panties to her ankles and says, "Can you take it strong?"

"Yes, I want it hard. Hurt me bad."

I might be full of anxiety but this is fucking hot!

"Can I have your whip?" he asks.

"Spank her first," I say, trying to gain a toehold.

"Count them!" he commands her.

He spanks her hard a dozen times as she counts them off with pained glee.

"The whip now!" Mr. That's Unimportant semi-growls at me.

"Not yet," I growl back.

He spanks her harder a dozen more times as she counts, and thanks him with more breathy pain and more obvious elation. I hand him the whip and without warning, he whips her once across the buttocks. I can tell it hurts. I'm thinking that I just might have to intervene when Laura says, "Oh, God. I need that. Please hurt me. Hurt me bad." My dick is rock hard in my pants.

Mr. That's Unimportant spends the next ten minutes teasing her with the whip, making her beg for it and whipping her. Usually

Laura says, "This is for you, Jeffrey. I'm taking this pain for you." This time I hear no mention of my name.

"Do you want to fuck her?" I ask. I don't know why I say that. I think it is just to break their rhythm.

"No. Not tonight. Maybe another night."

"Are you sure? She likes to be fucked. She's a great fuck. She's got a wonderful pussy."

"No. Not tonight. Maybe another night."

Laura says, "I want more pain."

For the first time ever with Laura I am jealous. I am on the outside of whatever they are sharing. In some twilight zone perverse logical way, I think if he fucks her, or has any kind of sex with her, the jealousy might go away.

"Maybe you'd like to have her suck your cock?"

"No, thank you," Mr. That's Unimportant says politely.

He never takes off his pants. We never see his cock. Maybe he is like Jake Barnes? Maybe he has a tiny penis? Maybe he has genital herpes? It doesn't matter. I am jealous.

Mr. That's Unimportant continues for another ten minutes, whipping her more than I ever did and harder. All I can do is stand there. I never before lost control of Laura in all our outings. I never felt fear when she turned a trick. This is something brand-new and ugly and it is not sex that does me in—but Laura's masochistic desires. She lets out half a real whimper and Mr. That's Unimportant asks her whether that is enough, and amazingly she says yes. I am relieved.

I smell foul from my own fear. My hard-on is long gone. All I want is for this evening to end. Mr. That's Unimportant puts out his hand and I give him the key. He unlocks her handcuffs and she falls to the floor theatrically, at his feet. She holds on to his feet and kisses them and thanks him.

I feel humiliated.

Mr. That's Unimportant bends down, thanks her, gives her one long tonguey romantic kiss, stands up, shakes my hand firmly, thanks me, and walks out of the room without making any future plans or asking for our number. Thank God. I'm afraid Laura might have given it to him.

"Was that good for you?" I ask, hearing a cracking lack of confidence in my own voice and hoping it won't telegraph to Laura.

"That was fabulous. Fuck me, please. Now I need you to fuck me." She pulls her knickers off her feet and lies on her back with her arms and legs outstretched to greet me.

I don't know whether I can get it up.

"I love you Jeffrey for letting me have that," Laura pants. "You are the greatest master. It's my pleasure to be your slave. Please use me now. Please use me now." Maybe she does sense something. Or maybe not.

One thing for sure: At that minute with her makeup smeared and what I have just seen, she is the ultimate slut-goddess. I undress, put my cock in her warm mouth, feel it grow hard, move around to put it inside her and fuck her hard and long, very long because my head is so full of psychic turds it takes forever to shovel them out and make room for an orgasm.

To Laura it is just a great long hot fuck that allows her to come about half a dozen times, but to me it is an uphill battle, wondering the whole time if she is making believe I am him. Usually, when we fuck after a scene I instant-replay the best moments with color commentary. This night I am silent.

Laura stops coming and hangs in there another ten minutes to get me off. Finally, after a rest stop and some amyl nitrate poppers, the real things, I come. It is not great. I feel cold and alone. Now, not only do I fully hate the coke, I half-hate S&M. Wherever Laura has gone with her "M" is no longer the complement to my "S."

It wasn't Mr. That's Unimportant; it was what she did with him. I was the outsider. I'd been with Laura while she thrilled to terrific orgasms with handsome men, and I never blinked. Like her coke habit, her sex trip had moved beyond mine.

43

S&M clarification

December 1982

For the first time down this road I find myself uncomfortable. Being an "S" in an S&M relationship sounds playful. Being a sadist sounds cruel. I need clarification, so the next day I go to the New York Public Library while Laura is seeing several of her clients.

I read that there are pathological sadists who like to inflict pain on the innocent, and sexual sadists who only enjoy giving pain to those who beg for it. At least I was in that latter group, rather than the first one with Ted Bundy and Dr. Joseph Mengele.

I find comfort in Havelock Ellis's classic, *Studies in the Psychology of Sex*. Ellis died just before World War II so he never went to Plato's Retreat, but his theories are helpful. He says sadomasochists want the pain to be inflicted or received in love, not in abuse. Ellis says mutual pleasure is essential for the satisfaction of both the S and the M.

Ellis says consensual S&M is not only pain to initiate pleasure, it's also violence—or the simulation of violence—to express love. Sadomasochism, Ellis believes, might appear to be controlled by the sadist, but it's really controlled by the masochist. That took the ugliest side away from it. And the part about Laura actually controlling it not only made me feel better, it was true.

I read that addictions are there to relieve and control psychological suffering. It may be a clumsy and dangerous answer— but it is an answer. I really do not know what Laura is working out, but at the beginning I bought the idea that I was helping her, that somewhere inside her was an intolerable pain that couldn't be soothed except by being a whipped sex slave.

The master-slave relationship Laura and I lived was nuclear synergy where one plus one equaled four. It was an explosive shot of adrenaline, like jumping out of an airplane or riding a huge draft horse at full gallop or performing on stage and basking in the applause of a huge crowd. It was living in the beauty and serenity of black and white and exploding to the vivid color and saturation of Kodachrome.

I left the library wondering if an evil person walks around thinking of himself as being evil. I thought not. So what was I?

44

New Year's Eve 1983

Little Richard meets the Sopranos: The wedding of Silvio Dante

After that night at Club O, we slipped back into our routine. Laura turned tricks and did too much coke; I continued my video apprenticeship and our sex continued to slide into S&M. I couldn't tell day-to-day that we were falling apart but month-to-month I could feel whatever we had getting smaller.

On New Year's Eve, 1983, Laura and I got a gig with the video company I'd been working for. The pay ($100 and a half gram of coke each) wasn't the draw; it was the chance to be part of a glamorous New Year's Eve party-slash-wedding.

Little Steven, a.k.a. Miami Steve, a.k.a. Steven Van Zandt, the lead guitarist for Bruce Springsteen's E Street Band, was getting married. Bruce Springsteen was the best man, Little Richard was the preacher, Percy Sledge would sing "When a Man Loves a Woman" at the kiss, and Gary U.S. Bonds and Southside Johnny were the wedding bands.

I was an assistant director so I went to the rehearsal a few days before the wedding with my boss, George. George was killing himself with cocaine and vodka, but he was brilliant and I kept learning the business from him while he remained alive. At one point during the rehearsal it fell to me to go over to Mr. Springsteen and tell him, most humbly, that he was standing in the wrong place. Springsteen was amazingly polite and shy. You could hardly hear his voice when he talked.

He didn't move much either until he started talking to a young black man, one of Little Stevie's ushers. The topic was dance steps, and the young black man said he'd never heard of the "Mashed Potato," so Bruce, with great flair, gave a demonstration. The rehearsal ended with many in the wedding party doing the "Mashed Potato."

If you could bet on whether celebrity couples would last, I would have bet that Stevie and Maureen would make it. The first time I met them they seemed like an old Italian couple with conspiratorial togetherness, deference and tenderness. They were a couple that didn't seem to need to work things out. And as far as the chemistry thing went, well, that was easy; Maureen was a slinky fox with such a warm smile that any man would enjoy being naked next to her.

This wasn't a normal one-camera wedding job. We would cover the wedding with four cameras. Each camera package was totally mobile with battery packs, cameraman, a grip with a hand-held Sun Gun, and a soundman with a boom. Each team was connected to each other by headset. And on a different channel the two assistant directors were connected to George. Two production assistants just charged, recharged, and ran batteries to the units. Unconnected to us was another company, an audio company with a mobile, sixteen-track tape deck in a truck outside that would record all the sound that wasn't synch-sound video. In total it was nearly the equipment, minus a live switcher, used for a small televised rock concert.

The New Year's Eve party-slash-wedding was held at the Knickerbocker Club and the place was grand. I heard the flowers alone cost $15,000. Huge exotic floral displays were everywhere and they made the entire hall fragrant, like what I guess the rain forest smells like when the sun comes out.

I was in charge of two mobile units. I followed George's

instructions over the headset and made sure what he wanted got captured on tape. Even when he was stoned on coke and booze his talent was formidable. With Laura holding one of my unit's Sun Guns, we covered the wedding from various angles, interviewed guests, and then shot the bands and the dancing. Stevie wore his trademark bandana. Maureen looked like a seductive pixie angel. I was surprised that Bruce Springsteen came without a date.

> "Little Richard said, 'Come over here and sit on my lap.' He was totally coming on to me, playfully." Laura remembers. "He was being very forward with me. I did go sit on his lap, and I was sitting there talking to people, waiting for the wedding to start. I thought he was gay but he was at least bisexual that New Year's Eve."

At midnight, just after I wished Little Richard "Happy New Year," and a belated happy birthday (we both are born on December 5th), I was looking into Laura's face and over the airways of our headsets we wished each other Happy New Year and said, "I love you." I did love her, but it was changing shape. George had given us each half a gram of coke. Mine was still in my pocket. Laura's was dripping out of her nose.

At 2:30 a.m. on New Year's Day 1983, Bruce Springsteen and the E Street Band took the stage and played for two hours straight. Springsteen, quiet as a mouse and slow as a sloth offstage, exploded as a performer. The entire room stood and sang every word of every song and at one point Bruce just took a break, and became Mitch Miller leading the sing-a-long.

> "Before that, I didn't like Bruce Springsteen's music," Laura confesses, "but then we were standing right on the stage watching them perform for two hours, maybe three hours and I was so taken with the energy. And the music just pored over me and I liked it. He was so quiet before he

performed and then when he got on stage and he was like someone else."

Twenty years later Steven played Silvio Dante of *Sopranos* fame. His wife on the show was played by his real life wife, Maureen. They did pass the longevity test.

45
The final chapter

Spring 1983

From that height the year gets worse.

Laura and I are spending less and less time with each other. With three residences it is easy to be somewhere else. I am spending more time alone in the country and enjoying it. When we are together I hardly ever see Laura sleep for long. She naps and then gets up and snorts. She hardly eats food anymore. She's become a jittery coke whore and is now anorexic thin. I've always been turned on by svelte and thin, even skinny, but Laura is emaciated.

Many in the crowd we hang out with are out of control. More people we know have nasal surgery because they've burnt out the center of their nose. I wonder how long it will take for Laura to burn out hers.

She is smoking freebase more frequently, often with George, the video producer I am working for. He is more strung out than she is and doesn't like to get high alone. He even goes to her house in New Hope when she is there without me. He provides the drugs.

George was a perfect example of a nice person losing his life to cocaine. Every film and video shoot he did, from car commercials and rock concerts to MTV music videos—including music videos for Aldo Nova, and Blue Oyster Cult's pyrotechnic laden "Burnin'

For You"—had drugs covertly written into the budget. It was where all the per diems, art supplies, and several other categories of money went and, as time progressed, most or all of the profit.

It finally got so bad that Jeannie, George's long-suffering partner and the rock of the company, plus many employees and a half dozen friends got together with George in an attempt at intervention. We all cried. George cried. We all promised to stop all drugs and go "Straight for George." He made all the worthless empty dope head promises that dope heads make. I think his rehab lasted two days. Then he was back on the grand slide.

George was so talented that his work, even a grade below his best clear-headed effort, was still brilliant. Along with the coke, he was drinking a fifth of vodka a day. And even stoned on coke, George could eat. Unlike Laura, who kept getting skinnier, George was a fat cokehead getting fatter. Not many people could be so hedonistic as to gain weight while nurturing a severe coke habit. Much of it was junk food, but a fair amount was lavish dinners at Cafe Un Deux Trois, where the video company and an entire hip entertainment subculture of New York City hung out. George always picked up the check. He was that kind of gracious, larger-than-life, super-talented, charismatic, suicidal man.

Every time I see Laura she is out of her head stoned. I still do coke occasionally, not often but in a group of people passing it around it's hard to say no. There is still something about the first twelve minutes of being stoned on coke that I like. I love the part about not wanting to eat. I just don't like doing coke for hours and hours. And I don't have the physiology that can withstand doing it for two days in a row unlike other physiologies that want more and more every day. This isn't a choice, it's biology.

Laura has gone from the optimistic cheerful princess whom I saw as releasing a damaged underside to being all damaged underside. Part of me wants to save the relationship and save Laura, and part of me wants out. This goes on for months, with our fights about her coke habit taking up half of our conversations. Sometimes Laura promises to quit. But it never lasts longer than a few days.

"Tough shit if you don't like it," she shouts at me. "You love me and it's the price you have to pay for my pussy. All pussy has a price."

That gives me something to think about. I do love her. That is a fact. All pussy does have a price. That is a fact. I am arrogant enough to believe I can get her off drugs. Maybe it is hubris or just naïveté´, but I keep thinking I can make the difference. I still love her enough to not want to love any other woman. Fuck another one, yes; be emotionally involved with another one, no.

We still have heat sometimes and still have warmth sometimes but in general we move to a lower temperature. There is less stuff traveling between us emotionally. We are wilting.

Outside in the real world it is the opposite. The buds are on the trees. It is unseasonably warm and after the hard winter it feels magical. I have spring fever. I am randy. I don't bring up the drug thing and try to concentrate on just having fun and sex with Laura. It is Friday night. I do coke with Laura.

We start off the evening with me hand-cuffing Laura's hands behind her back. I give her directions. Suck my asshole. Lick my feet. Suck my dick. When she begs for the whip I give her enough to bring her to a frenzy and conclude with a hot fuck.

I take off the handcuffs and we rest. She tells me she loves me more than ever, but I know it's not true. We fuck some more and whatever primitive coding we share takes center stage. Laura climaxes several times and then I come again. It is explosive and lifts my spirit. I nap for a while. I wake to Laura rubbing me and begging me to do more drugs so I can fuck her more. I do a line in each nose. I am careful not to do too much and lose my ability to get hard.

We go back to sex games. I put Laura on her knees, tie her up with long pieces of rope, and began to whip her furiously, which is to her liking. She has a collection of welts from her neck to her thighs. I stop whipping her and with her hands still tied, I fuck her. Then I wet her anus with my spunk and fuck her in her ass. It takes me forever to come and it is intense in the way orgasms you really have to work for usually are.

I have to piss, and since piss isn't part of our sex scene, I go to the bathroom, leaving Laura tied up.

I'm standing in front of the mirror. I look at the face in the mirror. I've got coke juice dripping down my nostrils and into my moustache. I still have the whip in my hand. The whole world stops.

I can't stop looking in the mirror. I'm spellbound. I notice every little line in my face, how big my nose is and my receding hairline. I don't know what it's like to be beautiful, like a model and enjoy your reflection, but sometimes I see enough character in the mirror to please myself. At this moment I've never looked uglier. Plus there is sadness in my eyes.

I hear Laura begging for more whipping from the bedroom. I look in the mirror. Now at the whip in my hand. I shake my head back and forth slightly and purse my lips. I look like my father for a moment, looking at me when I've done something stupid. Full of love tinged with disappointment. I stare at the face, and my eyes fill with water. Just looking. Really looking into me. I look at the coke dripping from my nose and the whip in my hand and say to myself with none of the humor with which you might expect the line to be read, "What's a nice Jewish boy like you doing in a place like this?"

I swear that is the line verbatim.

I cry. To say it was an epiphany is to give it too much religious significance. It was more like a drunk hitting bottom.

It isn't about Laura anymore. It's about me. At that moment I know I have gone too far down the wrong road. I don't blame Laura. It just has to end.

I go back to Laura and untie her and tell her I'm tired and need to sleep. She goes into the kitchen to do some more coke. I don't care. I go to sleep and sleep for a long time. I wake up and Laura is in my arms, naked and hot from her welts. I don't feel desire, but I do still love her.

I am scared about not being with Laura and I'm scared about staying with her. I am sick to my stomach. Like so many others who played with drugs or sex or gambling or food, I thought I could keep it as a preference and not an addiction and like most of them I was wrong.

I go out for a walk with Necort. It is still warmer than usual for early April. I feel sad, but the day is sunny. I walk to Washington

Square Park and watch the chess games and roller skaters. I walk to John's Pizza and order a veggie with anchovies and eat a slice on the way home. Laura is awake when I enter and she's hungry and eats.

No one says anything.

I speak first. "I think it's time we take a break from each other."

"You're right," she says without surprise. "We're not so much fun anymore. And I'm tired of fighting about coke."

"I'm tired of fighting about coke, too."

In her sober, humorless voice she continues, "Maybe I can't quit and maybe I don't want to quit but I know I don't want to fight about it with you anymore."

It's that quick. The team is splitting up. There is sad resignation in the knowledge that things will be different forever.

I move out of the apartment that day and Necort and I go back to the country. I cry more than once, but I never have second thoughts.

We were over. That's just the way it was. We talked a few times in the next few days and then stopped calling for a few weeks.

About six weeks after we split up, Laura and I bumped into each other at a mutual friend's townhouse on the Upper East Side. She looked great. She'd been off coke for a few days and had been eating. She said she was trying to get a handle on the coke thing and was only using when she was in the city. I'd heard it all before.

We decided to spend the night together there in our friend's guest bedroom. We made sweet love like old friends. We talked. We said we missed each other. We cried. We cuddled. We held each other tight. We ended like a tight band jamming, not on a pre-set cue, but where, in synch, together, we felt the end belonged.

The breakup with Laura wasn't like any I'd gone through before. There were no theatrics, no pleading and no mortal pain. I missed her, I suppose she missed me, but we knew we did the right thing.

"From the beginning," concludes Laura, "I never thought of us as being in a long-term relationship. It was definitely a fuck experience. I was in this decadent period of sex and drugs, mostly coke, and Jeffrey joined me in the middle of it. It was going on before him and it went on after him but all the time I knew this part of my personality was not going to go on and on forever.

"I remember toward the end, when we first started not getting along so good anymore, Jeffrey telling me his friend Jimmy said to him, 'You know this isn't a permanent thing; she's just with you while she's in this stage of her life. Soon she's going to change into another personality and she'll be gone.' And I remember Jeffrey telling me, in total shock, 'Can you believe he said that?'

"I said I thought Jimmy was right. It was so completely obvious to me that I was playing a role. I was just playing out one facet of who I was, and I couldn't be that part of myself forever. I could only play that one facet for a while. Jeffrey said he understood what I was saying and he could accept that but he hoped Jimmy and I were wrong. I think he was happy to settle for the incredible hot sex, and this bizarre, 90-mile-an-hour lifestyle, but I guess in his heart he hung on to a more long-term romantic dream of us until he didn't."

One morning I arrived at our friend's town house and discovered that Laura had spent the night there and just left. I went to the guest room, sank into the bed's fragrance and jerked off. I'd broken up with her but my pheromones hadn't.

She and I talked and met and continued to have sex occasionally. It was as though we were ex-lovers who still fancied each other, who'd spent three or five years after they split up resolving their turmoil and had become friends again, with benefits. Except we cut right to the benefits.

Our sex was more like our early days. Dominant and submissive, yes, S&M, no. We would look into each other's eyes and smile knowingly. We still thrilled each other's body but we both knew that the love that made orgasm spiritual was gone.

With Laura seeing different men all the time for money it was hard to tell if she was dating. I was somewhere north of curious and south of jealous. It wasn't uncomfortable and I never asked. In a few months Laura had a new boyfriend, a nouveau riche, Jewish, hippie-entrepreneur cokehead who had made a fortune in drug paraphernalia. He was a bit pompous, but seemed to love Laura and wanted to take care of her so he was okay with me. Every time I saw them they were zonked.

> Laura recalls, "George came to see me one night, in New Hope. All of a sudden he showed up at my house. I was like, 'What's up?'
>
> "George said, 'I just thought we might hang out.'
>
> "I said, 'Okay, okay...'
>
> "He said, 'Let's go get cocaine.'
>
> "I didn't know he'd just escaped from detox so I said, 'All right, let's go into town, and see if we can find some cocaine.'
>
> "We went into town and couldn't find any cocaine.
>
> "George said, 'Let's go up to the city...' I said, 'Okay, I'll drive.'
>
> "So I drove him to New York City, where he was dealing cocaine by the way, and he knew there was an ounce of cocaine, and he and I did an ounce of cocaine, in one night, and that's the most cocaine I've ever done in my life. And we freebased it at his apartment through the whole night. Then I got up, drove home back to New Hope and went to an acupuncture appointment, which was fucking insane because I was on cocaine and I hadn't slept."

The last time I saw Laura was six months after we split up at George's funeral. George's friend Sue, a madam who owned a big brothel, had gone on vacation for two weeks and left him in charge. At the end of each day, George was supposed to check in with her well-trained and reliable staff and collect the receipts. George collected and then spent every dime of the receipts on cocaine, which he boiled down to freebase and smoked. He inhaled close to $20,000 in ten days. The madam was understandably pissed. I think she threatened to have him whacked. She didn't need to. A week later George died of a cocaine-induced misadventure. At his wake, Laura was stoned on coke. I wondered how long she would be alive.

"George was dead. He was sitting back on a chair and threw up and suffocated on his own vomit. I took that personally, because I was the one who took him from the detox—that he had escaped from—and I took him to get cocaine in the city, which totally hooked him in again.

"It was horrible—it is one of the worst memories of my life.

"I'm such an idiot that I went to his funeral high on cocaine. I weighed ninety-nine pounds. There I was at my friend's funeral who died from doing cocaine, and this guy standing next to me, said, 'You know, you're next, you're going to die next.'

"I was like, 'Fuck no, man, I'm not going to die, I'm not going to die.'

"The guy standing next to me was part of George's film crew, and he said it again, 'You know it, you're next....'

"The second time that guy said to me that I was the next to die, it hit me. He was right. I could feel it. George was dead and I was next. I went back and told my therapist, 'I have to stop doing cocaine.'

"I finally could see that cocaine was fucking up my life. That was the main thing. I was fucking up my life and I was making choices to be with people who also did cocaine. I was choosing my friends for their drugs. I was not into getting off coke when I went into therapy; I just was going because of my bad relationships with men, and to figure out why I wanted to get hurt all the time.

"My therapist had me look deep into myself, because I

was the one hurting myself and the answer would be inside me. And if I didn't want to be hurt anymore, then I had to start with myself. You see, I discovered during therapy, with my mother's help, that when I was about one year old and my sister was five years old, this two-year-old boy came to live with us. And my parents said that I was in love with him. I followed him around and he ignored me completely. He was only into my older sister.

"Anyway, this boy lived with us for two years, so by the time he left I was almost three years old. For the two years that he lived there, I was in love with him—and he always loved somebody else. It was constant rejection and I guess I became hooked on rejection.

"Every man I ever lived with wanted to have sex with other women. My first husband always wanted to have sex with other women. He went to a whorehouse regularly in Manhattan. Jeffrey was always having sex with other women. He loved me but he ended up hurting me. Well, Jeffrey didn't reject me sexually, but he hurt me even if he only left over my doing cocaine. I think that kind of, well, it made up for my need to satisfy rejection, but I didn't recognize it until I went into therapy.

"So I established a pattern for my whole life of being attracted to people who rejected me. Or giving them a reason to reject me. It was ridiculous but I was stuck in it. And then I went from Jeffrey to another guy who wanted me and also other women. He wanted to be with whores, and me and whores, and whatever—and I finally realized that I had to break the pattern.

"So I went into therapy not meaning to get off cocaine," Laura laughs again, "and immediately I got off cocaine. Therapy was all about me getting healthy. And I was absolutely determined to get healthy. So I worked on it. It was hard to stop doing cocaine, but not all that hard. Not really. I've always given up things like that. When I gave up smoking, I gave it up fast. First I was smoking and then I wasn't smoking. So I gave up cocaine fast. I never got whipped by anybody after Jeffrey. It was just something I did because of what we were together. I still wanted real men, strong men, who were dominant. But I didn't need to get rid of any more pain. I got rid of enough.

"I remember that I just said to myself, 'I'm not going to do these things anymore. Never again.'

"And I was off cocaine. And I was done with being whipped. That was it. No more. Except in my mind when I masturbate."

Only the dead know Brooklyn

Early autumn 1983

A few months after Laura, I got inspired to change my life and find a nice girl, preferably Jewish, and maybe get married or at least achieve some kind of Certified Normality. I needed the absolution that only I could give myself by leading a less perverted life.

I wouldn't find a nice Jewish girl in Goyimville where I lived way out in the country so I had to figure out another way. I'd heard that the Village Voice personals were a great place to find romance. I even knew a couple that met that way. It seemed pretty easy. I wrote ads for a living. I'd take myself on as the client. I was determined to meet some regular women. Not crazies. Not hookers. Not cokeheads. I wanted to prove to myself I could enjoy healthy sex again. Well, at least moderately healthy sex. Maybe not vanilla but cherry vanilla.

And where was the line? Having a whip in my hand was across the line. Was a playful spank over the edge? Too many women liked to be spanked for me to go on the spanking wagon. I was a sinner looking for redemption faced with the common question every addict faces: How do I make a new life? How do I make a life without drugs? How do I make a life without gambling? How do I live without alcohol? And for me, how do I live without the adrenaline rush of S&M?

Would I need to be the alcoholic who has to completely give up alcohol? The heroin junkie who can't even smoke a joint once a year? Gambling, alcohol, and heroin are best left completely alone. I was more like the obese person who still needs to eat, just not to excess. I don't want to give up sex; I just want to take the violence out of it.

My parents raised me to marry a nice Jewish girl and deep inside me I had that notion, too. But this always worked better as a concept than a reality. Not many Jewish women were tall, thin and cheekboned unless their fathers had already married and converted a gentile with dominant genes or their great-great-grandmother had been raped by a Cossack.

I'd met a few full-blooded both-sides-for-generations tall slinky Jewish brunettes and even one blonde—a gorgeous, natural blue-eyed blonde Jewess who could have passed in Germany during World War II—but they were hardly ever demure and I like demure. The dictionary says demure means "disinclined to obtrude oneself." And obtrude means "to take usually unwarranted advantage." That says it for me. I always thought Jewish girls would make better business partners than wives. But throughout my life I intermittently kept up the search, and I was about to make another attempt.

The Village Voice might introduce me to more bohemian, less materialistic Jewish girls. It was worth the try. I wrote:

"Healthy fit brave & witty single Jewish male with riverbank cabin. 36, 6,' 175 lbs. In NYC weekly. Seeks tall trim Jewish female for passion, laughter & lasting relationship. Must send photo."

I filled out the form, sent in the ad, and waited anxiously till the issue came out. Then I bought a copy and read my ad maybe 240 times over the next three days. I liked it. It was tight and spoke of someone of serious intent with enough means for a country abode without mentioning money. The six feet, 175 pounds was a lie by half an inch and four pounds but I was close. The brave and witty part came from Norman Mailer, who wrote: "A hero exhibits a consecutive set of brave and witty self-creations." If I have a credo, that's it. Not that I always live up to it.

A surprising total of forty-seven responses came the first week. I opened them up as they came in but made no judgments until my mailbox had its first empty day and I had a total of seventy-eight replies.

Triage. Two piles. Potential and Fireplace.

All the letters, twenty-two of them, without photos went first. I might have missed the Jewish Wife of the Millennium but I had asked for a photo so I mistrusted or deemed too timid, aesthetically challenged, or a Luddite those who didn't have a photo or wouldn't send one. All the replies with pictures that made me squirm or wince, seventeen of them, went into the fireplace pile. Then all that were more than two pages, both sides, went into the fireplace unless the photo was simply outstanding—and there was only one of these.

One of the fireplace letters was only one page but I couldn't make out a single word including her name or phone number. Another one with a decent-looking photo of a very thin girl had ketchup stains on it and I figured she might be bulimic.

Then I threw out any (thirteen more) that were not Jewish unless the photo especially caught my eye and none did. Any that telegraphed psychosis, or mentioned their shrink or their mother or Thorazine or Stellazine went next.

I got down to about a dozen potentials. Three of them, who sent only head shots and said they were 5'3" or under and 140 pounds or over went next. Any woman who sends just a headshot and says she is 5'3" and 140 is at the most 5'2" and at least 150.

Three more were burned just on strange vibes. One that went into the fireplace was an outstanding photo of a Jane Fonda look-a-like in a bikini that to my dismay was accompanied by a letter that sounded like it had been written by a man. Another went on way too long about guys who hurt her and used her and I thought she might be hungry for revenge. The third letter just smelled weird.

I finished with five possibles. Two I spoke with briefly but we had nothing to say to each other. Fireplace.

One who sent half a torn photograph looked both pretty and hot on her Bahamas vacation wearing a sexy one-piece bathing suit.

Great tits, a real waist, longish legs, good muscle tone, warm smile. She wrote flirty elegant prose. I called and she was fun, and overtly sexual. But she had a high-pitched voice, not whiny, just torturous to listen to. Automatic disqualifier.

With the last two I had decent flowing conversations punctuated with laughter. Beth claimed to be not only Jewish but bat mitzvahed. She sent two photos of herself, which I thought was quite thorough. Tall with a large Aryan forehead and what appeared to be natural blonde hair, she was all dressed up in one photo, I think for a summer wedding, in a flashy strapless with lots of healthy tanned flesh and lovely boobs. The other photo was one of her skiing which spoke of athletic prowess and muscle tone. In both photographs she looked terrific.

I could tell from Beth's photos that either her father was one of those men who had married and converted a gentile with dominant genes or her Jewish mother had married a concentration camp guard and converted him, or there was a Cossack somewhere up her family tree.

We talked. Beth was an only child, had grown up in Manhattan, gone to college in London, and was an investment banker. We discovered that we were the same age and had lived in London during the same period, 1966/67. I'd gone to The Polytechnic on Regent Street; she'd gone to the London School of Economics. My favorite places were rock clubs like the Marquee Club and The Underground on Tottenham Court Road—where I used to see Pink Floyd play every Tuesday night for half a crown—and nasty dance clubs in Soho. Her favorites were shopping at Harrod's, tea at Simpson's, and posh dance clubs like Annabelle's, Pescadora, Sue's Soul, and Barbarella's, none of which I had ever been to.

She admitted to being a "Sloane Ranger," one of the trendy upper class birds who hung out or lived near Sloane Square; Diana Spencer before she married Chuck was the classic "Sloanie." Beth was probably too sophisticated—and too bossy for me but she was so good looking and her voice was so mezzo-soprano delicious that I wanted to meet her.

I gave her an honest description of myself, and she said it was to her liking. I asked her why she was available. She said she'd just broken up with a short, rich, Jewish investment banker-wimp and wanted to meet a taller, less conventional Jew. The conversation stayed buoyant, and there was obviously some sort of mutual interest.

Beth was going away for a "fortnight's holiday," so I took her address and sent my photos, two of them, one dressed in a tux for a wedding and one boxing. How many Jewish men have boxing pictures to send? My boxing photo was me at my thinnest, looking great, and landing a punch on a black boxer who later beat the shit out of me and bloodied my nose.

I phoned the other finalist, who was equally attractive, but in a slinky, bohemian, darker way. Her name was Helene and she was a social worker. She was twenty-nine and came from a middle-class Jewish family that sounded vaguely like mine except with two daughters instead of two sons. Her photo showed her in jeans and a cut-off New York Jets T-shirt revealing a flat tummy. She was luscious unless she'd gained fifty pounds since the photo was taken.

She said she was 5'7" and 125 pounds, which looked right. She had longish brown hair, a winning smile, no cheekbones, but a pleasing oval face. She said her hair was even longer now. I was looking at her picture, talking to her politely and wondering what her ass felt like.

I liked her voice. It evinced education with a hint of Long Island. It was cigarette deep and made me think she gave great head. She said she smoked pot; cigarettes only occasionally, drank wine, and didn't like coke. She'd done some speed and acid but that was history. She never mentioned any of the opiates, which I took as a good sign.

During the next day's conversation she said she loved sex, but never did it on the first date, so please don't even try. I didn't probe her on her sex likes/dislikes because I couldn't find a spot where it fit in. She did say she was "uninhibited." That's usually code for "likes anal."

She'd never been married and had been dating a gentile stockbroker for six years and just broke up three months ago. She ended it because she didn't love him anymore. She thought her love died mostly because they had almost no cultural intersections and in the long run that's what keeps couples together. It was her second long-term relationship with a shagats (a gentile man) that had ended thus. Like me, she wanted to try to find a Jew and settle down. We decided to meet for one drink with dinner optional. I suggested the Village and she suggested a bar on Seventh Avenue called Montana Eve named after a famous douche from the 1930s.

The first moment our eyes meet there is a little spark. Not a huge tractor beam but meaningful magnetism. I'd been working out everyday for months and felt confident. I wore my best chambray shirt that made me feel sexy. I had on my zip-up collarless, black leather jacket that was slimming. I wore my jeans on the smaller of the two belt holes I frequented, which gave me a mental edge.

She speaks first. "You didn't lie too much when you described yourself," she giggles. "You're actually better looking than you said." I'm stuck for something to say.

"You're just as lovely as I expected," I lie politely. She's actually not as pretty as her picture, but close. She's "photogenic," an odd compliment meaning one looks better in photographs than in person. Helene does have terrific skin, nice hair and sweet large brown eyes with a hint of hazel. And she's demure with a soft pleasing voice that's even throatier than on the phone. I bet she gives great head.

I hug her firmly and she responds in kind. I slide my hand down her lower back and just below—not so rude as to put her off—but enough to feel that her bum is firm. She's wearing a not-too-short tight black skirt, clingy black silk top, a lightweight very expensive-looking British racing green leather jacket and a yellow-accented Hermes scarf. She has two earrings in each ear, one a small ring plus a long, dangly thingy. Though she dresses well, she doesn't seem acquisitive and materialistic. She doesn't wear too much makeup or jewelry. Besides the earrings, she's got a single gold bangle bracelet and one simple semiprecious ring, probably her birthstone. When I compliment her clothes she just says, "Thank you," and doesn't go on about the shopping or bargains the way only Americans and arriviste Europeans do. Instead, she tells me she likes to paint and write poetry. Another good sign.

We easily slide past the drinks-only marker and decide to order dinner. We order medium-rare hamburgers, also a good sign. I've noticed that women who order their meat either very well done or bloody rare come with too many unresolved men issues. I don't know why. She eats politely but with gusto, with two hands. She smiles a lot and has a little laugh that is a fraction nervous. It's something that might become unendurable and drive me to murder her in twenty years but it's half-charming at this early stage.

Nothing automatically disqualifies her and usually ninety-eight times out of a hundred there is something that shouts "NO!" about a date that comes up and bites you within six minutes. It could be their looks, breath, hair, laugh, breathing, skin, voice, attitude or aroma.

Some women go to great lengths to smell good but to me their effort achieves the opposite. They use differently scented bath oil, soap, shampoo, conditioner, hair spray, powder, makeup and deodorant, and then add a splash of perfume plus a spritz of vaginal spray to create a well-meaning but horrible olfactory cacophony. It's an unpleasant barrage committed by women who are otherwise sensible enough not to wear stripes with plaids.

Helene smells only of Ivory soap and Chanel No. 5, one of my favorite man-made combos.

We spend a long time talking about the movie, "Tootsie." We both loved it and agree it's one of the few flawless A+ comedies we've ever seen. We talk about actors: Hoffman, Brando, Pacino, De Niro. I say that after seeing De Niro in "Raging Bull," a benchmark hundred-percent effort, I probably hadn't ever put more than seventy-five percent into anything in my life. Even my best fuck. I blurt out the "fuck" remark without thinking—but she smiles invitingly.

We keep the ball in the air most of the time, no stumbles, just a few awkward courting pauses that signal we fancy each other. The talk volley is whimsical, not competitive. She says she really must be going. She had a great time, would love to see me again if I were so inclined and would I walk her to the subway. And would I like to smoke a doobie on the way there. Okay, good. Yes. Of course. And for sure.

Evening has cooled off the autumn day just enough to make us button up our jackets.

We take a left on Charles to get off Seventh Avenue. Although we are in the Open-minded Free Turf of the West Village in the Liberated Zone that is New York City, smoking a joint in front of cops—and there are always cops near the subway in Sheridan Square—could get us in trouble—for hubris if not specifically for breaking the law. And to cops in New York, middle-class hubris, especially middle-class Jewish hubris, is a worse crime than smoking pot.

It is some tasty shit she is smoking. Very expensive. Good quality like her leather coat. Zaps me right away. Like Vietnamese killer weed that makes it nearly impossible to finish a joint.

The conversation drops away as we pay attention to the machine-rolled joint with an English-style cardboard filter. Lots of oows and ahhhs and a few wows and then we just saunter along the street like it is an amusement park ride. At one point she holds firmly onto my sleeve, our first post-hug physical contact. Usually I'm more aggressive, but I let her make the first move. It seems natural, like the way a lioness in oestrus parades her stuff to get the males going.

I'd made sure to have sex with my friend Erika The Cum Junkie that afternoon so I wouldn't be particularly horny. I had decided to play it cool and lay way back. The worst thing a horny man can do is wear it on his sleeve. Most women hate that on a first date.

Also, I take her No-Sex-On-The-First-Date literally. I'm looking for a wife, not an easy lay. We hold hands and rub against each other in a kind of walking cuddle. Then at the corner of Charles and Hudson without a word we turn around to go back to the subway and in mid-pivot when our eyes meet, we kiss.

Haimisha fireworks. Instant Jewish karma.

We kiss too long and gropey for a first kiss. In a pause she falls half limp into my arms like al dente pasta. Whatever her number is,

I have it.

We duck into a basement stairwell and dry fuck standing up. I feel her small soft breasts. I put my hand under her skirt and feel the wet on the front of her pantyhose. There are no panties beneath them. I lift up her skirt and feel her ass. It is heavenly. I hold her hand on my jeans just over my hard-on and she dances with it.

"Let's go back to my place in Brooklyn."

"What about the no-sex-on-the-first-date rule?"

"I lied. Sometimes I sleep with guys I like on the first date. Let's go get the subway."

"Fuck the subway. Let's catch a cab."

"The subway is faster."

"Yeah, but we can make out better in a cab."

I hadn't used the term "make out" in ten years.

We grab a cab and kiss and fondle our way south toward the Brooklyn Bridge. Hands travel underneath clothing. Her nails are sharp, and she cat digs them into the skin on my back just a little. Just enough to let me know she's hot as well as warm.

Over the East River I ask her if she would like me to rip a hole in her pantyhose. She says yes. I stick my finger in her. Fabulous vagina! Very wet. Nice contractions. Excellent viscosity. The Pakistani cab driver is watching the rear view mirror as much as the road. On the Brooklyn side of the bridge one of us, I'm not sure who, I think it was me, helps my penis emerge. She goes down to greet it. She gives great head! I knew it! I smile at the cabby who is watching my face and her head bob up and down and he gives me one of those grins that says, "Yes, I am knowing you are lucky man."

Her apartment building in Brooklyn Heights looks vaguely familiar. I think ten years before Andrea and I had gone to some orgies there given by a nice Jewish couple named Ken and Matty. We button up enough to keep clothed and get out of the cab. Helene unlocks the front door and guides me to the elevator. We take a long, civil, handholding, silent ride up with an older man and his smiling doggie going to a higher floor.

Her one-bedroom flat is large and fastidious, with a spectacular view that is ninety-eight percent Brooklyn and only a slight slice of the river and Manhattan. It's furnished like she dresses, tasteful, expensive and mostly black with lots of leather. The only thing I can smell is more Ivory soap and Chanel No. 5. The bedroom and living room are theatrically lit with half a dozen low-wattage hidden floodlight floor spots shining up the walls in an unconscious tribute to Albert Speer. Either she expected she might bring me back, or she lives like this and pays lots of attention to lighting. Either way is OK with me.

Helene pulls me into the bedroom and onto a giant slippery duvet on her queen-size bed so quickly that if I'd been a thief I couldn't have taken inventory of what was worth stealing.

She scampers into the kitchen and returns with a bottle of Asti Spumonti and two flutes. She pulls out another perfect pre-rolled joint and lights it as I open the Asti and pour. We pass the smoke, clink our glasses, smile and drink. We both undress to entertain each other. Not two dozen words have been spoken since we left Manhattan.

Helene rolls onto the middle of the bed and I get my first glimpse of her completely naked. She's slender with a magnificent ass, a pleasing combination of muscle and fat and firm and soft. Helene has a body I can adore.

She moves up toward the wooden headboard and spreads her legs and beckons me with her entire self. "Put it in me," she says. I like her more and more. Her skin is lovely. I feel empowered by my ancestors. I am hard as a rock. And with a hot Jewish Girl! Destiny calls!

I enter her and feel like Judah Maccabee after a successful day killing Philistines. We find our rhythm, slow exaggerated deep and round. Her fingers first dig gently into my back and then come around to my chest and caress my nipples. This girl is fun.

In a variety of positions for the next fifteen minutes I can tell she comes at least twice. Once when I fuck her from behind. Once when we are eating sixty-nine. Then I'm back on top of her. I can feel myself getting close to coming and exercise restraint. I slow the pace down. We are diagonal across the bed with her head near stage-left bottom corner.

"Harder! I want it harder," she orders.

I speed up. I slam into her a dozen times and we slide slightly on the duvet. I'm getting close to the point of no return.

"More hard!" she yells and each thrust takes me one step closer.

"Bang Me! BANG ME!"

She's writhing in her eleventh orgasm. I pull back, just ready to come, and hit my midsection against hers with enough force to move a professional football tackling practice dummy. We slide off the bed and she hits the floor headfirst with me still in her. Her neck makes a cracking sound you never want to hear. It's the crunch of a 300-pound defensive lineman who misses the sideline tackle and helmet-first hits the skull of a one-hundred-thirty-pound photographer.

Her head is bent over sideways.

Not breathing.

Eyes open.

Lifeless. I'm about to come.

I think I killed her.

My penis doesn't care.

It starts shooting.

What the fuck do I do? I've accidentally killed a girl. In mid-orgasm. I'm not a necrophile. How does one abort an orgasm that's achieved liftoff? The bottom half of me keeps moving like a headless chicken.

Two-hundred-and-forty-seven different thoughts collide.

What do I tell the police? I don't even know the exact address. Do I hunt around for some envelope with her address on it? Do I run naked through the halls screaming for help? Do I stay and wait for the cops or split? Will I go to jail? Does this say something about my future with Jewish women? Will I go to jail?

She doesn't move.

The devilpenis says she's already dead so just keep pumping.

Penis wins although I can't say it was one of my better orgasms.

I pull out on the second to last squirt with my what-to-do-next questions still unanswered.

I hover over dead Helene. I gather my wits. My mind aches. My body is still in afterglow.

CRACK! Helene straightens her head back to where it belongs. She moans. Cries. Screams. It's a good sign. She's not dead.

I'm glad I didn't kill her.

I didn't want to explain this to my mother. The police. Go to jail. End up as some giant tattooed biker's prison bitch.

"Can you move Helene? Are you all right?"

She's not screaming anymore. She's just crying.

Maybe she's paralyzed. Will that carry less jail time than killing her? Will I be spending every Sunday for the rest of my life visiting her in some hospital? How will I explain this to her parents? How will I tell *my* parents?

I promise to believe in God for the rest of my life if he makes her well again.

She moves. Maybe I won't go to jail.

"What happened?" she asks.

She blessedly sits up and rubs her neck.

"We slipped off the bed and your head hit the floor and your neck went sideways and you went out like a light for a moment. Should I call you a doctor?"

I thought it best not to tell her I thought she died.

"No. I think I'm okay. It's just that my neck is sore."

"You sure you don't want to go to the hospital or see a doctor?"

"No, I just want to go to bed. I've got a bad headache."

I'll bet she does.

I get dressed and for certain the mood is different. Somewhere deep inside her she knows I fucked her when she was dead.

We kiss perfunctorily.

I take the lift down, walk outside, and get a fix on where I am. I catch the subway to Port Authority in time for the last bus out to the country. It's a long fucking bus ride as questions ricochet around inside my skull looking for answers.

I thought that whatever potential Helene and I may have had was poisoned. Over. History. This would prove true with the lifeless phone conversation we have when I call the next day. She was polite but I could tell she wanted to get off the phone. Maybe by that time she knew I fucked her when she was dead. That could put a damper on any relationship.

A week later I called Beth. She loved my photos! I was much better looking and sexier than she expected, but—a big but—she'd met a man on "hols" and they were already half an item. His description matched her ex—short, rich New York City Jew. He was a lawyer and from her description he was as malleable as her previous wimp.

A few more replies came in over the next month but no one I found attractive.

Whatever was going to happen to me after Laura wouldn't be fast or easy. There wouldn't be a quick fix. But the good news was that just before I killed Helene, I was outside the fog of perversion and completely absorbed in a good old fashioned fuck.

And the better news was that I wasn't going to jail and I wouldn't have to be some big, gamy skinhead Neo-Nazi's anal slave. At least not now.

Afterword

Since then

About a year after we split up and a few months after George died, Laura changed her life and gave up coke. The next year she gave up whoring and studied interior design. The year after that she was not only clean and sober, but, get this, celibate. She said she had to do that to prepare herself for the love of her life she knew would come. Then she met him.

Today, twenty-seven years later, she's a healthy happily married, drug-free mother of three with a successful business and a beautiful country home. Her husband knows much of her history, including my part, and sees her past as a step she had to take to meet him. Whenever we've been in each other's company he's been warm and at ease.

Laura and I went through some kind of sexual healing that although bizarre, did lead each of us to external positive results and an inner therapeutic equanimity. Her submission to me, a beautiful sex slave princess adoring me, offering her pain as a sign of her devotion, forever erased some parts of my insecurities and raised my confidence level and not just with women. Laura, having divested herself of a physical manifestation of her psychic pain, evolved to the end of punishing herself and drug abuse, and forever gave herself a lighter load to carry and paved the way to her place in marriage, motherhood and as a successful businesswoman.

Laura is one of those people who can do whatever she sets out to do. She wanted coke and whipping and gangbangs and had that. Before that she wanted to be a Sufi vegetarian celibate acid freak and she did that. She was a great girlfriend for three and a half years. She was sweet and entertaining which is why Norman and Norris and Legs and my parents and all my friends loved her.

She was a great whore and now is a great mother and wife and cook and housekeeper and she'll be a great grandmother when she gets there. Her design business varies with the jobs and seasons but sometimes she has twenty-two people on her payroll. She is a winner.

A few years after AIDS made the headlines Laura and I both got tested several times and passed. Laura took her first test just after she became pregnant with her first child. She called me when she got her cherished negative. "I guess we got it all in under the wire, didn't we Jeffrey?" she said. "Yes," I said, "We did."

* * *

I was one of the horniest men I ever met. I'm not anymore. All the stuff in this book happened twenty-five to forty years ago. Today I'm just average for my age. Maybe a little bit higher. Hormone levels fluctuate with age and since hormones often reveal themselves as thoughts, there are some thoughts I don't have any more and many I have much less often.

For all my high hormone years, the real power behind the curtain, Testosterone Rex, turned me into its amoral endocrinological bitch and forced me to hunt for orgasms every day. It wasn't something I chose or that could be turned off. Lots of times, especially when I was alone and horny and had jerked off three or four times and the monkey was still on my back I daydreamed that there was an off switch I could throw.

There were, however, magic golden periods, like the apogee of my testosterone when I collided with Laura, an erotic outlier whose libido matched mine. I never once looked for the off switch.

Neither Laura nor I were involved with heavy S&M before we met each other and neither of us ever got into it with anyone else after we split. Neither of us have any residual shame or regrets or guilt. We are grateful we got to live our fantasies and make it out alive.

I suppose if Laura had died or ended up with mental or physical incapacitation, or we were shooting drugs and one or both of us got Hep C, if we had perished in a libidinous Gotterdammerung, then my retrospection would be different. But we both landed on our feet, we thrived and we earned the luxury of nostalgia.

After Laura, my life went in other directions with the same maniacal intensity. At thirty-seven, in 1984, I replaced Laura with a bass guitar and taught myself how to play. Badly.

I published a high-end hard-core erotic photography book shot in London, Paris and Los Angeles and got arrested for pandering while in L.A. The police were trying to skirt around the First Amendment and arrest pornographers under a Draconian anti-pimping law that carried a minimum of three years incarceration.

In London I looked up my ex-wife Tisha whom I hadn't seen in sixteen years and we fell in love again. Sometimes you just need a decade or two of space to work things out. I took the music I was writing and put together a band in London. I invented a publicity prone character, Max Gelt, Miami Beach deli owner. In my alter ego story Max invested with a group of English friends in a London rock band and was touring around with them when the lead singer broke his leg and Max filled in and the band loved him and he left the deli and his wife and two kids to become the lead singer of Max and The Broadway Metal Choir. (Google it. I found one of my albums for sale on Amazon UK for £8!) It was musical guerrilla theatre performance art and I was Max.

I got adopted by some great musicians who loved the concept. I even hired a bass guitarist because I was writing parts I couldn't play and I wanted to concentrate on being the lead singer. I didn't have a great voice but I had some character.

While I was Jeffrey in the USA, I was Max in England to the band, who all helped promote the fiction, and to the press, who never saw through it. I mean who would make up a lie about being a delicatessen owner? We got signed to a middle level indie label, Powerstation, and put out an album that went somewhere but not far enough for me to get a major deal and profitably continue.

Tisha saved my erotic life. She made my transition from kinky S&M to regular alpha male sex easy. Her emotional warmth, refined aristocratic attitude and her enlightened aromatherapist alternative lifestyle smoothed my way to the hard edge of hot but not decadent sex.

Tisha loved England and wouldn't leave. I was an American who knew what real food and real weather were like. This intractability brought me back home alone again in 1987. Tish and I remain friends to this day and forever.

The California Supremes overturned the pandering law as it related to pornography so I was off that hook. I needed a new gig, especially to pay off my lawyers (it cost me over $100,000 to be found not only "not guilty," but as the court papers said, "factually innocent"). I fell into direct response TV commercials and infomercials, where I made a nice living and which grew because while direct response doesn't get much respect in the production world, it's the only place where directors get royalties if the product sells.

A one-percent royalty doesn't seem like much. It's just $.75 on every $75 order for a steam iron or electric slicer or dicer or new design floor cleaner, but if a product sells $1,000,000 every quarter for a year or two, and some do, you get sent a check for $10,000 every three months for work you already did. A friend of mine, working on the first ab-exercise machine, a mammoth hit in the '90s made one percent of $120,000,000 over two years. That's eight checks averaging about $150,000 every three months. Sweet.

A few months after I came back to my cabin, one of my best

friends, a gorgeous, brilliant French artist and model, Juliette, came over to visit me for a month and we fell, if not into love, then at least way deep into friends and lovers. We lived with each other for four to seven months a year at my cabin, at her flat in Brighton and when either of us was working in Paris or L.A. One of Juliette's most remarkable erotic traits was sucking bisexuality out of women who might have thought about it but never expressed it so I was the lucky recipient of lots of waking up to a female on each side. While not being "in love," I didn't lack for sex, which allowed me to concentrate on growing my business.

In 1990 I married Bunny, a horsewoman, a tall, blonde shiksa goddess, and the chemistry of romance was back. I am sad to report that she was not bisexual and was very traditional about marriage and monogamy. But I really loved her, my hormones were cooling down, I was willing to try monogamy and we had very compatible country lifestyles. Around the same time Juliette met a guy in France and moved there and we drifted apart.

Bunny taught me to ride when I was forty-eight in 1994. Within three years of all-weather riding more days than not, Bunny and I became a noted cross-country team winning scores of ribbons and trophies at local Hunter/Pace and Paper Chase events riding our Tennessee Walking Horses. We bought a ranch for our five horses, which included a giant—an 18h2 2,000-pound Belgian that was going to be dogfood until I outbid the butcher by a penny at $.65 a pound. He was broke to ride and drive and soon I bought a cart and was doing both.

Bunny and I stayed together for seventeen monogamous years until 2007 when we divorced. In one of the few amicable divorces I know, we split the ranch and kept the team together.

Then I got back with, *Tada!* Andrea. My partner of 300 orgies and I, now in late 2011, forty years after that night at my first orgy when we met while eating carrots at the snack table, are heading toward our sixth anniversary. Andrea and I built a house on the ranch and share the stables and pastures with Bunny, our friend and neighbor.

Juliette, single again, and with Andrea's liberal erotic blessing, visits us for a few weeks every couple of months. Polyamory, no surprise, suits ex-swingers.

Andrea enjoys continued relationships and occasional vacations with a few of her ex-lovers and sometimes I travel to Paris to hang out in fancy hotels with Juliette, who paints and lives in Normandy. My goal in Paris is to walk and fuck enough to burn off the cheeses and the croissants.

On occasion you hear of men who remarry or get back with the same women one or more times but having done this three times I am one of only a handful of registered serial recyclers of lovers. We are a small cult who believe you must be decent at all times, no matter the circumstances or stage of a relationship, and never burn a bridge with anybody you ever adored.

The history of this book

In the late 1990s, as my testosterone ebbed—which gave me some free time—I wrote the first draft of an erotic memoir. My ex-boss, sparring partner, and friend Norman Mailer loved it. His agent loved it. Most editors hated it. Some wanted it but couldn't get their editorial boards to agree. Nobody bought it. I put the book away and returned to my life making infomercials and competing on my Tennessee Walkers in cross-country equestrian events.

But two or three times every year, Norman would urge me to finish the book. He'd give me editorial advice: cut certain characters, develop the Laura arc, avoid adverbs, read it out loud and edit with a brutal knife. A month before he died he suggested two methods to make my book publishable and to have the opportunity of financial success.

The first option was to change the word "Memoir" to "Novel."

Changing this one word, he hypothesized, would allow editors to do two things: separate my ego from the main character's, and not need to question my veracity. Norman knew I was truthful, but cautioned that others, in particular, editors, might not believe me.

The second option was to give the finished book to my ex-girlfriend Laura, the main character, and let her tell her side of the story.

During my last visit with Norman, a week before he died in November of 2007, he made me promise to finish this book.

I began rewriting when I retired in February of 2009. Norman's widow and my late friend, author Norris Mailer suggested I expand on my relationship with Laura, whom she and all the Mailers loved.

"Tell a love story," she said. I took her advice.

A year later when my part was done, I chose Norman's second option, and Laura agreed to reveal her side of the story in a series of interviews with pop culture oral historian, Legs McNeil.

Acknowledgments A

Thanks to Norman Mailer's family for permission to reprint parts of "The Best Move Lies Close to the Worst" from *Esquire* (1993) and his interview from *Puritan* (1981.)

Thanks to Joanna Poncavage for editorial perseverance, literary expertise and love.

Thanks to all the people who helped make this book better starting with Norris Church Mailer who was honest enough to tell me everything that was wrong and loving enough to tell me how to make it right. Also thank you to John Lotte, Paul Willistein, Richard Luksin-Cross, Tony Cardillo, Annick Portal, Arthur Powers, Peri Lyons, Diana Morse, Stephen Mailer, Elizabeth Mailer, Erica Line, Jan Cyrka, Bob Gruen, Tom Bowser, Robert Hoffman and Jimmy Haskett.

Thanks to Professor J. Michael Lennon for his early help, his later advice, his insults and praise through multiple readings, and his final line-by-line comma-by-comma edit which was so useful I shall be forced to treat him with deference for the rest of my life.

Thanks to Legs McNeil for having faith in this project, his slash and burn editing, his interviews with Laura, the huge amount of time he donated to this project, and for not smoking in my house.

And thanks to Laura for the wild ride then and for her courage now. —JM

Acknowledgments B

Ten things I learned from Norman Mailer

Norman Mailer's 1959 book, *Advertisements For Myself*, shocked me. I read it when I was sixteen in 1963. It is a collection of essays, fiction, polemics and autobiography, unfiltered to allow him to be seen equally as genius and fool, champion and clown. It was a kind of journalism I had never encountered; a mix of objective and subjective, a search for the truth no matter where it took him. It was the first journalism I ever read where the writer was a character in the story.

In the way the quick-cut editing of Miami Vice and MTV would later change television and movies, Mailer's book changed journalism, and laid the groundwork for what would be called the New Journalism of Tom Wolfe, Hunter S. Thompson and all who followed.

Mailer's 1965 novel, *American Dream*, also grabbed me. Flawed antihero Steven Rojack is a murderer, yet the reader cares about him. He's a proto-Tony Soprano, and it's no surprise that Norman not only liked *The Sopranos* but also considered it the television equivalent of The Great American Novel.

Norman's books alone would have only made me a fan.

What raised him to hero was that he crossed over to celebrity.

He was a two-fisted, bar-brawling tough guy Jewish intellectual, and the first to break the genteel mold of those like Saul Bellow, Arthur Miller, Norman Podhoretz and Isaac Singer. And while Arthur Miller, bless him, married Marilyn Monroe and helped to forever make Jewish intellectuals' penises more attractive to beautiful gentile blondes, Norman gave young Jews like me pride in being physical as well cerebral.

He was a cross between a longshoreman and a professor and as the military might of Israel's self-defense force in 1948, 1956 and 1967 helped wipe away some of the stigma of my tribe as sheep walking into Nazi ovens, Norman gave Jewish boys license to be fighters and thinkers, poets and warriors at the same time. It may not have seemed much to non-Jews then or to Jews today, but it was big stuff and quite liberating to me over fifty years ago.

I first met Norman when I was nineteen, in 1966.

I came to understand that his intelligence wasn't just a difference in quantity of brainpower: It was a difference in quality, a quantum change where a difference of degree becomes a difference of kind.

To explain: Put a salad plate on top of a dinner plate. The circumference of the salad plate is the limits of mental abilities of a normal person, even a brilliant one.

The larger dinner plate represents Norman. Now imagine a line running from twelve to six and another from nine to three. The twelve to six line represents kind and cruel and the nine to three line represents smart and stupid. Norman is bigger in every direction. Not only could he be smarter than you or I, he could be stupider; not only more kind but more cruel.

Norman taught me how to box, sail and rock climb, as well as how to navigate though our language from the formal to the obscene. Norman was a great buddy to hang out with who happened to be an oracle.

Here are ten things I took home from him in no particular order; some he's told many people and some maybe just me:

1. How to re-hydrate a stale bagel. Cut the bagel in half and finger paint the inside of the bagels with water and then toast

normally. It works every time. I call it *"Norman Mailerizing* a bagel."

2. Be professional. Take your job seriously. No matter what mood Norman was in, how drunk he got the night before (he stopped drinking to excess decades ago), whether he was fighting with a family member or someone else or even if he was feeling poorly, he dragged himself off to his studio and wrote if he wasn't on vacation from writing. He always showed up.

3. Do not allow self-pity. This is maybe the most useful thing he taught me. Self-pity can become an attractive melancholy comfort and you must avoid it. It's one of the worst vices because it not only keeps you from altering a situation you need to change, it's a magnet for other vices like gambling, alcohol and drugs. You can allow yourself sadness—with cause—for a certain time period but too long and/or too deep and it becomes self-pity.

4. How to make an unkempt house look clean in ten minutes. One afternoon in the summer of 1967 Norman got a phone call that someone important was stopping by in ten minutes. Norman shouted to all of us to set everything we could at right angles. It works. Squaring everything off visually makes a place look neat.

5. The best trick to making sure that what you write reads well is to speak the words out loud as you edit.

6. The most important thing in a book or movie is mood and it has to flow like a river. This is maybe the second most important thing I learned from Norman.

7. When writing, avoid adverbs, be scarce with adjectives, describe with nouns and verbs. Not so easy but I try.

8. *Good* is the enemy of *great*. I love this one. Good is so near great it makes us settle. Don't settle. Know the difference between good and great and if time and/or the money allow it—and it doesn't always—go for great.

9. How to get more comfortable in your own skin. When I was

twenty-two and having a bad time after my first wife left me and went back to England I asked him how one gets more comfortable being alone. He said much of it can come from aiming for success and achieving success. You gain comfort doing the best you can.

10. Avoid the instant karma of insulting a warrior with condescension. We were in the ring boxing two three-minute rounds on the day before his fifty-ninth birthday—January 31, 1982. I was thinking about cutting him a little slack when he delivered a right that smashed me back two feet, a left jab and another punishing right cross. I growled a silent "TO HELL WITH YOU OLD MAN" and went to work. I had broken two rules of combat and deserved the beating: never insult a warrior with condescension, and when you fight, don't think.

* * *

I visited Norman in the hospital in New York City near the end but he slept the whole time. His sister Barbara was there and said it was OK to wake him but I couldn't do it.

I came back a week later. He was awake but couldn't talk with all the tubes down his throat. I didn't know what to do so I held his hand and said hello, then told him I needed the men's room. I called his wife, Norris, for guidance. She said, "He's interested in your adventures so tell him what's going on in your life. And ask him yes or no questions he can answer with a nod."

I told him about my new horse, Pilgrim. I had him for a year but that morning was the first time I ever told him I loved him. My previous horse, Genius, the horse love of my life, had died suddenly about a year and a half before and it took me a while to fall in love with Pilgrim.

I admitted I was more promiscuous with my emotions with women than I was with horses. I'd told women I loved them either to fuck them or to make the fuck better but since there was no sex with Pilgrim because he was a horse, and more important a gelding,

I found myself adhering to a higher ethical standard. Even with all the tubes I got the big Norman Mailer smile and part of a laugh. Making Norman laugh was always rewarding and up till being in the hospital he had a bellow of a laugh. He wasn't just a great performer, he was a generous audience.

I asked him if he was still Norman Mailer in his head and he rotated his hand on its axis, the international sign for "sort of." I asked him if the doctors were optimistic and he gave me the same sign, this time slower and with a shaking back and forth of his head. He was down to 125 pounds and didn't look like he was going to get better.

A nurse came in and asked me to please leave soon so she could give Norman a respiratory treatment. She said it was OK to take a few minutes. She knew his condition and that his clock was running down.

He pantomimed like you do to a waiter when you want a check with air squiggles. I asked if he wanted pen and paper and he shook his head no. He pointed to me and motioned again and looked at me with stern eyes. I asked if he wanted *me* to write something down for him. He nodded yes, put his palms together and opened his hands like a book. I asked him if he meant my book (this book) and he pointed his finger at me with emphasis. He kept his finger stuck out and with a hint of strength jabbed it at me until I promised I'd finish it. Then he nodded his head with a smile.

I grabbed his hand and squeezed and told him that I loved him, even more than I loved my horse. He chuckled and coughed. Our relationship, as were many relationships others had with Norman, hadn't always been smooth. In the forty years we were friends there were sometimes months and years we didn't talk. But we always got back on track and it had been smooth for a decade.

With some torque still left, he squeezed my hand.

He let go and pointed his index finger at me.

Then he pointed his thumb to himself.

Then in the middle between us he made thumbs up.

"You. Me. We're OK."

I kissed his hand. We both had tears in our eyes. He knew. I knew. I kissed him on the cheek.

That weekend surrounded by his family he passed away. At the very end his son Stephen held his hand as he left this planet, which had benefited from his time here.

My favorite thing Norman ever said to me was a left- and right-handed compliment: "Jeffrey, you are the most improved person I ever met."

What even his genius may not have known was how much of it was because of him.

a note on the type

The main text of this book is set in Cycles, designed by Sumner Stone and first released in 1993. Laura's side of the story is set in Today Sans Serif designed by Volker Küster in 1988. The display type is set in Base 9 designed by Zuzana Licko in 1995. The book was designed by John Lotte for Blue Mountain Marketing Inc.

LauraMeetsJeffrey.com

Lightning Source UK Ltd.
Milton Keynes UK
UKOW032141261112

202822UK00002B/486/P